What the critics said about MARJE:

'An extraordinary biography'

– *News of the World*

'A tale to bring a tear to any eye'

– *Observer*

'A brutally honest biography . . . the real-life anguish of Britain's favourite advice columnist is laid bare'

– *Daily Mirror*

'Astonishingly candid'

– *Daily Mail*

'The disclosures may be her revenge on all those who thought only the young and beautiful have anything to hide'

– *Independent on Sunday*

'No holds barred . . . a full exchange of confidence – perhaps to repay all those given to her by her correspondents'

– *Spectator*

'Marje emerges as a warm and likeable person, worthy of her unique place among the glowing cockles of the nation's heart'

– *Sunday Times*

'The most shockingly sad story of the decade'

– *Sun*

'A remarkable life . . . Marje – the genuine article'

– *Star*

Former International Fulbright Scholar Angela Patmore has written twelve books, several of them with or about sports stars, including Mike Gatting and Alex Higgins. Her best-known was an in-depth study of the mental agonies of high level competition, *Sportsmen Under Stress*. She has also produced several books on her pet subject – dogs – including *The Mongrel* and *Sex Tips for Dogs*, the ghosted manifesto of the world's foremost authority on canine sexual behaviour, Randy Barker.

Marje

THE GUILT AND THE GINGERBREAD

The Authorized Biography

ANGELA PATMORE

WARNER
BOOKS

To Stanley, who died without me, 6 March 1992

A *Warner* Book

First published in Great Britain in 1993
by Little, Brown and Company
This updated edition published in 1993 by Warner Books

Copyright © Angela Patmore and Marjorie Proops 1993
Afterword copyright © Marjorie Proops 1993

The moral right of the author has been asserted.

A CIP catalogue record for this book
is available from the British Library.

ISBN 0 7515 0718 0

Typeset by Hewer Text Composition Services, Edinburgh
Printed and bound in Great Britain by
Clays Ltd, St Ives plc

Warner Books
A Division of
Little, Brown and Company (UK) Limited
165 Great Dover Street
London SE1 4YA

CONTENTS

	Acknowledgements	vi
1.	Beaky and The Voice	1
2.	No Sex and the Single Girl	15
3.	Worse Than Death in Bournemouth	32
4.	War Work	47
5.	The Herald Years	66
6.	The Hellish Years	88
7.	Mirror Mirror Off the Wall	111
8.	'Passion Put to Use'	134
9.	Aunt Misbehaving	158
10.	First Lady	184
11.	Caring Thatcher, Cuddly Wilson	207
12.	Magnum Ops	228
13.	The Arterial Aunt	249
14.	Bonzo	265
15.	Double Widow	286
16.	A Mortal Remains	313
	Afterword by Marjorie Proops	335
	Index	342

ACKNOWLEDGEMENTS

Marje Proops and I would particularly like to thank Lord Cudlipp for his invaluable help.

We are also most grateful to the following family members, friends, colleagues and dignitaries for their kindness and their time: Leo Abse, Lady Alma Birk, Tony Boram, Josephine Bourne, Ernie Burrington, Dame Barbara Cartland, Dame Barbara Castle, Hugh Corrie, Margaret Disher, Robert Edwards, Emma Field, Michael Foot MP, Geoffrey Goodman, Felicity Green, Len Greener, Roy Greenslade, Fiona Griffin, Bill Hagerty, Joe Haines, Susie Hayman, Gerald Kaufman MP, Cyril Kersch, Dr Tom Kraft, John Knight, Cissie Lewis, Des Lyons, Brian McConnell, Lord McGregor, Mike Molloy, Olumade Okubadeju, Robert Proops, Claire Rayner, Deidre Sanders, Doreen Spooner, Mary Stott, George Thaw, David Thompson, Penny Vincenzi, Don Walker, Keith Waterhouse, Audrey Whiting, Shirley Williams and Justin Wright.

— 1 —

Beaky and The Voice

*P*icture the scene, if you will. In the parlour of their house in Dalston, a small, very British Jewish family is waiting for Father to come home. (I can't tell you the year because the subject of this biography fears her readers might not heed her advice any more if they knew her age. She thinks they might say, 'What could she possibly know about my problems – silly old trout.')

Martha Israel, a nervous, fastidious lady with tiny feet and a fixation about appearances, is sewing an extravagant frilly dress for her dark two-year-old, Rebecca. Rebecca wears an enormous satin bow in her hair, which her mother feels helps her image slightly. The child, named Rebecca Marjorie after a character in a romantic novel Mrs Israel read whilst expecting, should have been blue-eyed and blonde, with ringlets, but turned out disappointing.

The parlourmaid (they later have a nanny) is preparing the evening meal, and Mrs Israel, pregnant again, is mulling over suitable fictional heroines' names for the impending child. Clarissa? Pamela? Shamela? By the fire sit Aunt Lilian (who lives with them) and Granny Annie Flatau, Martha's mother, who once caught herself and her nightdress ablaze in the cinders but who was to live for many years in one of the rooms upstairs, playing German whist. The women are silent, except for the occasional remark about a young local girl, no better than she should be, who is also having a b-a-b-y (the word 'pregnant' is never to be uttered in this household in front of children).

Where is Father? A jovial, generous, glamorous fellow with a moustache, Abraham 'Alfred' Israel is out doing a bit of business. He may be having a flutter on the horses – a besetting anguish to his wife. If he loses, he will make a joke of it as usual, and if he wins, which is marginally worse, he will come in lugging some expensive and unnecessary gift for Martha, when all she wants is a bit of peace and not to have to worry herself sick all the time. Father plunged the family into uncertainty by selling a perfectly nice greengrocery business in Woking to come to Dalston. Now what?

Eventually the door is flung open and in comes Father, tossing his hat on to the hook. 'Got a surprise!' he says gaily, swinging his precious child Rebecca Marjorie round and round in the air. 'Sold the place. Bought a pub in the East End. You'll love it. Anything for dinner?'

And so it was that young Rebecca Marjorie and her family came to live over a pub. Over several pubs, in fact, because Father could never stay in one place for more than a short time before his whiskers started twitching restlessly. The first was the Royal Standard, in rural-sounding Shepherdess Walk. 'Oh good,' said poor Mrs Israel, and 'Oh God' when she found out it was in Hoxton, which is not the end of the world but you can see it from there. Then came the Victory in Kingsland Road, Dalston. Then the Royal Oak at Clissold Park. Then the Fleet at Hampstead, then back to the Royal Oak. Followed by the Marquis of Lansdowne, Stoke Newington. The family feet hardly touched the floorboards before they were whisked off by eager Alfred Israel to yet another hostelry. His second daughter was born during the Royal Standard sojourn.

Rebecca Marjorie, who began this pub-crawl at the age of two, estimates that she went to 'about eight' schools, and was never able to keep up with the classwork. She remembers only the main ones: a dame-school near the Royal Standard; Packington Street LCC Elementary; Dalston County Secondary; and even, while they were at the Fleet in Hampstead, a convent school in Haverstock Hill, where she sat out the religious instruction with the other Jewish children but was lured by the sound of the catechisms: 'I was at an age when I'd begun getting very emotional and falling in love with things: I think it was hormonal.'

She was nine before it was discovered that she couldn't see the blackboard, and she was given – oh shame and worry to her mother – a pair of spectacles. These at least prevented her from missing her footing and falling down the stairs from short-sightedness, as had happened before, but they added nothing to Rebecca Marjorie's allure. She was already far too tall for her mother's liking. Both she and her sister had gaps between their front teeth and Mrs Israel consoled herself by saying, 'This is a sign you'll travel!' Not so promising, thought Mother, was the fact that Rebecca's teeth also jutted forth like gravestones. The younger girl, Josephine ('Jo-jo'), was fortunately very pretty, with light brown locks, a fact which comforted Mother slightly. She would dress both children in hair ribbons, frilly frocks and white buckskin shoes ('I think she had an image of us as dolls,' says Marje now) and hope for the best. She would push the girls forward in their Sunday-best dresses, telling visitors, 'This is Jo, she's the pretty one, and this is Rebecca, she's the brainy one.'

Under this burden of expectation, Rebecca would periodically come home from school in tears. Among other things she was assailed with cries of 'Becky the Jew-girl!' across the playground, which obliged her mother to start calling her by her middle name instead. 'Marjorie the Jew-girl' didn't have quite the same ring to it, and her schoolmates soon tired of their taunts. Father eventually decided that for the sake of a quiet life the family name should be changed from Israel to 'Rayle'. They were British after all, with British roots going back to the 1660s on Martha's side, and they weren't going to be singled out by hooligans and halfwits as undesirable aliens.

Mrs Rayle's concern for her daughters' social standing led to polishings, primpings and refinements. They had to dress prettily, wash behind their ears, develop accomplishments such as singing and playing the pianoforte, and learn quaint graces, such as deportment, considered appropriate for young ladies of that era. It was a cross between Emily Post and Jane Austen, a sort of middle-class finishing school. Marje's sister Jo (now Mrs Josephine Bourne) remembers:

> Although our parents weren't wealthy and worked very hard to earn a living, they did their best as far as our education was concerned. We learned deportment from a lady named Mrs Edwards, who lived in a charming cottage overlooking the New River in North London. We had to walk around balancing books on our heads, and we had to keep repeating 'How now brown cow' and 'Did you see Father pass the path' with lips pursed.

Marjorie tried and tried at her regular schoolwork but kept coming bottom. Father, whom she adored, would hug her and say, 'Don't worry about it, Marje – you've got hidden talents, my dear!' and in fact she had. Once she could read the blackboard she started to shine a bit at English, enjoying books and winning a poetry competition. But what she really could do well was to draw, the lines seeming to flow from her pencil with lightning deftness. It was a gift she would one day use to create a small caricature above her name: hair, glasses, mouth, cigarette-holder. It became her insignia as a newspaper columnist.

At the age of five, Marjorie had become a socialist. She and her sister were quick-marched through the pub on their way to their living quarters upstairs, but the observant young Marje had already made a note of the different rooms on the premises. One room always had cloth-capped clients chinning pints, and the other had suited City-types sipping shorts. 'Public Bar' and 'Saloon Bar'. She would ask her father what it was all about. 'Never you mind,' he said. 'You don't understand these things. Go upstairs.' But Marje kept pulling his sleeve.

I kept on and on nagging him until in the end he told me. 'The reason is that the men in the saloon bar are the well-off customers who can afford those little drinks which cost much more money. And the men in the other bar are not well off and can't afford the polished glasses and the small drinks and to dress well like the others do.' And that was really my first experience of haves and have-nots. And I was outraged by this, even as a very small girl. I thought it was absolutely appalling that there should be this difference in the lives of human beings all coming into the place where I lived. My father was a devoted Conservative. He'd have loved Margaret Thatcher, and if he had been alive during her reign we would have come almost to blows about Thatcherism because he would have admired all that she stood for.

The dilemma of haves and have-nots was not always seen from the painful end. When Marje and her sister eventually went to secondary school, they soon discovered

that Dalston Grammar was divided into two streams, A
and B. Jo remembers it like this: 'We all wore navy-blue
gymslips, cream blouses and panama hats, felt in winter.
The A-formers were clever girls who had won a scholar-
ship so that they didn't have to pay. We were in the
B-stream. We had to pay. And even though most of the
B-stream were absolute dunces, we used to look down on
the A's because we thought we were "it".'

Another haunting sight for the infant socialist being
quick-marched through the pub was what her father called
the Guinness Girls – Ena Sharples types who sat in the corner of the public bar and hardly spoke. They wore mangy
fur tippets and stared blanky into their stout, ignored by
everyone except the publican, who was kind to everybody.
The thought of lonely, unwanted women would always
trouble and frighten Marje very much. She would go out
of her way – a long way out of her way if necessary – to
avoid being one. When her mother told her to 'Eat up that
last slice of bread or you'll be an old maid', Marje ate up.

Mrs Rayle was full of old saws, most sadly no longer in
vogue. If Marge spilled something on her dress, Mother
would say, 'Blind man would be glad to see it!' Such
sayings came thick and fast. 'Ne'er cast a clout till May
is out' was one that Marje struggled with for some time,
thinking it referred to their Auntie May. Meanwhile her
education broadened.

Granny Flatau, upstairs in her room, was a veritable
fount of dirty language and rude songs. There she lay,
propped up in bed with her proudly arranged white hair
and her lace-trimmed pillows, telling yarns and teaching
the girls to play German whist (Marje rather hoped it
was poker) for money. If they heard Mother's high heels
tapping along the linoleum towards the door, the pennies
and cards would be stashed under the covers and Grandmother would recite something from her repertoire, such

as *Little Red Riding Hood*, without the swear words. 'Come down now, girls, for your banana sandwiches,' Mrs Rayle would say. Or else their cucumber sandwiches. They ate decently but never kosher, except for Grandmother, who was more exotic than the others.

As the girls grew into their teens, Mrs Rayle began to worry more than ever. Firstly there was Father's Jack-the-lad behaviour. Quite apart from his dragging the family round London like gypsies, his wife never knew what he might get up to next. One day he surprised her with a bull-nosed Morris car. Another day it was a blue and gold dinner service (for twelve) from Harrods, which she was far too frightened to use.

Despite being a Tory, he seemed to have no proper respect for his money, putting their livelihood at stake in public houses. Who could say what might happen? They'd lived through air-raid warnings during the First World War at the Royal Standard, hiding in the cellar holding sing-songs and giving the children Bath Oliver biscuits to keep them from worrying. It was all very dangerous, Mrs Rayle felt, investing in pubs and frittering away the takings on lavish presents for people. You had to watch your ready cash. She did her best, using her dressmaker's skills, to help the family budget. 'Only the rich,' she told her girls, 'can afford to borrow. If you have money in your purse you can be a respectable solid citizen. You can look the rich in the eye when you meet them, and even feel morally superior.'

And then there was this other dreadful business. Marje explains:

My father was a punter. He used to buy the midday paper and sit there in the pub in his shirtsleeves marking off the horses. Every now and again he'd go to the races. He'd be at Ascot all dressed up and looking absolutely

stunning because he was very good-looking. He and my
mother adored each other and I never remember them
quarrelling, but she did worry about his gambling.

She did have a lot of worry in her life. My strongest
recollection of my mother was of this small, refined,
anxious woman who worried about everything because
that was her nature. She was very neat and precise,
and very very timid. I think that fear must have been
engendered in her somewhere even before she met
my father, and the life she led with him afterwards
didn't help matters. Really what she should have done
was to marry a nice comfortable shopkeeper – the
greengrocer, perhaps, that my father failed to be –
so that she could live a quiet lower-middle-class existence. I hate to talk about class, but it counted in
those days.

The family background encouraged a feeling of protectiveness. Marje's cousin, Cissie Lewis: 'Children of our
generation lived a very sheltered life. We hardly mixed
with non-Jewish children other than at school, because
there was such a lot of family. We were always having
birthday parties for the various children. We called them
all "cousins", and their parents were "aunties and uncles"
and treated with a great deal of respect. I have a couple
of in-laws now who never could get in, because it was an
enchanted circle.'

The girls were allowed out and about, doing charity
work. They sold roses in the foyer of the Alexandra
Theatre in Stoke Newington, the proceeds going to the
Metropolitan Hospital, of which their father was a life
governor and supporter. Every Christmas Mr Rayle would
appear in the children's ward laden with an enormous
stocking, sewn by his wife, full of gifts, toys, fruit, sweets
and handmade presents for the small patients.

But Marje and Jo-jo were never permitted to go swimming for fear they might drown, and Marje never travelled on public transport until she was sixteen. They were allowed to do amateur dramatics, and to play tennis at a small club in Clissold Park, but never to take lifts from anyone they met there. Disaster stalked them everywhere, in Mother's view. They certainly weren't allowed to go into the bars – or, heaven forbid, behind them – while they were young. When Mrs Rayle had to do it, pulling pints, for this publican's wife, was like pulling teeth.

There were no boyfriends for Marje, only boy acquaintances, and the excitement of mingling in the road with acned pupils from William Ellis School, round the corner from the convent ('I expect we'd all have been expelled if the nuns had known!'). For her pretty sister Jo-jo, however, life was rosier. She was thirteen when she stepped out with her first boyfriend. Jo:

His name was Sidney. I wasn't allowed to go out with him on my own, so if he ever invited me for a walk in the park – in those days all you ever did was to go for a walk in the park – my mother always insisted Marje come with us. I can remember once, we were walking along Green Lanes where we lived, with Marje there as usual playing gooseberry, when Sidney said to Marje, 'Walk behind us, please' because he wanted us to be on our own. Every time we were out, Marje had to trail behind us.

Marje was permitted one social solace. Her father used to take her to smoking concerts – amateur talent evenings – and Marje would sing to her own piano accompaniment. She had a thrilling contralto voice which issued from her mouth like a stranger's and surprised her audience. Marje was unpleasantly surprised by it herself. Her father, whose party stage-name was 'Alfred Lester', used to sing and dance occasionally, but all his admiration was reserved for his daughter, warbling her heart out in her glasses and frilly frock.

The family loved to entertain themselves at weekends by having their many 'aunts', 'uncles' and 'cousins' round for smoked salmon or cucumber sandwiches, bananas and cream, and entertainment. Jo-jo strummed the ukulele, Marje sang and provided keyboard accompaniment, and the dog Mick howled behind the piano. And whenever Marje's voice rang in the ears of Aunt Lilian, an opera buff, she would tell her sister it was something special. Mrs Rayle had to agree, and sought to nurture the child's talent more conventionally by employing a voice coach and a piano teacher, the appointment of the former leading to national competition. Marje should tell you the story.

I was still at school, about fourteen and in my gymslip, tall, skinny and gangling, a very shy, plain child with this enormous contralto voice, and every time I sang I'd listen and shudder because this voice was somebody else's, and what I longed for, the same way I longed to be blonde and small and pretty, was to have a coloratura voice, very high and beautiful. And of course nature had provided me with this great big contralto voice instead, which I hated as much as I hated my glasses and my teeth, but my mother was very proud of The Voice, absolutely delighted and thrilled with it. So I had singing lessons with a lady near the pub, which I found boring. Part of my brief musical education with this poor woman was that I had to learn scoring. I composed a few pieces, nothing very much but at least romantic. And then one day she announced that there was to be an All-England contest for contralto singers that she would like to enter me for.

I went through the heats, and I won the London one and qualified for the finals, which took place at the Kingsway Hall. And the song that all the contestants had to render was Handel's 'Oh rest in the Lord'. There were ninety-eight performers, but I was the only child, and I was the third contestant to sing. So I got up on the stage and delivered my 'Oh rest in the Lord' and when I'd finished I went back to my mother and my singing teacher.

'Can we go now?'

'Sshhh!!!'

So I had to sit there through all the other bloody contestants, listening to ninety-odd versions of 'Oh rest in the Lord'. And when this ordeal was finally over, six or seven musicians, including the distinguished Herbert Voss, adjudicated. The chief adjudicator made some wearisome speech about the quality of the contestants' singing and said that he was reluctantly awarding the medal and diploma to the contestant whose rendering was the worst of all, but who had the best voice, the purest contralto sound they'd heard all morning. And on and on he went about this poor creature, and I was feeling ever so sorry for her until I discovered it was me.

My mother was outraged, taking the view that if I had this pure beautiful contralto voice and sang so badly, whose fault was it but this poor wretched teacher's? So the teacher was immediately sacked.'

A grander replacement was employed, and soon afterwards the family had a visit from the renowned Carl Rosa Opera Company. They had something very important to tell Mrs Rayle. 'They offered to take me into the company, to train The Voice and continue my education. They would guarantee that I'd be looked after, and in due course when this voice had developed properly and I was old enough, I would be given minor and hopefully major roles.'

Mrs Rayle listened to all this with gathering gloom, one tiny foot tapping slightly, and finally made her announcement. She couldn't possibly allow her daughter to go away from home and travel. Why, she might have to go all round the country. Or to foreign parts. 'And I wasn't to do that,' says Marje. 'The same sort of thing as the swimming.'

Any newborn dreams of Tosca or Aida that Marje might have nursed were immediately stifled in their cots. She wasn't brokenhearted, since The Voice belonged to a stranger anyway. But it was another sign of her mother's fierce protectiveness towards the children, and of the growing sense of timidity and terror of the outside world which would eventually develop into agoraphobia.

Marje carried on singing as a hobby, joining a local operatic company and doing Gilbert and Sullivan: all the contralto leads, beginning with Princess Ida. She loved the mischievous lyrics of G & S, but she would really have liked to have tackled grand opera, like her heroine, soprano Amelita Galli-Curci. Marje and The Voice actually performed at the Fortune Theatre near Covent Garden, as well as in a charity concert at the London Palladium. 'All I can remember was standing on that huge stage in that vast auditorium, belting out something or other – it wouldn't have been "Oh rest in the Lord" – and not being able to see the audience but hearing the noises and coughs and shuffles. I don't think I was frightened because to me singing was like breathing. Out came The Voice.'

Oddly, in view of what had happened, Mrs Rayle still cherished Marje's musical talents, and did her best to develop them at home. This was to have startling consequences.

One day, Marje arrived home from school to find a strange and very handsome man sitting in the parlour. He was the new piano teacher. He spoke with a mysterious accent, possibly Austrian, and looked like Chopin, or some equally heart-thundering romantic creature. He was very distinctive, very artistic. Marje thought at the time he might be 'about forty' (he was probably about twenty-five). He was enormously charming and courteous, and music flowed from his fingertips on to the keyboard as though from heaven on high. His name was Joseph Barer, and young Marje, who had never thought of herself in the feminine until this moment, fell silently and violently in love with him.

He was the first man I ever loved. I think that for the first time I felt like a human being and not just a plain schoolgirl. All I remember was sitting at the piano and being beside him, and feeling the excitement of sitting beside him. He smelled of eau-de-cologne and had lovely hands, and I can still see those brown hands going up and down the keyboard as he taught me. I played the piano reasonably well and if he'd told me to practise twelve hours a day I'd have done it. I'd have done anything for him. I was responding to him in a way that I recognize now, but didn't then.

If those days had been today, I'd have been writing to somebody like me saying, 'I'm in love with this dishy music teacher and I dream about him all night.' You couldn't say anything to him about it. He was the object of your 'happy ever after'. I still think about 'happy ever after'. I still want life to be 'happy ever after' for everybody. And I know because of my job, and because I'm not entirely impractical and stupid, that it cannot be, and that for a large number of people it never ever has been and never ever will be. But I will never give up hope. And I think it all started over Joseph. I never dared ask him about himself. He probably had four children.

Marje never said a word about the matter to anyone, other than to her sister Jo-jo, who was also smitten with the Barer phenomenon. Jo and Marje had a sparring sisterhood, biting and clawing and rowing in their room. There were affectionate interludes, of course. Jo's nickname for Marje was 'Beaky' (after either Rebecca or her nose), and when Marje talked at the top of her voice in her sleep and sat up frightened, Jo would say comfortingly, 'Hold my hand, Beaky.' But most of the time they were rivals.

Their mutual hatred was sparked off by their parents' favouritism. Father favoured Marje; Mother favoured Jo-jo. The jealousy that these preferences aroused has haunted the sisters to this day, although they are now sufficiently close friends to be able to laugh off most of the hurt. Marje had no way of winning her mother's favour, for she couldn't be pretty. Only talented. And Jo-jo longed to be idolized by her father and admired for something other than her looks: it took her years to find the confidence to become the clever businesswoman she is now. Parents are always amateurs at being parents, and can do a lot of damage while they are learning the trade.

2

No Sex and the Single Girl

I already realized how plain I was compared with my sister. Wearing glasses was one more blow. My sister's front teeth were beautifully straight. Mine were crooked, and they stick out a bit – I've always dreamed of having Chicklet teeth. So my sister had all these advantages. She had lovely hair, lightish brown. Mine was dull off-black. And my eyes have always been shrouded with glasses. As I grew older, I drew caricatures of myself and learned to laugh with other people about the way I looked, and even to be amused by the enormous contrast between the pretty blonde daughter named Marjorie that my mother imagined I was going to be and the way I turned out. I no longer have hang-ups about it – if one ever does get rid of one's hang-ups. But my mother was really, I think, mainly responsible for the misery that I felt when I was young. I think her perception affected me in all sorts of ways my whole life. I think if she had realized for one instant how it hurt me, for years and years and years, she'd have been horrified.

Racial prejudice has taken a bit of a bashing since Marje was growing up in London, when you could taunt a little child with 'Becky the Jew-girl' and get away with it. Not so, facial prejudice. Discrimination on grounds of looks is as strong today as it was then, when Marje's mother was introducing her in conciliatory tones as 'the brainy one' rather than 'the pretty one'. Facial prejudice has not been legislated against; indeed, it is being constantly reaffirmed by powerful screen and newspaper images in case the message should have escaped anybody. When Marje's unconventional features began to be plastered over the *Daily Mirror*, cheerful blokes felt compelled to write in: 'If I had a face like yours, I'd wear a mask.' Because unlike racial and class discrimination – now considered not quite cricket – facial prejudice is still openly or covertly accepted as having some justification. It is one of the few genuinely unapproachable and unacknowledged subjects of the twentieth century, the last unstormed bastion of human nastiness.

The subject of 'ugliness as sin' remains hidden away in the postbags of advice columnists like Marje herself, where it causes untold pain and misery. Only with the bargepole of humour is it touched. The world and his wife have written books on human beauty. Human ugliness, quite as intriguing and quite as decisive in influencing our affairs, has either been ignored altogether or mentioned only in passing wind. Several hundred years of literary endeavour have not advanced our understanding of the subject much beyond the Ugly Sisters and the Ugly Duckling and the reason is as plain as Jane. Most influential writers have been men, and most men, being connoisseurs, have thought beauty a desirable thing in women and nature, if not in their good selves.

As Marje the advice columnist points out to worried female letter-writers now, the majority of women are, like her, not particularly pretty. She tells them not to fret. Yet the edict has undoubtedly gone out from somewhere that women should 'make up' whatever their faces lack, starve themselves into proportion, and be surgically adjusted in order to look like the 'model' girls set before them. And it takes a shrewd lady, like Marjorie Proops, to see the 'birds or bags' mentality for what it is.

Martha Rayle was not particularly shrewd. But in introducing her daughters as 'the pretty one' and 'the brainy one', she should not be judged too harshly. She was doing her best, seeking to promote her girls as best she could according to the rules of society, and she was very afraid that Marje's face would not fit. She told Marje to stand on her own two feet, fearing that because of her looks, she would have to. The fact that she was wrong, and that Marje's inward beauty was eventually to triumph over all the odds, is a mark of her daughter's own courage and character. But it hurt then, and the memories hurt still.

Marje dreaded dances and parties where her partners usually came up to her shoulder – 'If I was lucky!' Some nestled in her bosom. Rarely did she find one upon whom she could nestle. She was good at school sports, 'not because of any outstanding ambition to be the fastest thing in black stockings in North London, but just because I happened to be rather freakishly long-legged.' She gave up all her sports apart from tennis for fear of developing sinews, and she learned not to beat boys at the game either, in case she muscled in on their egos. She says she only learned to play tennis in the first place to impress 'some dish' at the tennis club, but that he lost interest after being aced.

Marje would one day confide to her readers, 'When I was a teenager I wrote reams and reams of sorrowful poems, all about my unrequited love for the spotty youths I worshipped from afar. They, alas, saw only this plain, bespectacled face of mine instead of the beautiful soul behind the glasses.' She lost many a potential boyfriend

to her sister. And even if Jo-jo didn't pinch them, they
would be quietly pinching Jo-jo, or chatting her up behind
Marje's back. Jo:

> I remember one, Harry Rosen. He was taking Marje
> out but he was always grabbing me. I must have
> been fourteen or fifteen, and I hated him – he was
> horrible. We never did anything like that, you see. We
> weren't allowed to wear make-up until Marje was about
> seventeen. But we'd bought a lipstick between us which
> we applied in the street, and also a red handkerchief,
> which we used to wipe it off before we got home. Once
> our mother found a lipstick in Marje's room which
> she promptly burned. They were very strict about our
> upbringing. If we kissed a boy, that was as far as it went.
> Marje and I were both virgins until we got married. We
> wouldn't have dreamed of having sex. We didn't think
> much about it, in fact we were quite ignorant about
> these things really.

It is a minor miracle of sorts that Marje became the first
journalist to use the word 'masturbation' in print. When
she was an adolescent, sex was, like Essex and Sussex,
remote. She did manage to preserve one lipstick from
confiscation by hiding it in her navy serge drawers, but
puberty itself was a penance. Marje:

> I menstruated late – I was fifteen going on sixteen –
> and at the time I thought I was dying. My mother
> never told me anything at all. There I was, bleeding
> to death as I thought. Just to mention it would have
> killed my mother. She wouldn't have been able to say
> the word.

Little did Mrs Rayle know that Marje would shortly be

looking at real, live, nude bodies. What's more, it came about with both her parents' compliance, one of fate's saucy little tricks.

> When I was approaching sixteen, the head teacher at Dalston Secondary, who must have been a very sensitive, intelligent woman, asked my parents to go and see her. She was worried about what was going to happen to me when I sat metriculation, because she knew that I would fail everything except drawing and English. And she thought that the best thing that my parents could do would be to remove me from school before I had to sit the exams, and put me in an art school.

This is what they did. Marje was sent to the Hackney Technical School, now Hackney College. For good measure she enrolled for evening classes there as well. She reckons she was one of the original Beatniks. At Hackney Tech she learned the techniques of drawing, at first from what were called 'antiques' – plaster casts of the human body, noses, heads and feet. Once students had grasped the basics of anatomy and the mysteries of curves and sweeps, they progressed to drawing from life – nude models, mostly women of various shapes and sizes. Marje only vaguely remembers drawing nude men:

> Probably did. They'd have been wearing something over their willies. And the women were nude but wore something round their whatnots. Pubic hair remained a mystery for a long time. I think that my art training was probably the most useful grounding for anyone, though, because my familiarity with the human body was ingrained very early on. After I left art school, I was never ever nervous about it. That familiarity

with unclothed bodies has stood me in good stead
in my job to this very day, because I can discuss the
way bodies work. I've always been easy about bodies.

One of the things Marje learned was that women were
not all perfectly formed: indeed, that she herself, with
her svelte figure and long legs, was formed better than
many. This gave a much-needed boost to her confidence.
She also learned that she was a naturally gifted artist.
Where this talent comes from is anyone's guess, but her
father could draw, her sister sketches, her son Robert is a
designer, and her grandson Daniel, a former Goldsmiths
student, is a professional artist. Samples of his work hang
on the walls of Marje's home in Barnes alongside her own
remarkable paintings and portraits. As Marje says, 'Some
of his work is very exciting. Some I don't understand at
all, but I love his still lifes, and his nudes are beautiful,
wonderful. He's never happier than when he's up there
in that rather grotty little studio with his canvases stacked
all over the place and in the bath, simply painting.' The
life that Marje might have lived, perhaps?

During her arty period, Marje acquired her first admirer,
a fellow student. She would never invite him indoors in
case his eyes lighted upon Jo, but he used to carry Marje's
portfolio, and accompany her to her doorstep from Hackney Tech. Sometimes they would go all the way to a coffee
shop. They never held hands, but discussed art and life
as best they could without a language between them. He
was Polish and handsome. 'He was a very gentle, elegant
boy; very protective towards me. And he had this rather
romantic Polish pallor and shiny dark hair.' He was about
nine inches shorter than Marje (already five foot seven),
and her portfolio must have been a struggle for him, but
he was always charming and courteous. She never knew
his first name, referring to him quaintly as 'Mr Pogerelski',

the way Jane Austen's characters refer to their men as 'Mr Darcy' and 'Mr Bertram'. (Even Marje's husband Sidney Proops would always be known as 'Proops' or 'Proopsie', never 'Sidney'.)

At all events, Mr Pogerelski was Marje's first romance, as distinct from her first 'pash' on the piano teacher. She can't remember who left whom, but it was Paradise Lost in any case. She'd had the sleepless nights and the starvation languor, and she'd dreamed impossible dreams about being short and blonde and racing into his arms. One never forgives such a disappointment. Thirty years later, in a piece in the *Daily Mirror* on Bonfire Night and guys, she described some little lad's straw-and-sacking effort she had seen on the way to work which 'resembled a boy who once jilted me'. Whether this was Pogerelski or some other suitor, she gave the child a tanner and said, 'Burn him real good, boy.'

Father didn't help. Mr Rayle would crack jokes and tease. On one occasion he found out that Marje had brought home an opera buff. Father greeted the young man with his usual frivolity: 'Come in and make yourself at home, Madame Butterfly!' It was the kiss of death to that particular relationship. Marje thinks her father was 'probably very possessive'. She was reading a lot of romantic literature during this period, from the Brownings and Shakespeare's Sonnets to *The Sheikh*, a torrid roller coaster of a novel crammed with Mills-and-Boon-style sensuality. Marje has never despised Mills and Boon pap: she feels it gives weary housewives fantasy and romance. 'I quite liked detective stories, so long as they weren't violent and to do with people being chopped up. I still can't look at a television programme where somebody sticks a knife into somebody else and blood spurts out.'

Meanwhile Jo-jo had gone to secretarial college, and was doing some freelance typing. She was to be paid per 1,000

words, and asked Marje to help her work out what the job
was worth. Her sister was always truly bad at maths, but
covered a page with figures. Jo: 'In the end she said to
me, "You're going to get £35,000!" Of course I got £5, so
that was the biggest load of rubbish I've ever heard.'

Marje was getting restless about her own career. After
three terms at Hackney Tech she started scanning the
classified ads. Her cousin Cissie knew she was up to
something because she had seen her standing outside
fashion shops sketching costumes in the window displays.
She had also begun to affect strange arty habits, such as
painting the frames of her glasses with red nail polish.
On holiday with the family at Cliftonville, the girls were
all at a seaside Pierrot show with their Aunt Lilian when
Cissie swivelled her head to behold her cousin with a
cigarette in her chops. 'We all looked at one another,
horrified – we thought it was absolutely dreadful. Aunt
Lil idolized Marjorie and would never correct her. And
there she was, smoking in the theatre.' It was only the
odd fag. Marje didn't suck weeds in earnest until she fell
under the influence of her first boss, a woman artist by
the beautiful name of May Rose.

The job was acquired for Marje by her father, who paid a
premium to one of his pub customers in the print trade, a
Mr Walker. Marje knew nothing about this money changing
hands and would have been pink with shame about it. But
she made her way to work on her first morning down Long
Lane in Aldersgate and through Smithfield meat market,
where she heard her first F-word from one of the porters
lugging huge carcasses. She didn't know what it meant
but it was evidently inoffensive and part of the normal
parlance of 'blokes'. Marje and the meat porters were soon
on cordial terms (Marje has always got on well with 'blokes')
and they would regale her with 'Fucking nice day, Marje,'
or 'Looks like it's genner fucking pour, dunnit Marje.'

In the midst of this proletarian hubbub was a small fashion studio over a butchers' supply merchants. 'It was called City Studios,' says Marje, 'and it was very grotty. The artist in charge was a rather mad-looking character, probably in her late thirties, smoking away.' This was the remarkable May Rose, and Marje thought her 'the most glamorous thing since Marlene Dietrich'. Her most striking features were a pudding-shaped hat – she had a colourful collection of felt sou'westers – vivid blue eye make-up and peroxide blonde curls. One of Marje's duties turned out to be bleaching her roots while she worked. May Rose ruled the studio with a rod of iron. There were four artists in an open-plan office with a partition that didn't quite reach the ceiling. Without warning May Rose would stand on a chair behind this partition and glare at her staff through the gap at the top. The habit struck terror into young Marje, who was only just finding her way in the art world.

> I wasn't considered to be an artist, just a messenger and odd-job girl. One of my jobs, apart from making tea and doing May's roots, was to clean up the drawings of the real artists. They would do their sketches first in pencil and then Indian ink them, and I had to rub out the pencil marks. I also had to pack and mount their work, and deliver the drawings to clothing manufacturers round the city, like the Brenner Brothers. Gradually I was allowed to do one or two drawings myself. The first I ever produced was of a baby in a woolly outfit and bootees that appeared in some catalogue or other.

Marje was paid a fee for the drawing of 5s. 6d., which compared favourably with her weekly wage of fifteen shillings. 'Of course I thought I was a genius then, and a success.' No one was prouder than Marje's mother. Mrs Rayle could now introduce her daughter as 'Marjorie, the artist', and this was a huge step forward in their relationship. As Marje says, 'I desperately wanted her approval.'

One of the other artists captivated Marje's imagination because he appeared to have plucked eyebrows. He was embroidering designs on a satin wedding dress. 'I was dumbstruck because I'd never ever imagined a man sewing. I'd grown up in pubs where the men were hard drinkers, and my father was a very very masculine man. But this young man was something again. I guess, looking back, that he was probably the first gay I ever met. I don't remember being embarrassed. I don't have any embarrassment about people's sexuality. He was a lovely man, very sweet and very feminine.' One day he advanced on Marje with some tweezers, saying, 'You've got very untidy eyebrows and I think they ought to be straightened out a bit.' Marje ended up with 'rather surprised' brows, similar to his.

Under May Rose's spell, Marje began to shovel on make-up, wear felt hats, swear and smoke heavily. She copied everything May did – 'You see, I had the kind of mother that a young girl wouldn't want to copy' – and became very arty-crafty, going to the theatre with May and following May's fashions, despite the fact that her inspiration was short and rounded and Marje was tall and svelte ('I did have a pretty good shape in those days'). The studio was very successful, but Marje wanted to do more with her life than rub out other people's pencil marks and have her eyebrows plucked. She was to remain lifelong friends with May Rose, but after a few months she decided to move on and freelance.

She heard of a studio for rent in Wine Office Court, off Fleet Street. It belonged to a lettering artist by the name of Bliss, and the accommodation turned out to be a tiny room at the top of a rickety staircase, with a desk, a table and a sooty hob. Just as well she didn't have to live there. The rent was 3s. 9d., and Mr Bliss, taking a shine to the determined young tenant sketching away in his garret, offered to act as her business manager. Soon she was introduced to an agent, Douglas Mount, who began to hawk Marje's growing portfolio of drawings round London for a 10 per cent commission. He got her some decent assignments: the *Daily Express*, the *Daily Mail* and women's magazines all used Marje's drawings, sometimes at 7s. 6d. a shot – more than enough to pay the rent. She was on her way.

In her leisure hours, though, Marje was still going nowhere. Mr Pogerelski had long since vanished and Jo, with whom Marje shared a bedroom, would sometimes come home late at night from her various dates and wake her sister up. Marje would sulk for days. To console herself she would read in bed. This infuriated Jo, who wanted the light out. Marje read all the more. Novels, George Bernard Shaw, H. G. Wells, the Brontës, poetry. Her favourite poem was Elizabeth Barrett Browning's heartbreakingly beautiful 'How do I love thee?' from her *Sonnets from the Portuguese*. She still keeps a copy of it in her handbag, and cannot read it without tears.

> How do I love thee? Let me count the ways.
> I love thee to the depth and breadth and height
> My soul can reach, when feeling out of sight
> For the ends of Being and ideal Grace.
> I love thee to the level of everyday's
> Most quiet need, by sun and candlelight.
> I love thee freely, as men strive for Right:
> I love thee purely, as they turn from Praise.
> I love thee with the passion put to use
> In my old griefs, and with my childhood's faith.
> I love thee with a love I seemed to lose

> With my lost saints – I love thee with the breath,
> Smiles, tears of all my life – and if God choose,
> I shall but love thee better after death.

One day, she would find someone for whom those words
were fit.

It wasn't a happy time for anyone Jewish in Britain,
because if they opened a newspaper they kept seeing the
name of Adolf Hitler, whose notions of racial purity had
gained considerable credence in the higher echelons of British society. In January 1934 even the *Daily Mirror* printed
an article, 'Give the Blackshirts a Helping Hand', signed
not by some political hack but by its press baron Lord
Rothermere. It ridiculed 'timid alarmists' who criticized
the activities of Oswald Mosley. Marje carefully steered
her imagination away from the Blackshirt drum marches
in the streets not far from the pub. She couldn't bear to
listen to the broadcasts of Mosley's massive London rallies,
and would rush to turn off the radio. She did not know
that Jo-jo was equally petrified, because her sister kept
her terror to herself. During the War, Jo was to see at their
local cinema the harrowing film footage of the liberation
of Belsen, which affected her so deeply that she became
desperate, unable to speak or sleep. Marje:

> I had no idea that Jo had these horrors, but I can tell you
> that I had them too. Still have. And I don't think there
> can be many Jews who have not been affected in some
> way or another, even Jews who have never been at the
> other end of prejudice. I think it's the fear of belonging
> to a minority. So that if you're Jewish, you're born to
> fear persecution. And in a curious way, you feel guilty
> about being Jewish, because you believe that so many
> of your Protestant and Catholic and non-Jewish friends
> hold you personally responsible for the death of Christ.

And it's a very basic guilt that not many Jews express. I've thought about it a lot because I'm analytical, and I believe that Jews always have this fear of persecution – of never feeling quite secure in life. I feel British to my bones: our first ancestor here was a Spanish doctor who settled in England in the 1600s, and one of my cousins traced our family tree. So I'm probably more 'English' than large numbers of English people who are second-generation Irish or Scots. And yet I still have this feeling that I'm a foreigner.

By now, the family were living over the Marquis of Lansdowne, on the corner of Arcola Street near Green Lanes, Stoke Newington. Marje and Jo had always played tennis in Clissold Park, and Marje was keen for them to join the Hillside Tennis Club at the top of Green Lanes, but Jo was now a secretary and her social life was busy. So Marje often had to go to the Hillside club on her own. Her mother was undoubtedly beginning to worry about Marje's wifely prospects. The family were not orthodox and there was no question of an arranged marriage, but matchmaking certainly went on in the Jewish community, the hope being that a daughter would marry Jewish and 'marry well'. Marje:

'Well' meant marrying somebody who could set the girl up in a three-bedroomed semi in Golders Green. And if they had two or three daughters and one was seen to be getting past her sell-by date, then they would try to do a bit of matchmaking. It would always be the women, who on the whole were manipulative and clever and researched the field pretty well. The men simply stood back from all this and let the women get on with it.

Marje's sell-by date having loomed fairly large, Mrs Rayle

was no doubt urging her elder daughter to eat up that last slice of bread at breakfast on Christmas morning 1934. Despite the freezing weather and a streaming cold in her nose, Marje fully intended to go to the Hillside Tennis Club and look for someone to give her a game.

Not surprisingly the place was as dead as a doornail. Gales blew small quantities of sleet across the courts, and whistled through the clubhouse. Hillside club members were sensibly lying abed, or stuffing their turkeys. Marje, the fool, was sitting disconsolately in her shorts, blowing her nose and staring at her reflection in the Coke bar, wondering if she should paint her glasses a brighter crimson to cheer herself up, when in walked another being, looking for bridge partners.

It was Sidney Proops. Marje had seen him before but never spoken. He was older than the other boys, with thick dark hair and a good set of whiskers like her father. He was beaky in the nose department, but not unpleasantly. Shorter than Marje, of course, but that didn't matter either. Marje didn't play bridge at the time, so she couldn't be of assistance cards-wise. Later on he would drum the game into her, and she would show him up with impulsive bids. He bought her a hot lemonade. They talked. He was a nice fellow, very genuine, very clear in his ideas, a humanist, a thinker. He considered Jesus of Nazareth to be the first socialist, and admired him very much. Despite being Jewish himself, he criticized his race for their part in Jesus's downfall.

Marje aired her own socialist principles and romantic notions, which he considered very attractive, and her long bare legs couldn't have done her any harm either. She made him laugh – she had always been a wag – and her very unusual style and character impressed him so decisively that he determined to marry the owner as soon as possible.

The pair discovered that they had both been invited to the same party, and Sidney offered to escort Marje to the bash. As she already knew a couple of Sidneys, she would call him 'Proopsie' to avoid confusion. For their first date Marje dressed up, without asking, in one of her sister's party frocks (after all, Jo pinched her boyfriends), and they had such fun stepping over the prone bodies ('the party was full of other kids necking like mad') and discussing politics that Proopsie took her next day to the pictures. One other date followed, and then after a long preamble, in which he summarized all his faults so that she would not be wooed under false pretences, Proopsie proposed. Marje said, 'I'll have to think about it. I'll let you know in two or three days.' She didn't want to fall off the tree into his basket. She also wanted to know how he voted – that was very important – and she stipulated that she would want to carry on with her career, married or no (Marje's mother always had 'help' around the house and Marje didn't care much for kitchen drudgery). Proopsie, waiving the conventions of the day, agreed that he would support her in everything she did, and being the sort of man he was, he meant it.

Three days later they were engaged. Marje's cold had turned chesty, and her mother was liberally rubbing in the Vick when Marje made her shock announcement.

'I'm engaged, Mother.'

'Drink that milk before it gets cold,' said Mrs Rayle, rubbing more fiercely.

'To Sidney, Mother. You know, Sidney Proops'.

Proopsie had not been invited in prior to the engagement for fear of Jo-jo's allure, but Mrs Rayle knew who he was.

'I expect it's pneumonia. Fancy going to play tennis in this weather. You'll worry me to death, you and your father.'

'Sidney's asked me to marry him, and I've said yes.'

'I'll leave the Vick by the bed. Breathe deeply, dear, and get the vapours.'

When the news finally broke over Mrs Rayle's bows, she took a very dim view indeed of Sidney Proops's ancestry. Despite being Jewish, he was 'marked down as Dutch'. Marje explains:

> There was this extraordinary snobbishness on my mother's side of the family [the side that arrived in Britain in the 1660s]. My father's family was of course disregarded in this, but my mother's people were Sephardic Jews. Which meant, I think, that they originally emanated from Europe, and that they were mostly Spanish or French. They undoubtedly regarded themselves as socially superior on this account. They were snobs. My mother would have had kittens if either myself or my sister had taken home for her approval, say, a Polak – that means a Jew, however good, decent, intelligent and nice, who happened to emanate from Poland or any part of Eastern Europe. He would be quite beyond the pale. Mr Pogerelski would have stood absolutely no chance!
>
> Now my mother wanted to know, from very very early on in the game, where Proopsie's family came from. And I had to find out. And it was pretty plain that they came from Holland: Proops is a Dutch name. Proopsie's mother's maiden name was De Jongh, and there were Van Gelders and a few De Jongh cousins knocking about as well. So he was on the fringe. He wasn't quite up to scratch. Jo-jo and I used to fall about laughing over this, of course. We thought it was hilarious.

Another worry for poor Mrs Rayle. True, Proopsie had the most charming parents, Joe and Dinah. But they had a draper's shop in King Henry's Walk and a little stall in Ridley Road market, and Proopsie was very proud of his father's business endeavours. Mrs Rayle would have advised them, if they'd asked her, to lie about this, and say Proops Senior ran Harrods or something. But they didn't ask. Well, they wouldn't, being of Dutch descent. You can't teach blood.

By strange irony, one that was to cast a shadow over Marje's marriage, Proopsie's family were in fact extremely strict and traditional in their proprieties. His son Robert would one day learn just how fierce and strict. Robert Proops:

> My father came from an old Dutch Jewish family, a strong, patriarchal community run with a rod of iron from generations past, where there was a Head of the Family – not just of the nuclear family but of the whole family group. He was almighty in this situation, and he was called Uncle Sam. My father had to show Uncle Sam the ring before my mother saw it. And if Uncle Sam approved, he could show it to my mother. It was a very interesting psychological structure, one that broke down totally as my parents' generation grew up. But for my father, it never broke down. It's odd, because in many ways to the outside world, my parents were the ultra-modern couple. But their roots were somewhere else, particularly my father's. He believed in the old Head of the Family tradition, and he saw himself eventually taking on that role.

It was Proopsie's misfortune that he was a liberal man, saddled with these deep patriarchal beliefs. Marje was to find in him an honourable, honest, caring husband – and, when crossed, a tyrant.

3

Worse Than Death in Bournemouth

arje's generation believed that marriages had 'made in Heaven' stamped on their bottoms. Many newlyweds reeled in shock when all they got was the do-it-yourself kit. These days we are generally less romantic, or less daft. If a young woman wrote to Marje now and said that she was getting engaged to a man she had known for just three days, the World's Greatest Advice Columnist would tell the girl she was barking mad, and to find out more about the intentions of her intended. But Marje had to learn the hard way.

Her mother warned her, goodness knows. Mrs Rayle considered Marje was marrying beneath her, and would drag her own family's seventeenth-century Spanish doctor-ancestor into the conversation at every opportunity. Nobody was good enough for either of her girls, least of all Dutch stock with a haberdashery stall. Now, this Sidney Proops was in his twenties and apparently in the building trade. He'd started with Bovis at sixteen making tea in a bucket for the painters, and was now doing estimating and going to evening classes to get engineering qualifications. He hadn't got them yet, mind you. These things had to be thought through. How would Marjorie manage her home? She did housework with a bad grace if she did it at all, and couldn't boil water. Aunt Lilian, or cook, or the parlourmaid had always been on tap to do chores. And Marjorie wouldn't have a modest flat over a pub like her poor mother; oh no. She was going to live in a mortgaged three-bedroomed semi in Dunstan Road, Golders Green, like a regular Jewish housewife. Oh well. At least this Sidney hadn't got horns or two heads. Perhaps they'd be all right. Mrs Rayle bit her lip and hoped for the best.

All the couple's wooing took place at the Marquis of Lansdowne in Stoke Newington – despite their socialist principles, in the saloon bar. They talked about politics and religion. Proopsie wasn't in the least embarrassed about the prospect of having a wife going out to work; he was proud of her talents and wanted to foster her career. But he was a devout atheist, whereas Marje likes to keep all her options open ('I think he thought that I was a bit lily-livered,' says Marje).

They discussed socialism – a key issue for them both. Marje was devoted to fundamental Labour Party ideals. Proopsie said Marje was 'a sentimental socialist': one who felt sorry for dustmen and people who didn't need her pity. Proopsie was too busy trying to find ways to put his beliefs into practice to worry about leaving tearstains on the dustbin. He could be very fierce. Many years later, when Marje was a famous columnist, the pair were at an informal reception at Buckingham Palace, and to Marje's horror Proopsie got into a heated gesticulating row with Prince Philip about the ethics of selling off land belonging to a housing charity, and would not shut up. Next time Prince Philip saw Marje, he greeted her cordially: 'And how's that bloody argumentative husband of yours?'

Sentimental socialist Marje may have been, but being a socialist of any description was considered very queer indeed in the Rayle household. Her parents and her sister, Tories to the bone, did not like to hear Marje

discussing such topics as she flashed her pearl and diamond engagement ring. Neither did friends or cousins,
preoccupied with make-up, marriage and men. 'Most of
my middle-class friends weren't the least bit interested,
and thought it was utter crap,' recalls Marje. Her cousin
Cissie Lewis, a *Telegraph* reader, explains:

> My brother was a socialist. I can't think why. I didn't
> have any political leanings in those days and I don't
> suppose I thought much about it. But some of his
> friends called my brother the Red Dog or the Old
> Red Bull. You see, we were all very English. I don't
> know why my brother and Marje started thinking
> about socialism. Perhaps it was because the politics
> of the country began to worry them. Because Jewish
> people between the two wars, until we were thrust
> into this other dreadful war, I don't think were really
> political creatures. I suppose we lived a very sheltered
> life, with family get-togethers where we ate smoked
> salmon and had maids. When Aunt Martha used to
> find someone in the pub to run up half a dozen
> dresses, we all used to laugh about it. My generation
> knew nothing about our parents' financial affairs. We
> were never concerned about money. Money never came
> into it.

Stories that Marje was a 'wartime teenage bride' have
appeared in print in various articles, one or two of them
claiming to quote from the horse's mouth. This myth is
wholly without foundation, and one suspects it got about
through confusion over the lady's age, which Marje has
been careful to encourage. Marje and Proopsie were in
fact married out of the pub on a grey 21 November
1935. Marje joked that the Marquis of Lansdowne was
coming to give her away, but he proved unavailable.

She was done up, no doubt under mother's influence, in orange blossom and billowing tulle and satin. She was about to put on her heavy tortoiseshell glasses but thought better of it and left them on the dressing table – 'hideous things'.

We got married at Shacklewell Lane synagogue in Dalston, in traditional style to please our parents, though even they weren't the slightest bit orthodox. I don't remember us ever going into a synagogue to pray. But we would go there for ceremonies like weddings. I think that both my parents and Proopsie's, like many other Jewish families at that time, were more superstitious than religious. It was like throwing salt over your shoulder to get married in the synagogue – known as 'schule' in the vernacular. I believe the synagogue where we married is now a mosque. At any rate we had the traditional bridal canopy, and the glass wrapped in paper or cloth which the bridegroom stamps on at the end of the ceremony for luck. He's supposed to splinter it and crush it at the first blow, and I think that if you cock it up and have to have two goes, your luck is uncertain. But Proopsie did get it in one blow, which just goes to show what a nonsense it is, because he didn't have much luck.

The peering bride managed to manoeuvre up and down the aisle without mishap – 'taking the serious risk of marrying the wrong chap' – though signing the register proved a touch challenging. Everyone remarked that she took the ceremony very seriously. She was in fact studying Proopsie's new haircut and wondering whether kippers should be boiled or fried. She was filled with gratitude to Proopsie for not having preferred Jo-jo when he met her, and was determined to honour and obey:

After the register was signed, we got into the leading bridal car and the procession moved off towards
the reception, to be held at Monnickendam's catering
establishment in Victoria Street – the site is now a block
of flats. And there I sat in my bridal finery, white gown,
big bouquet and with this new ring on my finger, and
when we got to Trafalgar Square, just ahead of us, two
cars crashed. And there was a hoo-ha and noise, and
Proops immediately leapt out of the car in his top hat
and morning suit and strode towards the scene, leaving
me on my own in the bridal car.

A taxi drew up alongside and a man got out of the
cab and put his head through the window. 'Are you
all right? Not hurt or anything?' he asked. I said no,
no, I was fine. And he got in the car and sat there
talking to me – he didn't hold my hand so far as I can
remember, though I dare say I was a bit disappointed
– until Proopsie had clearly got it all sorted out. And
this was the first demonstration I had of Proopsie taking
charge of something that was nothing to do with him at
all. And that was very much the sort of man he was. He
took charge of everything all his life, including me. In
his own little sphere of operations, he was a law-maker,
and expected people to conform to his rules. I was really
quite frightened of him.

The honeymoon spot was Bournemouth – in November.
This unusual choice was a result of the bride's attitude to
aeroplanes: she would sooner fight two sabre-tooth tigers
and swim round the world than fly. The trip was in any
case foredoomed. The couple had spent nearly a year
discussing their social and political leanings but had never
mentioned sex. Pre-marital experimentation was out of the
question. Proopsie, if he knew anything, was not letting
on, and Marje knew damn all about such practices. Her

mother had never breathed naughty words: Marje thinks that Mrs Rayle was the sort of woman for whom sex was a duty to be endured with her eyes closed. And to cap it all, Marje now developed an itchy nervous rash, requiring the application of an evil-smelling lotion.

Marje's new husband, faced with this stink-embalmed, shy, spotty and scratching bedfellow, was not himself the most sensitive of lovers. His main concern during the trip seemed to be ringing the office every day. For Marje, with her head full of romantic hopes and dreams, their new sex life was upsetting and shocking, more like being tortured than made love to. The horror of it was to give her powerful insight and compassion when she eventually came to advise on other people's sexual miseries. No prissiness on the part of her biographer should pretty up Marje's experience:

I didn't honestly know what to expect. Technically I was a virgin, and knew nothing about sex. I'd readily co-operated with fumbling boys who got under my bra and into my knickers, but I was virgo-intacta on my wedding night. In fact I thought my body was rather disgusting and horrible. These days, of course, girls experiment when they are much younger, so that the bodies of boys they have a relationship with aren't so mysterious. For me it wasn't like that. When it got to bedtime, I was confronted by this great big ugly penis which terrified the life out of me when I saw it. And Proops was dressing it up with a condom before pushing it into me. It was a tremendous intrusion, and it was frightening, disagreeable.

And I think that if you are introduced to sex like this, you feel from very early on that you are victimized. You don't think about it as a man loving and wanting you, and needing to express that love in a physical way, and

needing yourself to express love for him; you literally do
lie there and think of England. Or think of something,
anything, other than what is happening to you. The
whole thing was such a hideous and very very painful
experience. And it really did hurt terribly every time.
He continued to use this condom for quite a long while
until in the end it became obvious even to him that I
was finding it unbearable and unendurable.

Proopsie eventually discovered a woman gynaecologist,
Dr Helena Wright, who specialized in the latest contraceptive devices. Marje was prescribed the precursor of the
coil. It was a bowl-shaped object, made of rubber, and had
a hard rim which the wearer was required to pinch together
before insertion. Marje: 'Looking back, I don't know which
was worse: having to look at this penis being dressed or
having to put the ring inside myself. You inserted it when
you went to bed, sighing with resignation at the thought
that this was what you'd got to endure, and then you
removed it and washed it in the morning, powdered it
and put it in a little box. I used to be so relieved when
my period arrived so that I'd have a few days of glorious
freedom.'
  The device helped both as a contraceptive and a painkiller, and Marje endured her connubial duties for a long
time like this, without complaint. Fortunately for her,
Proopsie appeared to have a low sex-drive. 'He preferred
bridge to bonking. That's why during our long marriage he
never looked elsewhere. He'd rather have dug the garden.'
He knew nothing about his new wife's sexuality. Every
month she would have to conceal the 'little secret' of her
menstrual cycle, hiding her sanitary towels so as not to
offend or embarrass her husband. It was not done for a
young woman from Marje's background to allow a man
to contemplate this odious business. It was considered

unclean. Childbirth was another such mystery that happened to women. Marje thinks that if Proopsie had been present at the birth of their son in 1941, he would have run screaming from the room, or fainted dead away.

Out of bed, married life was more pleasant. She gradually found out the rudiments of housewifery – such as whether you put peas in cold or boiling water – not from her mother, but from her much more relaxed and forthcoming mother-in-law, Dinah, a former schoolteacher. Marje loved her in-laws like a daughter and keenly visited their little parlour over the haberdasher's shop ('It rang with laughter and merriment'). She thought the Rayles were lucky to know such fine people, and she made a lifelong friend of Proopsie's sister Queenie, a linguist. 'In fact the Proopses were far superior when it came to grey matter, so my mother should have been very thankful to Proops that he was prepared to marry beneath him, in terms of what goes between the ears.'

On the career front, she continued to rent her tiny studio in Wine Office Court, where until early in 1939 she did knitting illustrations and fashion drawings and paid 10 per cent to Douglas Mount to secure her commissions. Marje would produce what were known as 'specimens' ('not in a bottle'), and Mount would put them in a portfolio and tout them around London. She even submitted small items of prose to the women's page of the *Jewish Chronicle*, based on her ongoing political and social talks with Proopsie, though she never considered herself to be a writer.

Apart from society and politics, Proopsie and Marje were also discussing their feelings for each other. Marje wanted to know why Proopsie chose her from the bunch when he could have had someone much prettier and much more well-groomed. Proopsie said, 'You were the girl I wanted to marry.' 'But why me?' probed Marje. Proopsie answered simply: 'You were the one that I wanted. You were the one

I could talk to.' Marje herself certainly never analysed what she was looking for in a husband, but she was well content with Proopsie's sterling character:

> He was very very definitely a man of the highest moral standards. I never knew him to cheat or lie. Despite being an atheist, he was in a funny way more religious than many believers – in so far as being religious means being kind to your neighbours and leading an honourable life, and doing your best for other people in less fortunate circumstances. He was the epitome of such a man. His main fault was his temper – he was bad-tempered and irritable, and more so when he got older. And he interfered. He interfered with everybody, and had this rather godlike view of himself, that he knew better than everybody else, including me. And particularly me.

Proopsie, the know-all, was studying for his engineering degrees alongside his full-time job at Bovis. Despite having left school with not a skill to his name and worked his way up in the building trade from painters' tea-boy, he now set out to qualify in construction engineering and electrical engineering, and to become an MIHVE (Member of the Institute of Heating and Ventilating Engineers), an FIOB (Fellow of the Institute of Builders), an MRSANI (Member of the Royal Sanitary Institute), and later on an MBIM (Member of the British Institute of Management). It was the best he could do in the circumstances. His dream had been to become an architect. Marje remembers vividly the iron determination of the man, and also the growing sense of fear with which she now regarded him:

> He continued to study at home after our marriage. I

used to have to sit in our parlour in Golders Green, when we'd got our statutory suburban three-bedroomed stucco-fronted semi with mock-Tudor beams, in complete silence. I was not allowed to open a newspaper because the rustling disturbed and distracted him. We didn't have television then, but I wasn't even allowed to listen to the radio. I was mad about jazz, but I couldn't listen to records because he was studying. I used to creep about like a mouse. If I made a sound he would look up and frown at me and say 'Sshh!'

Proopsie was clearly in command at 65 Dunstan Road. Though their home had the unusual 1930s luxury of partial central heating, he liked the bedroom window open, even in the snow, and no hot-water bottle. Marje sometimes had two. Perhaps in an effort to keep warm she was already lighting up forty Senior Service a day, and Proopsie resented the fug that this caused in the bedroom. He himself was a pipe man, and more meticulous about his smoke. Proopsie, a sturdy Taurus, never did anything without a Proper Plan (his proposal of marriage was the only impulsive thing his wife ever remembers him doing). Marje was more flash-bang, a passionate Leo. However, they both loved animals. Marje's family had favoured fuzzy-faced wire-haired terriers, but the newlyweds' very first dog was a wild, mad, shiny black mongrel called Jock, who was very frisky and playful, and who once showed Marje up by plunging into the synagogue along Dunstan Road and racing about during a service. As time went on, the family would adopt all manner of dogs, cats and other creatures and cherish the lot of them.

The couple had an affinity, too, about something else. Proopsie was deeply ashamed and miserable about his large hooter. Marje:

Much as I detested everything about my looks, he detested his nose. From the very early part of our marriage he talked about having his nose fixed. He hated it so. But he was horrified at the thought of a nose job and wouldn't have surgery. I wish he had, for many many reasons; professionally he would have been more confident. I think it affected him all his life. He endured it, but I know he hated it. I never quite knew why, either, because Proopsie had secrets not just from me, but from himself, and I don't think he could admit to the feeling of inferiority that it gave him.

Being nasally handicapped did not affect Proopsie's confidence in running the marriage. One of his requirements was that Marje should immediately learn to play bridge. He was very devout about bridge, and exceptionally good at it. Marje would learn to play and they would make up a foursome with another young married couple, Proopsie decided. There was no question of Proopsie discovering Marje's hobbies and taking an interest in those. Marje would be taught to share his interests. 'The warning bells should have rung from that very first meeting,' says Marje. 'Proopsie and his bridge friends took it all very seriously: he would sit there pondering and working it all out.' Marje's reaction was to bid from the gut, whereupon Proopsie would fly into a fury, and lecture Marje on how important and serious it was. Marje would say, 'Well, it's only a game, dammit!' Nevertheless, bridge became quite an important part of their lives right up until Proopsie died.

Marje was prepared to struggle along at cooking when she came home from sketching assignments at her studio, with the help of recipe books and the appropriately named Dinah. Proopsie regarded kitchen duties as loathsome chores. Marje:

Although he was very good later on, he was completely undomesticated at that time of our lives and he was very spoiled by his mother, who used to pick up after him. And when he married me he used to step out of his underpants and leave them on the floor. I used to step over them. It took me a long, long time to get him round to the idea that it was not unmasculine to dry up a cup and saucer and help. He assumed this was what all women did. And this assumption remains today, really, despite all this nonsense about equality – that only happens in very small pockets of middle-class upwardly mobile society. The huge majority of the people in this country still have the same attitude that Proopsie had all those years ago, and that Proopsie's mother had, and my mother had. My mother was quite shocked about my efforts to domesticate Proops.

An interesting sidelight on the Home Front in the war of the sexes comes from ninety-year-old romance queen Dame Barbara Cartland:

I've known Marjorie for many, many years and I think she's marvellous because she tries to make people happy. But I've always been amused by the fact that Marjorie's husband was expected to share the house-work, and as you know, I've always disapproved of that! Husbands should not have to cope with such things as housework. Not even if the wife goes out to work, no. It's a case of making enough fuss of your husband. You have to look after him and make him feel masculine and keep saying 'You're wonderful.' If you constantly tell him how wonderful he is, you'll never lose your husband.

Proopsie, by this reckoning, was cruelly put upon, with

all his building work and engineering studies to do. But gradually he began to help a little around the house, and a succession of au pairs and housekeepers eased the couple's workload. Marje fully intended to pursue her career, and on this one issue of housewifery she would not submit. She had warned him when he proposed. 'I simply could not end up being a good little Jewish housewife. I could not have settled for such a life.' Proopsie bore all, and smoked his pipe. He shone at the more masculine tasks. Gardening he loved. Marje could never get his nose out of a new seed catalogue. And as Marje's career flourished, Proopsie defied all convention and supported her to the hilt, as he had promised to do before their wedding.

It is interesting, considering Marje's later reputation as a placard-waving feminist, that like many liberated women she secretly longed to follow the Cartland Code, and that in fact she obeyed, awe-inspired, just about every important man who entered her life, from her father onwards. Proopsie was one of these leading men:

He was a terrific organizer. He organized my life, and when our son was born, he organized his as well. He was very, very protective towards me, and very possessive. He never lost these qualities that I valued and loved about him. He was the sort of man who took charge. I am a feminist and I have always been very active indeed campaigning for a better deal for women. Nevertheless, Proopsie directed my life, and I let him! It wasn't that I *admired* it, so much as I *needed* it. It was a cop-out, it really was, not having to make the decisions. But I was grateful for it. I was grateful to have a man to look after me. I wasn't a strong-minded girl. I was only strong at my job. When I got home to Proopsie, I'll always be grateful for the fact that he took charge. Grateful all my life.

Anything presumably, rather than end up like those lonely Guinness Girls.

Marje and Proopsie knew that war was imminent and the young Mrs Proops felt a sense of urgency about having a child while they could. Proopsie was more circumspect. Chamberlain was proudly rattling the piece of paper on which he had obtained the world-famous Adolf Hitler's autograph, but no Jew living in London woke up in the mornings without a sense of foreboding. Proopsie, if not the world's greatest lover or dishwasher, was a highly principled person and told his wife that if war broke out, he intended to volunteer for army service. Jewish refugees were flocking to England from Germany, and Proopsie wanted to strike back at the Nazis with his own hands. He felt that this was his duty as a British Jew. Soon after the outbreak of war, Proopsie qualified as an engineer with letters after his name, and since he was in what was known as a 'reserved occupation', there would be no question of his being called up. He would go of his own accord.

Early in 1939, as these black war clouds were gathering on the horizon, Marje was doing a rush sketching job at her wobbly desk in Wine Office Court, when she got a call from her agent. Douglas Mount was at the *Daily Mirror*. Said Mount, 'You're to come here right away.' Marje, expecting to sit all day sketching, was wearing a manufacturers' give-away porridge-coloured suit miles too big for her, with a jacket that bagged at the back ('It made me look as if I had a huge great bum'). She was covered in ink, doing these very urgent drawings. Marje explained to her agent that she couldn't possibly go just at the moment. Mount said, 'Come here, whether you're covered in ink or not.'

Marje rushed as instructed to the office of the woman's page editor, Esme Zelger, where the perfectly groomed

Miss Zelger sat leafing calmly through Marje's portfolio. She liked Marje's work so much that she was going to show it to the features editor, and disappeared from the room. Marje rubbed at her ink-blackened fingers. She hoped they would ask her to do a fashion drawing in the *Daily Mirror*. She also hoped that her bum didn't look too enormous in this suit. At last the door flew open and in walked Ms Zelger with a 'terrifying-looking' man. He had a jutting chin, a shock of wavy hair driven back off his forehead and gimlet eyes, with which he examined Marje ferociously. He then strode towards her portfolio and scanned her work.

'Are these your drawings?'

'Yes.'

'Walk across the room.'

Marje dragged her porridge-suited body up and down as elegantly as she could.

'Do you think you could represent the *Daily Mirror* at Ascot?'

Marje thought of her father all dandied up at the racetrack. She knew Ascot was a racetrack.

'Of course, yes.'

'Start on Monday,' said the man. And out he went.

And that was how Marje came to work for the great Hugh Cudlipp.

4

War Work

The *Daily Mirror* in 1939, when Marje first caught the steely gaze of Hugh Cudlipp, was a far cry from the newspaper appearing under that name today. To understand how Marje felt about it at the time, we need to know a little about the paper's past.

The *Daily Mirror* (i.e., 'the daily looking-glass') was originally launched as an idle rich ladies' journal in 1903. Lord Northcliffe, whose simply topping wheeze this was, had set it up in a building like a wedding cake in Fetter Lane, called 'Geraldine House' after his mother. The paper was such a fiasco, and Northcliffe was so badly scorched by the experience, that he said he had learned two things: 'That women can't write, and don't want to read.' Relaunched along more commercial lines as an illustrated daily for both sexes, it meandered half-cut about the political landscape for thirty years, flirting with fascism, arguing against the granting of votes to women, and boldly going where most other papers had gone before under the guidance of Northcliffe's brother, the first Lord Rothermere.

Two men commandeered this wandering journal and turned it into a trendsetting, plain-speaking, notorious, mass-circulation, campaigning socialist newspaper, one that championed ordinary people and was adopted by

Britain's rank-and-file servicemen and women during the
war. The first of the *Daily Mirror's* commandants was
Harry Guy Bartholomew, a hard-driving, hard-swearing
newsman who believed in pictures and as few words as
possible, some of them printed in heavy black type. He was
too busy getting his 'human interest', crime and sex stories
to worry about politics. 'Bart' was editorial director in 1934
and became chairman in 1944. Marje was given the job of
'resident fashion artist' midway through his blaspheming
rise to power.

The other mover and shaker was Hugh Cudlipp, now
Lord Cudlipp, often referred to as the greatest tabloid
editor Fleet Street ever saw. One of three gifted newspaper-
editing Welsh brothers, Cudlipp was twenty-one when he
joined the *Mirror* in 1935 as features editor. In 1937, two
years before Marje met him, he had become the youngest-
ever editor of a national newspaper (the *Sunday Pictorial*,
now the *Sunday Mirror*). His role on the *Daily Mirror* was to
get hold of news and injustices, and to hit people with them
as hard and as sensationally as possible. He had a brilliant
'nose' and didn't mind who he upset – Churchill once tried
to get the paper banned. Cudlipp was the man behind what
is probably the most famous front page ever to appear. It
was aimed at bellicose Soviet premier Khrushchev during
the 1960 Paris Summit, and it said, in mammoth type, 'MR
K: DON'T BE SO BLOODY RUDE. Who do you think you
are – Stalin?' There wasn't any copy to follow. That was it.

There were various other VIPs in the building when
Marje got her job: the tall and aloof future chairman, Cecil
King; the scowling literary genius Cassandra; the scathing
cartoonist Philip Zec; the flame-haired Forces correspondent Barbara Castle; even the strip-cartoon 'Jane' lurked in
the corridors somewhere, peeling her clothes off as usual.
But Marje's career at the *Mirror* would chiefly depend on
one man: Hugh Cudlipp. 'He invented me,' she says now.

And in those early days she was on far from familiar terms with her inventor. If she was unlucky enough to meet him in the corridor she would scuttle past, eyes averted, 'And I never lost my awe of him.'

Cudlipp didn't in fact send her to cover Ascot as implied at their first meeting. He decided instead, with Esme Zelger, that the new fashion artist should go to Paris, sketching hats. In the meantime she could illustrate pieces at home, starting with one on low-budget fashion to be written by Kathleen Pearcey. And another thing. Marje could not possibly sign her fashion drawings 'Marjorie Proops', either. He would think of something more suitable.

The first sketch Marje did for the *Mirror* appeared on 4 September 1939 in a piece headed, 'That's the way your money goes!' It carries a drawing of a blonde (Jo-jo?) in a tight-waisted coat with buttons aligned in a 'V', and with black astrakhan hat, collar and vast muff to match, a 'dream' outfit most women readers could not afford. The drawing is signed 'Silvaine'. Marje blenched when she saw the name. 'I was horrified. It made me sound like a flower shop and I hated it.' Still, at least it was the right sex. William Neil Connor was saddled with 'Cassandra', after the ancient Greek prophetess ('I've got an idea Hugh was responsible for that, too').

Marje was scuttling down the corridor one day, hoping to avoid her mentor, when she noticed Cassandra's door ajar. Through the crack she could make out the great columnist, who kept a harmonium in his office, wrote acid bath articles, and whose glance could turn small journalists to stone. He had his feet up on a stool and appeared to be in pain.

Now, Marje had to make a decision here. She could either walk past and never find out anything – which is what her timid mother would have done – or else she could be a gambler like her father, and radiate friendliness towards

all and sundry. True, you might get hurt or humiliated,
but the reward for such conduct, if successful, would be
the one Marje craved the most: to be liked, and confided in,
and needed. So there was really only one choice. She would
see if she could remove the thorn from the lion's paw. She
would try to help (she would *always* try to help). She stuck
her head round Cassandra's door:

My first impression was one of terror. I was just the kid
with a desk in the office next door, meeting somebody
hugely important. But I asked him with great temerity
if he'd got some trouble with his feet, and he told me
that he had gout. He said that some days the pain was
bearable and some days it wasn't. And then I realized.
When he was in great pain with his gout, he wrote those
savagely bad-tempered articles. The classic was when
the war was over, and he began his column, 'As I was
saying when I was rudely interrupted . . .' I don't know
whether he was an irascible man anyway: I didn't know
him well enough, because he was way up and I was on
the ground. But when I look back on it now, I see that one
of the reasons for his irascibility was the pain he was in.

I don't think many people were aware of this. Journalists have this rather strange tunnel vision. I think it's
partly to do with training: you home in on somebody
when you're interviewing them and you think about
nothing else except that person: what you know about
them, what you've read up about them, what you're
going to get out of them. But things can be happening
all around that you don't even notice. So in a curious kind
of way I would say that the journalists I've known don't
seem to have much curiosity about life, about people,
about anything other than their job, which they home
in on. They're very single-minded about that. It's a very
tight, narrow little world.

Marje would not be narrow; she would be caring, and curious. And as a result of this encounter, the great Cassandra seemed to take a shine to Marje. Somehow he found out that her first name was Rebecca, which he thought very beautiful, and he would say, 'Rebecca, let us go for a jug!' – a jug in this instance being a jug of orange juice, or perhaps a cider: Marje has never been a drinker.

Marje went to Paris as assigned, though her proud mother must have had blackouts at the thought of such travel. Marje wasn't much more confident, but she negotiated the ferry and the French francs, and even managed to order herself meals in restaurants without starting an international incident. She discovered a white wine called Sylvaner, sketched twenty-two mad hats in snobby couturiers' salons and sent the drawings back by airmail. Particularly nerve-racking, to a girl who had never been anywhere grander than Sainsburys, was going into the deep-carpeted and chandeliered salon of sensational milliner Erik, where Marje's entire wages wouldn't have bought so much as a pillbox. When she earned more, she would begin to collect the sort of creations she saw there. In any case she came back to London feeling more like a real fashion artist.

Cudlipp liked her hats. He and Esme Zelger decided that 'Silvaine' was ready to tackle a new challenge. She would go to America with Miss Zelger and sketch things to do with the World Fair. Now, Marje had not been on a bus until she was sixteen, and she explained to her boss that she was a bit worried about the flying – well, she was sick with terror as a matter of fact. Cudlipp, whose ferocious aspect concealed a pitying heart, said very well, they would fly there, for speed, and sail back. Indeed, so protective was he of his new protégée that he would allow her to do this on all her trips, no matter what extra cost to the *Mirror*. Marje says she would sometimes be in transit for weeks coming back from places like Australia, with berserk news editors shouting 'Where the fuck is she?'

How Marje managed her first flight she doesn't know, or wish to recall. She doesn't even like to get out of her seat whilst airborne, in case the imbalance causes the plane to crash.

Unfortunately, whilst in New York, Marje the fashion artist, who had been getting on so well at her job and learning not to look down on herself, suffered the indignity of being given a tough assignment for which she had no training. This was an interview with the actor and film star Frederic March, who at the time was sticking on his false eyelashes in his Broadway dressing room. The man was so rude, and so cruelly dismissive of the inexperienced young woman's questions, that Marje panicked. She came away with very little, other than a hatred of Frederic March, and began to wonder if she was cut out for this newspaper lark after all. When Marje and Miss Zelger sailed back to London just after the outbreak of war, it took Hugh Cudlipp to restore her self-esteem. He paid attention to her talent. He said she was 'perceptive'. He believed she had great potential. He told her years later 'that I had certain qualities that he knew would make me significant in some way or another'. And when Cudlipp sensed such glimmers in a journalist, he burnished them until they shone.

Because of the imminent threat of war, Cudlipp was obliged to lay off his fashion artist. There was nothing much new to sketch except gas-masks. But to demonstrate his faith in her he paid her a retainer of six guineas a week not to work for another newspaper (she could freelance for magazines). He also gave Marje three pieces of advice about being a journalist, which she has tried faithfully to follow ever since. First, never use a three-syllable word when a two-syllable word will do. If possible use a one-syllable word. Second, if you *must* use a cliché, rewrite it. Third, and most important: never tell anyone your age. Marje:

> This was the most extraordinary thing to say to somebody as young as I was, and I was mystified and asked him why. He said, 'Because one day I believe your name will be in the record books and in the cuttings, and you'll reach the age of sixty when you will still be young for your age because of your energy and your determination and enthusiasm, and you will not want to retire and go home and put your feet up. You'll want to go on working. And if you've let them know your age and you're on somebody's payroll, you won't be able to. You'll have to give up whatever job you're doing.'

Marje has kept her age a closely guarded secret ever since. You won't find it in *Who's Who*. She will not even tell passport or hospital officials without a fight. She has told me, but only because I'd found out already, and my lips are sealed – careless talk costs lives. What is still more extraordinary is that Marje even goes to some lengths to conceal the ages of other people. 'When I was finally a reporter, I was always in trouble with the news editor because I would go and interview somebody and come back and do my piece, and he'd say, "What was the age of this person?" "I don't know," I'd say. "I never asked." I've always thought dates are irrelevant.'

No doubt Marje was following the Cudlipp canon here. No doubt, too, she is concerned to relate to her readers of all ages, and doesn't want to appear 'an old trout'. But her son Robert thinks there's a deeper explanation. He says simply, 'My mother has always been totally afraid of death and of advancing years.'

At home in Golders Green, Proopsie was planning to put his life on the line against the Third Reich. Mosley's black-uniformed army was goose-stepping up and down the London streets, occasionally set upon by offended Jewish citizens, and the atmosphere was very ugly. Marje was much more afraid of Mosley's rabble-rousing than of air raids – bombs, like accidents, were rather unreal things that befell other people. But Mosley and his troops were real. His crowd-pulling speeches in Trafalgar Square were real. His persuasive hatred and intelligence were real. His appeals to unite Britain with Nazi Germany and cleanse it of its foreign blood were real. And Marje, who hated no one, other than rude and cruel film stars, withered in the blast.

The *Daily Mirror*, on 4 September 1939, published an article which Marje still keeps in a carrier bag full of important cuttings: 'Battle Cry to Jewry'. It refers to the New Zionist Organization with an important message for Britain's Jews: 'A brutal enemy threatens Poland, heart of the Jewish Diaspora for nearly 1,000 years, where over three million Jews dwell in loyalty to the Polish land and nation . . . England has decided to make that fight her own, and we Jews shall, besides, never forget that for twenty years until recently England has been our partner in Zion. The Jewish nation's place is therefore on all fronts where these countries fight for those very foundations of [a] society whose Magna Carta is our Bible.'

Proopsie signed up for the Royal Engineers, and was quickly dispatched to the Midlands, either by Bovis or the army, on military construction and engineering assignments. In 1942 he would go on active service, entering the ranks as a second lieutenant because of his distinguished engineering qualifications, but for the moment he toured the Five Towns, helping to build munitions factories and other top-secret installations. He came home at weekends, but Marje missed him terribly.

She longed to have a child now more urgently than ever, and had stopped using her rubber contraceptive device for quite some time. She had begun to feel a failure at sex even for procreational purposes, though Proopsie's low sex drive undoubtedly made things more difficult. 'When we made this decision to have a baby, we airily assumed that we'd go to bed that night and the following morning I'd be pregnant. Not realizing that it wasn't going to happen. And then sex was even more awful than before, because it became Sex With a Purpose. And I simply felt like a vessel, a breeding machine.' She didn't attempt to dissuade Proopsie from joining up. She admired him, and besides, 'He was so positive and bossy. Once he said he was going to do something, that was it. There was never any question of holding committee meetings about it.'

Marje decided to do her bit by becoming an air-raid warden. There was a shelter in the park just behind their house and she was put in charge of it, keeping a ladder at the bottom of the garden. Marje: 'My job was to herd these citizens down into the air-raid shelter and stand outside the entrance, and if I saw any stray passers-by, I was to garner them up and suck them into the shelter with everybody else. I used to wait outside for the bombs to drop, wearing this horrible tin helmet at a very rakish angle.'

Marje has never liked living alone, and with Royal Engineer Proopsie away in the Midlands, she was miserable. There was only one thing to do: become a camp follower. So Marje let the house in Golders Green, and packed bag and baggage to follow Proopsie on his assignments. The towns were often depressing dumps but Marje would rent cheap rooms or lodgings near the site and attempt to earn a living as a freelance artist, as she had done before. One day, sketching away in her humble digs while Proopsie was working on a munitions installation in Staffordshire, Marje had a strange sensation in her stomach. She had missed a couple of periods and been to consult the local quack, who seemed to think she was pregnant. But after two years of trying to start a family and failing, Marje was sceptical. It was then that this strange thing happened:

> I felt this funny little flutter. I didn't recognize it until it was repeated a little later, a bit stronger the second time. And suddenly I realized what it was. And it was a magical moment, to me even more magical than the actual birth. Because from that moment on, you protect this little flutter, like butterfly wings, and you cherish it inside you, and hold it to yourself, and love it before it's born. And I think that any woman who has been through that experience, whether or not she realizes it, is bound to be left with that feeling for the rest of her life. She may transfer it, for example to the man she loves. But it's there; even for women who've never had children, the potential for that feeling is there, because their bodies prepare them every month. So it's no good Germaine Greer and company burning their bras and making empty gestures about things that are meaningless. Because that feeling of protectiveness is as strongly a part of the female spirit as any possible thing can be.

Baby Robert Proops, seven and a half pounds, was born on 7 October 1941, at a nursing home in a village called Weeping Cross, near Stafford. Marje never had postnatal depression but she was pretty fed up in general. Proopsie was working at a site in Stoke, one of the Five Towns, each one, according to Marje, more grim and dismal than the last. 'They might be lovely now, with theme parks, but in those days they were miserable and sad, with everybody out of work, everybody poor. I knew that Proopsie was going to be posted overseas, and there was great tension and fear in the country. We were waiting for the worst to happen.'

The expectant father sailed through the pregnancy with scarcely a whimper. Not being a great one for fussing over children he was 'casually cheerful' about the whole thing. He had told the midwife, 'I'm not one of these anxious husbands – I'll ring up in the morning to see how she's doing.' Marje had been pretty mad about this nonchalance, and was secretly delighted when events left Proopsie a nervous wreck.

The birth was not a pleasure. Marje's fifty-six hours in labour were the result, or cause, of a retroverted womb. She would need corrective surgery and, when that failed to stop her haemorrhaging later on, a hysterectomy at an early age – a bitter blow to a woman who desperately wanted more children, and who longed for a daughter all her life. Marje had no curiosity about the newborn infant, apart from asking the question most mothers ask: 'Is he all right?' She certainly didn't want to see the babe until it was 'nice and tidy and dollied up in its nightshirt', as Marje had a horror of nature red in tooth and umbilical cord. She was equally delicate about the process of childbirth, which is why she didn't want Proopsie present (supposing he could have remained conscious for the occasion). Marje:

I think the reason I didn't want him there was that childbirth, to me, is a very private, personal struggle for a woman. There's also an element of – I was going to say indecency. It's not exactly indecency. But I wanted to be on my own for this primitive experience.

Memories, perhaps, of Mrs Rayle talking to Aunt Lilian all those years ago about the b-a-b-y. Interestingly, long after her own 'primitive experience', Marje the journalist was required to see the graphic colour film *Helga*, which broke all taboos concerning cameras at the business end of childbirth. Far from being shocked, Marje found the film so moving and exhilarating that she went to see it again.

Proopsie, who never showed any desire to pick up the infant or cuddle him, received with manly calm the news of his army posting (to India and Ceylon, although Marje could not be told). The only thing he wasn't sure about was his uniform, and the military conventions attached thereto. On one occasion he and Marje were walking down the road, with Proopsie feeling very awkward and strange in his new gear, when suddenly he started behaving oddly. Turning to Marje he commanded, 'Stay where you are!' and dived into a shop doorway. He wouldn't come out until two soldiers had gone past, because he didn't know what to do if they saluted.

Proopsie spent his embarkation leave looking for lodgings where Marje and their new dwarf would be safe from bombs. He eventually found a smallholding called Grange Farm in Slough, not far from Stoke Poges, which seemed ideal. The fact that it was to receive a direct hit that would cave in one of the bedroom roofs could hardly have been foreseen when Proopsie found the place lying amid the sunlit meadows. The owners, a Mr and Mrs Marshall, were delightful people, and Marje would have a lot of nice animals to keep her company during his absence. Marje and baby Robert saw Proopsie off at King's Cross station, wishing him luck as they waved him goodbye. To the last he remained tight-lipped about where he was going, but his wife noticed that the clothes he took were for a hot climate.

Little did Marje know then that when her husband returned four years later – having risen in the ranks to major and acquired some of the haughty habits of the Raj – he would be, to all intents and purposes, a complete stranger.

She would sit in Stoke Poges' famous churchyard reading

that most moving of socialist poems, Gray's *Elegy* (which was written there), and scribbling long love letters to the distant Proops. She bought an old bicycle, and would 'wobble perilously' along the country lanes, or go by train with baby Robert to visit her sister Jo and her parents. On one occasion she had the child in a carrycot in a railway carriage full of soldiers when she realized it was time for his dinner. 'Excuse me,' she told the troops, 'but I have to feed my baby, and I don't mean with a bottle.' The men obligingly wandered off or stared out of the window.

At home on Grange Farm, Robert would be seated in his highchair throwing food while Marje attempted to earn a living. She had her Forces pay and her *Mirror* retainer, but she was always short of money. Rationing meant that you were only allowed eight ounces of sugar a week, and two ounces of tea, and there were no luxuries at all. You couldn't buy pencils, then, or toys: Marje had to improvise with cardboard cartons and cut-outs for her little boy. But she was still sketching with a pen and ink. She was doing a lot of drawings for women's magazines and some of these were extremely complex illustrations for knitting patterns which drove her mad, and which required extended captions. She was doing wartime knitting herself, including weird Balaclavas for the troops, and she also tried to make garments for Robert. But she was not gifted, and the child had a pair of woollen leggings with both feet facing sou'-sou'west.

Marje is not a pastoral person, and she found life on the farm very dull. She loved Mrs Marshall, who was everyone's vision of a maternal farmer's wife – white-haired, plump, rosy-cheeked and a terrific worker. There were two merry daughters, one called Bee, and everyone laughed good-naturedly when a bomb destroyed the roof and fell on Bee's bed while she wasn't in it. Marje warmed to them all; she was particularly fond of a brown Jersey cow among

the smallholder's herd of black-and-white Friesians. This
particular cow was very feminine and docile, with huge
dark eyes and long lashes, and she was called Griselda.
Like her namesake in Chaucer's tale, Griselda was patient
and long-suffering. Marje:

> I always felt that somehow Griselda and I had a lot in
> common. She was a lovely coppery colour, and I used to
> sit in the meadow with her very often, doing my freelance
> work for magazines or writing to Proopsie, which I did
> almost every day. And Robert, my little toddler, would
> be playing about, running around in the field or diving
> between Griselda's legs. Griselda was terribly gentle and
> she always reminded me of women generally. She had
> this expression of patient resignation and beautiful eyes.
> She and I used to look at each other and I felt we had
> this bond of understanding, a recognition between two
> women who submitted to men.
>
> And I once saw Griselda being served, as they called
> it, by this huge great black bull in another field. I didn't
> know if this consummation was the first time Griselda
> had been mounted by this enormous animal, but when it
> was all over I looked at Griselda and shook my head with
> pity and said, 'You didn't enjoy that, did you?' And the
> look on her face confirmed that there was no pleasure in
> it at all. I'll always remember that.

Letters came back from far-off Proopsie with strange post-
marks, smelling of curry. Her husband was apparently
keeping his matches dry in the jungle by wrapping them up
in his shirt during the monsoon, and he'd had diphtheria.
He was evidently not in the Ardennes then. Marje began
to worry about the dangers of dusky maidens and Jap
bayonets jabbing through the undergrowth. She would
show Robert a photograph of Proopsie in uniform while

the child was straining on his po, saying, 'Look at your daddy!' and doing goodness knows what damage to the young psyche during this crucial Freudian phase. Marje says of her adult son: 'Robert is always telling people now, "I got a lot of shit from my father."'

Robert was once almost attended by the Queen's physician, while Marje was visiting Jo-jo and her parents. Jo had by now married a chemist, David Bourne, who was abroad in the army, and Jo, who was soon to have a baby of her own, was living with mother and father over a posh pub in Windsor called the Grapes, right opposite the castle. Yes, Mr Rayle had sold up yet again, and this time he seemed finally to have hit the jackpot. It was a charming rural pub and Jo-jo helped behind the bar. Marje herself was staying at the Old House Hotel, just by the bridge at Eton, when little Robert took sick. Marje rang Jo-jo and asked if their family doctor could possibly pay the boy a visit, as he seemed dehydrated. The regular family GP in Windsor happened to be the illustrious Dr Francis Leslie who was off somewhere, probably treating the Queen, but his partner, Dr Concannon, agreed to go out of his way to see this patient indisposed at the Old House Hotel. Jo-jo:

When the doctor arrived, Marje had all her drawings and paintings around the room – she was an artist then, rather than a journalist – so we were chatting away with Dr Concannon about all this and Marje asked him if he'd like a coffee. The conversation had been going on for about an hour when suddenly Dr Concannon looked at his watch and said he was late for another appointment. It was only after he'd gone that we realized he'd not even seen the patient: poor Robert was outside in his pram. I had to phone and ask for the doctor to come back.

Not being an *Archers* type, Marje wasn't hitting it off very well with the rural folk around Stoke Poges. It took her at least a year to get the hang of village life. She had the impression the locals thought she was a refugee with a criminal background. She bravely joined the Women's Institute but never quite mastered jam-making and had to chuck her bottled gooseberries in the pig swill. Her WI function was to send pithy reports to the local newspapers about their jam-making and flower-arranging competitions. This was thrilling work in itself, but even more exciting were the WI meetings, about which Marje wrote many years later in her *Mirror* column: 'Speakers gave us nice talks guaranteed not to bend our tiny domestic minds. If anyone had mentioned intercourse there would have been a run on the smelling salts and injunctions from husbands to stay away from such wanton gatherings.'

She received cool but gracious nods from the lady of the manor, who eventually invited her in for tea. Marje was worried about what to wear, and turned up in her best tweed suit. Her ladyship wore an old baggy skirt and a rustic sweater with buckshot holes in the elbows. She was very charming. Marje quickly caught on that looking scruffy was the key to local acceptance, and fared much better in the village after that. But she never liked the country life: the lonely landscape, the bird squabbles at dawn, the smell of new-mown dung.

She fervently looked forward to occasional trips to the war-torn West End for a bit of jazz, or a tea dance at the Café de Paris, with Mrs Marshall kindly babysitting. Like other great survivors Marje became an accomplished bomb-dodger. Most of all she loved visiting her father's bijou new pub opposite Windsor Castle. The Grapes was very popular with the GIs from the nearby American base at Ascot, who also used to tour Stoke Poges admiring the famous churchyard and the girls' legs. Sometimes they would come to the Grapes bearing gifts – steaks, chickens, apple pies, that sort of thing. Mrs Rayle would get very shirty and tell her husband to give the stuff back, whereupon Alfred Rayle would sensibly hide it somewhere until the generous Americans had returned to base, and then bring it out for supper.

One GI, Delmer Wright, became a lifelong buddy to Marje: he and his wife Alice, known as 'Happy', used to visit and write to her for years after the war. He would come to Grange Farm of a Friday to share their egg and spam rations and tell Marje about American politics. She liked the Yanks in their neat berets and nifty uniforms. 'They were much smarter than the British soldiers and they also had much more money. They had nylons and goodies for the girls, and the girls would take down their knickers any day for a pair of nylons. I didn't take my knickers down for Delmer, no!'

Marje was an innocent bystander – 'I didn't have the kind of wild life that many other young females had at the time because I wasn't into promiscuous sex' – but she couldn't help noticing that things had changed in wartime Britain. There was a devil-may-care hedonism among men and women who accepted the possibility of being blown to bits at any moment, and whose loved ones were far away. She says there was an atmosphere of 'take what you can get while you can, because you may not be alive tomorrow'. People were hungry and lonely and frustrated. They grabbed at sex and any other pleasure they could lay their hands on.

The young Mrs Proops, though, was more concerned about her career than her loins. She had done some superb knitting illustrations and fashion sketches, but where was she going? 'In those days I used to be scratching about, not earning much money, doing the best I could. I used to work every evening after I'd put Robert to bed. There wasn't any night life in Stoke Poges and I had nothing else to do with

myself, so once he was in bed I used to draw, picking up a
few quid here and there with my sketches.'

It was a knitted cardigan that changed Marje's life. She'd
had terrible trouble with the detail and the buttons, because
if you drew it even slightly wrong, thousands of women
would be knitting up cardigans with teapot-spout sleeves
or neckholes like horse collars. The only enjoyable bit was
writing the long captions underneath. Marje delivered the
drawing, part of a series commissioned by Julia Cairns,
editor of *Good Taste* magazine, and Miss Cairns remarked
that Marje's captions were unusually good.

'Do you write, Mrs Proops?' asked the editor.

'Oh yes – I write to my husband every day.'

'No, I mean do you write articles?'

Marje searched her imagination. Best to keep mum about
the jam-making reports.

'No.'

'Well, why not do a piece for us, let's say a thousand
words, on what it's like to be a young wife and mother in
wartime Britain. Do you think you could do that?'

Marje couldn't wait. She also couldn't type. So she
scribbled the piece in longhand with Robert squawking
in his highchair and then cycled at breakneck speed to
Windsor to see her clever secretarial sister. Marje wasn't
sure if you counted the full stops and commas as part of the
1,000 words. Jo looked heavenward for strength, but typed
the article in a flash. And of course, when Julia Cairns saw
it, she knew that she had a writer on her hands. True, the
piece may have needed tightening up a few notches, but it
bore all the hallmarks of real journalism: it had the words,
the wit and the wisdom, and it had Marje's very own vision
of things.

Julia Cairns commissioned regular monthly 1,000-word
articles from Marje which, when they were seen, earned
her more work from other sources. She was now a writer

and illustrator, and she was asked to help produce a government booklet on wartime parenthood, both illustrating and editing the text. *You and Your Children*, as the publication was called, sold millions of copies and went on selling steadily when peace broke out. The text was by a psychiatrist, but the drawings of children were pure Proops and most of them – even the little girls – bore a striking resemblance to Robert. Sadly, all copies have long since vanished. Perhaps there is one in your attic.

Another important government publication followed, this time an information booklet for servicemen and women on the dangers of VD. Not being in the know about seamy sex, Marje had to go to her doctor to ask for reading material on the subject. The GP thought Marje had been 'up to some hanky-panky while Proopsie was away', and 'had a fit'. He was relieved to hear she was doing official research, though the material he gave Marje to read provided her with a bit of a jolt. She would never see sex in quite the same romantic light again.

Marjorie Proops, writer and artist, was now all set to fulfil Hugh Cudlipp's predictions, and her hopes were high that when the war was over, and Proopsie came home, they would be a happy and successful family. And then, as so often happens when one's ship is under full sail, a very ill wind blustered across her bows. The news came that her father had had an accident. He had fallen down into the cellar at the pub and had been rushed to Ashford General Hospital. Though he was badly hurt, his condition was not critical. The real casualty was Marje's mother. Mrs Rayle, who had been so dreadfully frightened for so many years that something terrible would happen, was now afraid to go out of doors.

5

The Herald Years

Marje's father never really recovered from his accident. He suffered extreme pain and ulceration of the leg which, after a period of retirement in Shepperton with his daughter Jo-jo's family, turned gangrenous. Alfred Rayle died in Ashford General Hospital two days after an amputation to save his life. He never lost his sparkle and to the last was cracking jokes to the nurses about his stump and laying odds on the outcome of his operation. But to Jo-jo, who was able to visit him every day, he also expressed his fears about being disabled. And he told Jo, and the nurses, and everyone who came within range of his bed, that he was deeply proud of his daughter Marje, and tickled pink about her career success. Jo went home and sobbed. She believed she had never amounted to anything in her father's eyes, and felt like Marje's 'country cousin'. Forty years later, when Marje rang her sister to ask her about those hospital visits for this book, she could hear Jo crying on the phone. Marje: 'The damage parents can do to their kids is absolutely unending and indescribable.'

Both Marje and Jo-jo missed their father deeply, but Martha Rayle, to whom he had been married for forty-one years, was devastated by the experience. She was now imprisoned in her home, crippled with agoraphobia, having lost her lifeline to the outside world. Her condition had been gradually deteriorating for some time. Marje recalls: 'I think that as she got older she got more and more afraid. She was afraid for us children, afraid to let us go anywhere out of her sight, and then when we grew up and got married she began to be afraid for herself. I think that this was the basis of the agoraphobia. And it got worse after my father died.' Mrs Rayle would sit petrified indoors, unable to venture out of the pub, or out of her daughter's house. Like other agoraphobics she avoided looking at the sky, as though the very sight of it might make her fall off the planet into nothingness. What happened at Alfred Rayle's funeral is therefore all the more remarkable:

Although we were non-practising, my father had a Jewish funeral, and by tradition the women didn't actually go to the grave or the cemetery. So all the females of the family were sitting in Jo-jo's house, with Jo and myself on either side of our mother, comforting her and keeping an eye on her. And she was suddenly aware that all the men had got up and were moving out of the house to go and join the funeral cortège. And she leapt to her feet, rushed out of the room and down the garden path, and ran along the road, shouting, 'Alfred! Alfred! Take me with you! I can't bear to live without you!'

How a severe agoraphobic could bring herself to do this, even in extreme distress, is something that Marje has sought to understand both as a daughter and an advice columnist, for many of her letter-writers are agoraphobes (Marje often refers them to the Open Door Association). Years afterwards her sister too began to suffer from fear of open spaces. Marje was terrified that Jo-jo would end up like their mother, but Jo courageously fought her way out of the illness to pursue a career as a sales representative, and she is now completely cured. One of Marje's own professional advisers, Harley Street psychiatrist Dr Tom Kraft, explains:

Agoraphobia is much more common in women than in men, and it tends to get passed down from mother to daughter. So that if the mother shows agoraphobic symptoms, then very often the daughter who has been constantly in her company somehow identifies with the mother and develops the same sort of problems. Oddly, it doesn't usually transfer from mother to son. The behaviour of Marje's mother at the funeral is not unusual. I have a patient who can't go to her front gate, yet travels here for her treatment sessions, a distance of forty miles. Because it doesn't matter how agoraphobic you are: if there's an emergency, you can do it. If there's a reality issue, the agoraphobe *can* go outside. The fact that Marje's mother ran out of the front door means that as far as she was concerned, that was *real*. She had to go after that cortège. Phobic disturbance is to do with the sufferer's fantasy and inner life. It has to do with symbolic meaning, rather than real fears.

During her father's illness Marje had been living and working in London, which was why she couldn't visit him at the hospital every day. Preparing for Major Proopsie's homecoming as the war drew to a close, she had moved herself and little Robert back into their semi in Golders Green, and Esme Zelger, former fashion editor at the *Mirror*, had told her that there might be a job for her at the *Daily Herald* after VE Day. Sure enough, there was. In 1945, Esme Zelger became the *Herald* woman's editor, and Marje, amicably ending her retainer arrangement with Hugh Cudlipp, was appointed fashion editor at £23 a week, both writing and illustrating under the overall editorship of Cudlipp's brother Percy.

The *Daily Herald*, based in the Odhams building in Endell Street near the old Covent Garden market, was an important newspaper, jointly funded by Odhams Press and the TUC. Both the *Mirror* and the *Herald* were watchdogs for the working classes. But whereas the *Daily Mirror* was a socialist pit bull, free to bite the Conservatives and Labour as well if it saw an exposed backside, the *Daily Herald* was the Labour Party's sheepdog. In 1946 Marje was writing proudly to Delmer, her GI buddy, 'The *Herald* is in fact the official organ of the Labour Party, and, therefore, of the Government. It suits me – I am even stronger, if anything, in my Labour sympathies. I don't think I could possibly work for one of the reactionary papers.' She adds now, 'That's why it was so wonderful for me to get on the *Herald*: I really thought in those days that I was part of the great big socialist surge of excitement.'

Looking back, she explains the difference between the two famous Labour newspapers: 'The *Herald* had a much older, very serious readership. The *Mirror* had serious things in it, like Cassandra, and the leaders, and Philip Zec, who did those celebrated war cartoons. The *Mirror* was always a very painful thorn in the side of authority and bureaucracy. But that sort of thing would never have appeared in the *Herald*, which was more polite and gentlemanly.'

Percy Cudlipp, the editor, was indeed a gentleman, intellectual and a lover of poetry and chivalry. He never quite galvanized Marje the way his fierce brother had done, because she responds to red-blooded males. Percy was somewhat porridge-coloured. When she was eventually promoted to woman's editor in 1950 after Esme Zelger left, Percy would gallantly rise from his chair if the *Herald's* only woman editor entered the conference room late. 'If I went in after the men had seated themselves, this meant that all the others would then have to stand up with the editor. I was very embarrassed and self-conscious about this, and I used to make a point of getting to the conference early.'

It was on the *Herald* that Marje cut her teeth as a newspaper journalist, learning strange skills such as doorstepping, phoning over copy from call boxes and going down on the 'stone' to 'sub' (see below). Nowadays Marje would probably walk through picket lines to do her advice column and expect her secretaries to do likewise, but the young Marje joined the National Union of Journalists and was even to become, at some stage, a chapel father, or rather, chapel mother – 'which was regarded as a great joke. The other members of the chapel were very sexist in those days, women being a rarity anywhere in Fleet Street, and they used to call me "Mummy".' Now Marje is an honorary life member of the NUJ.

At a time when printers ruled the presses and had more privileges than a sultan, innocent Marje once forgot the rigid print-union protocol and almost caused a shutdown of the paper. She should tell you the story:

It happened one day while I was stone-subbing on the *Herald*, which meant that I had to go down to the stone where the paper was actually made up and the type set in hot metal. And there were these elderly – mostly elderly, it seemed to me – compositors, known as the 'comps'. And the job of the stone-sub was to get the copy to fit, and to cut where necessary. You had to learn to do that there and then, and I could read the metal upside down and back to front, and I could 'cut on the stone', as they called it. Mostly, though, we had proofs pulled to see how the columns would look and if you were three or four lines over, you would cut the copy down on the stone.

Anyway, on this particular occasion I had a very old

comp indeed who was potteringly slow, and I was always in trouble anyway because the page for which I was responsible was invariably late. And there was what they call a stick of copy beside the bed, and there was a hole on the page where this little piece of type was to go. It was all ready to go in. And this ancient comp was scratching his head, and looking at the type, and looking at the hole on the page. And I got very impatient and suddenly said, 'That's where it goes!' and picked it up and put it in the hole.

Now, one of the greatest sins that any sub or indeed anybody else could commit was to pick up a piece of type and handle it. Only the comps were allowed to touch the type. And this old boy slowly put down his tweezers and his little tools, and said in this lugubrious voice, 'Send for the father of the chapel!' And they all downed tools and marched away to the far end of the room for a chapel meeting, called on the spot. I was terrified. I thought, 'This is the end. If the paper is stopped through me, I'll get the sack, and I'll deserve it. Whatever will the editor say?' I was in a dreadful state.

Marje had to grovel and wheedle, and ply the printers with all the feminine wiles she knew, saying she was just an ignorant girl and would never ever repeat such a wicked, thoughtless act. Finally they forgave her. But she was never permitted to touch the stone again, and had to stand there in future with her hands behind her back. Brian McConnell, now with the *Mirror*, was working in the Odhams Press building at the time and thinks Marje handled the situation remarkably well. 'Normally there would have been shouts and screams and an immediate walkout – trade unions were as disputatious as that – but Marje had this enormous presence and she placated them. I've never met anyone in my life who could have done it with so much charm and diplomacy.'

The nub of Marje's job in the early days was fashion. 'It was very important to me before I learned better,' she says now. Her work included 'fashion reporting on the news side', involving trivial pursuits. In June 1947, for example, when Princess Elizabeth was attending an NSPCC meeting, Marje was sent to record not what was said but that Elizabeth was wearing 'a silk summer outfit'. Visiting female celebrities, such as Betty Hutton and the teenage Joan Collins, were attended in their hotel suites, but only to see what garments they had in their suitcases. Utility styles and clothing coupons were discussed, but the *Herald* fashion expert was also very pro-fur. In a London street in 1949 she gleefully counted 21 out of 118 women with animal skins on their backs, a sign of high fashion tuning.

Paris designers commanded women to have twenty-inch waists, and that Spanish Inquisition corset the 'Waspie' was considered indispensable. Marje wore one to the office, and generally advised women against shedding their 'foundation garments' – despite fears being expressed by the medical profession around this time in the *Lancet* about chlorosis – 'fatigue, fainting, faddishness about food' – among corseted girls as young as fourteen. So powerful were the corset manufacturers in those days that they would hold audiences spellbound with their lavish shows. At one London parade that Marje attended, held in the dark, the models were dressed in phosphorescent nylon to give the impression of disembodied bras and girdles going up and down. Sometimes Marje sounded a note of rebellion about women being 'slaves of the silhouette', and asked dress manufacturers to consider women who didn't fit the mannequin mould. But her job meant that she couldn't take such criticisms to their logical conclusion, or be too catty about the catwalk.

Government-sponsored export drives called 'design weeks' and 'fashion fortnights' involved Marje in mind-numbing receptions and parties, with 'endless gin flowing' and cocktail chitchat with MPs and assorted dignitaries. Margaret Disher, a former member of the Council of Industrial Design (now the Design Council), found Proops of the *Herald* a sterling supporter of her British *haute couture* group, but remembers her chiefly for her irreverent sense of humour. 'In those days the models struck up rather ridiculous poses by today's standards – largely because the photographers wanted this exaggeration – and there was Proops striking identical poses, with wrists arched and fingers spread over her face, taking the micky out of the whole fashion hype and being caught in the photographers' pictures without her realizing.' At a lunch with Proops and Esme Zelger, Margaret tripped a fellow customer with her umbrella and was appointed 'Member of the Clumsy Women's Club' by Marje, who told her, 'My husband only married me because I could play the piano, which saved the cost of records.'

Marje's fashion calendar was dominated by the Paris collections, with which British designers had to compete or compare. Dior was 'a god' who couldn't show himself without mobs of admirers fainting, bursting into tears or climbing over seats to caress him. Marje got her hat knocked off in the throng, bruised shins, and on one occasion a glass of champagne in her lap. Dior's various 'looks' and 'lines' were fiercely protected from wholesale pirating. You were not permitted to photograph or sketch them on the catwalk, and Marje would surreptitiously jot down a few lines and fill in the detail with brush and ink once she got back to her hotel.

Despite bitchiness behind the catwalk curtain and what

Marje considered irrelevant 'lip-smacking speculation' that all the males in the business were gay and all the mannequins lesbians, out front she found her fellow fashion writers and artists – particularly the *Daily Express* team of Ann Edwards and Andrew Robb – a friendly bunch. They never looked down on her despite her mere three months at Hackney Tech. 'I hero-worshipped them, and felt such an amateur in comparison.'

Yves Saint Laurent and Jacques Fath were only a little less hallowed than Dior. At one of Fath's shows, held in a garden, Marje and her fellow fashion writers sat goggling at his garments whilst being bitten to death by mosquitoes. Marje's favourite among the design gods was Coco Chanel. 'I always thought Chanel was the greatest. She was knocking on when I met her, yet she was petite, trim, a little frail but with a lovely, soft, wrinkled face and keen, sharp eyes. She was "Madame" always. I think she was classical, in the way that some great painters become classical artists with work that will always remain supreme. Chanel in her way was a draftswoman, with a vision, and her influence persists today. The first chain handbag I ever saw was at Chanel's, and the first chain belt.'

Our fashion expert was constantly being confronted in this job by visions of loveliness – models, actresses, film goddesses – and she was required to talk non-stop to her readers about beauty and glamour, not an easy task for a woman who thought she was plain and who believed women were sentient creatures rather than daubs in a gallery. Imagine Marje Proops writing now, as she did in the *Herald*, 'Show your emotions too energetically and you're heading for lines and wrinkles before your time . . . Any woman can look animated without pulling faces and encouraging wrinkles!' Her beauty Waterloo came when she was sent in 1949 to interview seventeen-year-old Elizabeth Taylor. You can just detect the catch in her voice when she looks back on it:

> She was very young and she was so exquisite that it was like looking at a beautiful painting that wasn't real. The eyes were particularly wonderful – violet – and she had this very lovely creamy skin and all this magnificent dark hair. She was so nice – we got on well together and had lots of laughs and giggles. But I'd have given *anything* to look even a hundredth as beautiful. She was flawless.

Years later she was to write in the *Mirror* that the experience 'made me feel as plain as a steak and kidney pud'.

One person who thought Marje immensely more beautiful than Elizabeth Taylor was her son Robert, being looked after in the Golders Green semi. He rarely gave trouble, but one day the *Herald* news desk received a call from a small child claiming that his mother worked at the paper and that he had a very important news story to impart. His duck had laid an egg. This was a truly sensational story because they lived in town, and the duck normally didn't lay, so they should put it in the paper. It took the news desk some time to work out who 'Robert Proops' was.

Marje still couldn't type: 'I got all sorts of girls to type my copy and nobody realized for years.' She couldn't do shorthand either, and relied on longhand notes and a magnificent memory. Her job had made her highly fashion-conscious, and also rather posh. She still smoked heavily but had taken to using a cigarette-holder for elegance, which preserved her nail polish and ever-growing spectacle wings from the tar. When she was promoted in 1950 to woman's editor, she was put in charge of a small section of the paper called 'Womansense' and given a very wide remit, going over to Paris in hobble skirts and spectacular spectacles to sketch highlights from the couturiers' shows,

doing book reviews, general reporting and even – because
of her piano and vocal training – acting as deputy music
critic, with the occasional tiny by-line 'MP' after her short
opera or concert reports. She used to have to scribble them
in the dark, and then rush over to the nearest phone box
to transmit her hot comments to the copytaker.

She would also give her readers tips on etiquette (consulting the standard work on the subject by American Emily
Post) as well as her regular advice on beauty and fashion,
though her Womansense headed notepaper carried the
disclaimer, 'While trying to assist readers the *Daily Herald*
cannot accept legal or other liability for advice given.' This
sideline was to prove significant. When the newspaper's
'agony aunt' died suddenly of cancer, Marje was to take
on that onerous job, as we shall see.

By 1953, Marje was telling Delmer, 'I am now writing a
column for the *Herald* – "Labour's own Girl(!) Columnist" is
what my buddies call me. It's a pretty big headache, along
with all my other work, however I enjoy it because I've been
given a free hand and can write as the mood takes me – as
long as the mood takes me regularly once a week. My new
work means plenty of social engagements – boring cocktail
parties to meet boring celebrities. Meanwhile I'm preparing
for my Paris trip next month. Between fashion shows I shall
rush round the art galleries or sit in bars on the Left Bank,
goggle-eyed at the Existentialists. And best of all, I can buy
ridiculous hats I can't wear when I get back to England.'

She thinks the reason she got so much work was because
there was a shortage of staff after the war, but really her
talents spoke for themselves. Besides, she got on well both
with men and women, was never pushy, and hoped, like
her father, to make friends with everyone. Marje says that
her confidence as a journalist grew gradually; she began by
'inventing an image that would give me the self-assurance
that I needed to compete in that hard world', and ended

with the genuine article. 'You can see as you go through the cuttings that there's more and more confidence in the way I expressed opinions. In the end I was laying down the law – I got quite like Proopsie!'

I have been through the cuttings – all of them – and this is true. It is also true that, had Marje remained the fashion writer she was in the 1940s, we should all have forgotten her long ago. But Marje was too perceptive, too witty and too humane to go blathering on indefinitely about corsets and flounces. Gradually her *Herald* column began to shift focus to reflect her own wider interests and her deep social and political concerns. Pieces popped up on 'progressive' education (letting children do as they liked, which Marje tried out rather disastrously on Robert), on having a baby on the NHS ('The Health Scheme is for all of us'), on children in desperate need of foster parents, and on the National Marriage Guidance Council's conferences and debates.

She condemned the mounting cost of living and protested that housewives could no longer buy the family groceries. In 1954 a letter from a mother who couldn't afford a school uniform for her child brought forth some towering comments from the erstwhile fashion writer. 'No child,' stormed socialist Marje, 'should have to bear the kind of shame that the little girl from Lambeth endured.' And being as good as her word she sent the mother five pounds – a lot of money in those days.

There were thoughtful pieces on divorce (one in six marriages), on the 'little cruelties that ruin a marriage', on teenage dating, on the need for fathers to do their fair share of parenting, and on the newborn feminist movement – though in those days Marje was far from convinced of women's entitlements. In 1953 she was writing, 'I do not go in for all this equality business. I don't want to be equal. I don't want to lose all my feminine privileges just because

I help with the breadwinning.' She likes to be given a seat, she says, and flowers, and 'I am sad because when sex equality came in the door, courtesy flew out of the window.' There are some surprisingly un-Marje comments on a 1952 play, *Two Loves I Have*, which dealt with the subject of lesbianism. Shown at a private club, the production did not require a licence from the Lord Chamberlain. 'This sort of play is unhealthy,' booms the headline. Followed by, 'Do we want plays on the British stage with perversion as their main theme . . . the unhealthy passion of one woman for another?'

Overall, though, there emerges the recognizable style of Marje the social commentator, Marje the compassionate counsellor, Marje the wag. All the charactistic touches her readers would come to know and love were developed in these columns. 'Women are the worriers of the world,' she writes. 'They add to their daily burdens by loading themselves up with small anxieties about things that might never happen – often never do. There is a woman whose letter is on my desk as I write this: worrying because she doubts if her husband loves her. If he does, she says, it's not in the way she wants to be loved.' On books: 'Experts say if parents read pulp fiction, kids won't appreciate good books. What nonsense some of these people talk. Most of us, highbrow and lowbrow alike, want and need a little escape. Frivolous reading provides it.'

A professional controversialist, she tells the truth and shames the devil. Brides were accustomed to being told their matrimonial duties, so Marje puts forward some suggestions for grooms: 'Ready boys? We'll start with advice from Proops. You'll promise to share with her your worldly goods. That doesn't mean a grudging paying-out of the housekeeping money as if you are bestowing a great favour. Whatever she gets from you, she'll earn.' On a swivel armchair someone has invented to save craning one's neck to see the television: 'I intend to invest in one so that I can go the whole hog and swivel right round with my back to the TV – which is all it so often deserves.' And so on. Her *Herald* column is spiced, as her *Daily Mirror* one would be, with amusing glimpses of Marje's family life: 'When I discovered my eleven-year-old under a cloud of smoke at the bottom of the garden with two butt-ends at his feet and a third in his mouth, I said, "Smoking, huh? Next it'll be blondes." Instead of imparting the swift punishment expected, I offered the by now greenish boy another one. "No thank you," he said, vanishing behind a bush.'

Someone who remembers her journalism in the *Herald* period is retired Labour leader Michael Foot MP, who was writing the paper's trenchant political stuff:

> The old *Daily Herald* was really a very fine paper although it was eventually pushed out of existence by financial extremities and political pressures and other shocking interventions. However, just about the very best of all the correspondents who wrote for it was Marjorie Proops, and we were all very proud to know her then and have all boasted about our association with her ever since, because although she has written some splendid columns since then, and although she built up her reputation as the best of all the columnists doing the kind of business she did, some of us also remember that the foundation of it all was that she was a great reporter on the old *Daily Herald*.

But Marje was still doing what many will see as the demeaning side of her job, following fashion, and running after royal attire. On and on went the Womansense pages about the trivia of the coming coronation ('the Queen chooses make-up for the day') and about the 'waxy orange-blossom British satin gown' with its ten layers of stiff petticoats.

Coronation Day, 2 June 1953, was to see the *Herald*'s Proops
in a small stand overlooking the procession. Marje:

> My station was in Whitehall, near the Horseguards, in
> a box on top of one of the stands with about half a
> dozen reporters penned in – one, I remember, was an
> American. And there was a loo somewhere at the back.
> When any of us wanted to go to the loo, the others
> would make the necessary notes. And I had to be there
> at about four o'clock in the morning to start doing
> the 'colour', and the crowds. There were hundreds of
> thousands of people swarming about Whitehall, taking
> their positions, and reporters stationed all along the
> route. We stayed there all day in that cramped little
> box, finally emerging at about four in the afternoon. I
> had to walk miles to find an empty phone box and with
> a crowd of irritable people waiting to get in, I rang the
> copytaker at the *Herald*, put my story over, and then had
> to carry on walking to my office in the rain. I wonder
> how we did it in those days, at great speed, and with
> no comfort, no support, eating soggy sandwiches that
> we brought from home, and taking it in turns to go to
> the loo. It was bloody good training, learning to do it
> the hard way. I suppose I got about three lines in. And
> no by-line.

Marje was getting quietly sick of fashion in general. 'To
readers, the whole thing was wonderful,' she says now.
'But to the people involved, and the journalists, it was hell.'
By the January Paris collections of 1954, the *Herald* fashion
expert was letting her feelings show. What followed was
a taste of the real Marje Proops, though no doubt many
a Womansense reader at the time fell face forward in her
breakfast cereal with the shock of it. Hold on to your hats,
fashion fans:

I am writing this, jammed up so that I can hardly breathe, in a tiny back salon where the temperature is about eighty degrees. It is ten o'clock at night. The show was scheduled to start an hour ago, but still we wait, knowing we will be lucky to get away by 1 a.m. Wild-eyed young workroom girls in shabby blue cotton overalls are dashing into the mannequins' dressing room with just-finished models over their arms. As the door opens, I catch a glimpse of the tall, haughty beauties being hooked into tight corsets by distraught young men. Jacques Fath himself, wearing an Edwardian suit with drainpipe trousers, lends a hand with the hooking. Meanwhile, screaming socialite guests quarrel with journalists over seats with a good view. Place cards are surreptitiously moved.

While all this goes on, girls with large businesslike sprays are dosing us with Jacques' newest perfume. I feel like a greenfly being murdered by the gardener. At last, when I am about to pass out with the heat, noise and overwhelming perfume, Jacques, white-faced and excited, rushes out and says, 'Shush, shush, shush.' The arc lights are on, and we are off. Four of the haughty beauties, seeming at least seven feet tall, sway disdainfully through the salon.

Marje had started, so she'd finish. She proceeded to lay into the boned and strapless corsets 'that push up their bosoms, encase their ribs and pinch in their waists to about eighteen inches'. A whaleboned garment 'looked like a straightjacket'. Marje turns to the woman beside her. 'How would you eat?' she asks. The fashion follower stares at her with scorn. 'I gather,' says Marje, 'that those who are dressed by the Master must starve, if need be, to maintain the correct shape.' The skinnies swirl past. 'My eyes are closed, my feet are swollen. On come the evening dresses. Someone claps and there are cries of "Charmante", "Delicieuse".' Finally, at 2 a.m., the *Herald* fashion expert gives up and goes home. She would never be taken in by this flimsy fandango again.

Marje still gets a 25 per cent discount from Jaegar, dating back to her days as a fashion editor. But she says she wouldn't walk down the road in a Vivienne Westwood creation, however 'great and original', and would think it obscene to spend a queen's ransom on a model gown. She did a twirl on the catwalk in a recent television *Clothes Show*, and still dresses elegantly in her Jaegar suits and frocks. That's enough for her.

What did Marje look like in those *Herald* days? Tony Boram, now busy trying to sort out the *Daily Mirror*'s pension fund fiasco, used to be sports editor on the *Herald*: 'I can remember her sitting by a window near a rather cramped corridor – it was an open-plan office and she didn't have her own room – sketching her bits and pieces, looking over her shoulder as you went by. She looked rather like the drawings she did of herself later on at the *Mirror*: you couldn't miss her.' Oddly, considering Marje's vision of herself as not unlike the milkman's horse, passing males seemed to find her quite toothsome. The *Sunday Mirror*'s Cyril Kersh: 'She looked well: she was tall, slim, dark-haired, had a rather large nose but was quite attractive, and she had a certain style about her. There she was with her cigarette holder and her cigarette, and those glasses, and she self-consciously, if you like, created that image.'

Mirror Group ex-chairman Ernie Burrington used to be the *Daily Herald*'s chief sub-editor and, later, night editor:

I'll always remember Marje umpiring a cricket match at Richmond, in which I played, I'm sure, a nondescript part. There was a London *Daily Herald* team, led by editor Percy Cudlipp, against a Manchester team. And Marje was a striking figure at the wicket, if not striking the ball, striking in appearance. She usually wore the most extravagant spectacles, which drew attention at all times to her quite interesting looks: large spectacles, with huge horn rims. I don't think they'd reached the stage in those days of having glittery butterflies on them, but she was only a touch away from that kind of exotic eye-wear. And there was the cigarette holder, another exotic touch. I don't think anyone would have imagined, looking at her then, that she would finish up the revered agony aunt of all agony aunts!

When she was writing her column for the *Daily Herald*, at the head of the column you saw these disembowelled spectacles, and a charcoaled signature, 'Marjorie Proops'. It was a 1950s bit of typography and display, but it was an echo of an old *People* newspaper column entitled 'Cyclops', which I think had a pair of spectacles and a legend, which was later bowdlerized in connection with something else, 'In the eyes of the blind the one-eyed man is king'. So there was Marje as umpire with specs, and there was Marje on the page with specs and charcoal signature. Whatever she did was a bit – well, I've got to be careful now, because I don't want to dishonour her – just a touch flash. She was there to be noticed, Marje. She was a young woman, and she cut a dash at the wicket, and wrote bright, exhilarating, highly readable features.

In 1953, Marje had another quite striking aspect to her appearance. Marje:

Gradually I became aware that my neck was looking a bit peculiar. It turned out that my thyroid gland had a growth on it. I went into hospital in Hampstead and was put on a ward with a lot of other women similarly

afflicted. We were known to the surgeons as the Goitre
Girls. We all had our operations, which meant that your
throat was cut right across, and it had a very ugly
dressing. And because I was always aware of the uplift
that clothes give women, I asked somebody to bring me
a length of ribbon, quite wide, that I could tie round my
neck and make into a big pussycat bow. And all the other
Goitre Girls felt that this was a marvellous idea and they
all got visitors to bring them pieces of ribbon as well. So
we all sat there in bed with our bows. And although we
were outwardly cheerful, we were all frightened out of
our minds in case we had cancer. You had to wait nine
days after the operation for the biopsy results. But one
morning the surgeon stood in the swing doors to the
ward, smiling broadly, and announced, 'I'm very happy
to say that none of my Goitre Girls is malignant!' But I
had to take thyroid pills and medication for quite a long
time afterwards.

Marje's worries about cancer may well have been triggered
by events at work. The *Herald* had a woman advice
columnist by the real or fictitious name of Mary Marshall,
whose column dealt with readers' personal problems in
a conservative, no-nonsense manner. Whilst not as well
known as some agony aunts of the postwar period like
'Evelyn Home' and American Dorothy Dix, Mary Marshall
had a regular, mainly female readership, and she was
quite bold in her advice. She would not shirk from telling
readers to behave responsibly, or to grow up. A wife who
wrote saying her husband had fallen in love with another
woman and wanted to share himself between them both,
was told, 'Your husband is behaving like a spoiled child.
He has no right whatever to expect you to put up with such
nonsense. He must make up his mind and decide which of
you he loves.'

Some time after Marje was appointed woman's editor, Mary Marshall died suddenly of cancer. When Marje passed the door of her darkened office she could see the piles of letters gradually building up on the desk, unopened. Nobody touched them. A newspaper building is not a dogs' home, and no hard-boiled journalist likes to be lumbered with bleeding heart surgery. As the *Sunday Times* once so appositely put it in an article on what it called 'Aunt Fannies': 'To most people there is something faintly ridiculous about the whole business.' Soon the Mary Marshall letters began to land on Marje's desk as well, sitting there silently pathetic, like little strangled cries. Marje already wore about five hats to work and was frantic with all her existing jobs, but she became increasingly worried about this misery mail and thought somebody should try to deal with it. At the very least the writers should get some sort of explanation or apology. So Marje took a pile of the letters home to see what she could do.

Fortunately she was sitting down when she opened them. Because anyone who has seen these much-derided 'agony' letters – and I have seen some of Marje's unpublished ones – is struck by one thing. The writers have tried everything, *everything*, before making this pitiable, last-ditch appeal to a perfect stranger, and however hard you may think you are, they contain words which shatter your reserve. Marje:

I was horrified. Absolutely horrified. It never occurred to me that people were writing letters like this. And I decided I must make an effort to answer them, to give whatever little bit of comfort I could – and it was really comfort more than help, because I knew nothing. All I had going for me was Hugh Cudlipp's kind compliment that I was 'amazingly perceptive'.

Next day Marje called Harley Street psychologist Eustace
Chesser, author of several well-known books on sex
and relationships, and poured out her problem to him.
Dr Chesser invited her over for a lunchtime bowl of
soup, and the two of them sat in his consulting rooms
examining Mary Marshall's cries from the heart. Chesser
was to say, many years later, that he was impressed by
Marje Proops's humility in seeking professional advice.
Normally journalists 'knew all about' human psychology,
or thought they did. Many similar lunch sessions followed,
Marje turning up with another sheaf, and the psychologist
helping her to sift through and analyse them.

Chesser didn't attempt to tell Marje how to answer the
letters. Instead he sought to give her a crash training course
to enable her to answer them herself. She was given a long
reading list of standard works on psychology, psychiatry, marital breakdown, phobias, dreams, sex and even
etiquette. She was told which authorities and experts to
consult on particular problems. She was sent on a National
Marriage Guidance Council course. She was shown what
to look for in the handwriting and in the presentation of
the letters themselves, and she was taught how to retain
emotional detachment, so that she didn't simply drop more
tears on the pages.

And so it was that Marje Proops became that comical
thing, an agony aunt, working under the name of her
dead colleague Mary Marshall at the *Daily Herald*. The
more she did the job, the more committed she became
to helping people 'out there', and protecting her readers and letter-writers from derision. In May 1954 she
launched a rocket in her column entitled 'He Need Not
Scoff'. It was aimed at her fellow *Herald* journalist George
West, who had attacked agony aunts in his Monday slot.
Without revealing her special interest in the field, Marje
sounds off:

Every week, thousands of women – and men – turn eagerly to the page of their magazine or newspaper that deals with human problems . . . Some like to read about other people's affairs because they are just normally curious. Others read because they, too, have some kind of problem and seek comfort from the advice given to those with similar worries.

I am one who reads the human problem articles. So, it seems, is Mr George West . . . Mr West, however, takes a different view from mine about problem pages. I read them sympathetically. He sneers. 'Each week,' he wrote last Monday, 'I scan through twenty or thirty agonized pleas, hoping that one of the oracles will slip up . . . I hope no one follows the advice of these women. I know no one who takes them seriously.' Well, now, Mr West, let me introduce you to one of the women and two of the men who conduct problem pages.

Marje goes on to refer Mr George West to Evelyn Home, with 60,000 letters a year; Mayo Wingate, a psychologist who answers hundreds a week, and A. J. Brayshaw, secretary of the National Marriage Guidance Council which has helped 'thousands' of couples to overcome their difficulties. And she says these advisers who reach out to 'the lonely, the troubled, the neurotic, the misfits' are doing, in spite of what Mr George West might think, a cracking good job.

Marje didn't stay long at the *Herald* after that. Editor Percy Cudlipp had left, and she felt somehow rudderless without him. Perhaps, too, the *Herald* was getting a little too genteel for her liking. When her old mentor Hugh Cudlipp saw her at a party and said, 'Why not come back to us at the *Mirror*, Marje?' she was off like a ball from a cannon.

6

The Hellish Years

While Marje was at the *Herald*, she painted on a brave face about life at 65 Dunstan Road. Her little boy was being minded by a 'mother's help' so that she could go out to work, and Robert was wondering why she couldn't be at home like other mums, 'making cucumber sandwiches'. Later on Robert came to understand the many benefits of having such an in-demand mum, but when he blurted out his accusation about the sandwiches Marje cried into her pillow and seriously considered giving up her career. She had other reasons for the painted smile as well. Worse reasons.

Proopsie's homecoming was after VJ Day. He didn't return until mid-June 1946, because victory in the East took a little longer than in Europe and Major Proops was based in India. Marje had gone up to Liverpool Docks to meet him, having begged the news editor to get her a press boarding pass because she wanted to go on to the troop carrier to greet the conquering hero. Five-year-old Robert was being minded, and Marje was as excited as a child herself as the ship berthed and she watched all the other wives waving at their menfolk from the quayside. She had written Proopsie love letters almost every day, and she hadn't seen him for four years. Would he still have his whiskers? Would he whirl her round and round in the air? Their reunion promised to be a scene from *Gone With the Wind* at the very least. Marje recalls the great day:

I was terribly thrilled and excited and triumphant to be going on the ship. I did have a few pangs about being the only civilian privileged to go on board, but I squashed those feelings of guilt and went up the gangplank. And there at the top was Proopsie! Although I didn't know it, he was Officer of the Day. I didn't even know what Officer of the Day meant; I still don't really know. But when he saw me, his face hardened, and he made a dismissive gesture, as if to push me aside with his arm. Clearly, the message to me was 'Go away!' And then he turned round and marched down a gangway of the ship and I didn't see him again until he came back to London.

Marje was felled. When Proopsie arrived home, he explained that because he had been Officer of the Day he had had to maintain the discipline of his regiment on board ship, and had been deeply embarrassed that his wife had been the only person allowed up the gangplank when all his men had loved ones waiting on the dock. The last thing in the world he wanted was to be seen pulling rank on his troops and enjoying special treatment. Marje understood, but the damage was done. She had been crushed and hurt and humiliated. Worse, the romantic had had the gilt taken off her gingerbread.

It very quickly became apparent that small Robert and large Proopsie did not see eye to eye. Proopsie was not about to cuddle or cherish his little boy, since children tended to get on his nerves and whatever his inward affections, he was not a sentimental father, any more than he was a sentimental socialist. Robert, for his part, had been sleeping for five years in his mother's bedroom, at first in a cot, and then, at the farmhouse, in a little bed next to hers. Now he was suddenly chucked out and supplanted by a tall dark stranger of whom he had no personal recollection, but of whom he had heard tell whilst on his potty. Marje: 'Robert was terribly, terribly jealous of his father, and his father was terribly, terribly jealous of Robert. There was enormous hostility between them. It never went away, right up until Proopsie's death, though it was not overt any longer by then, and they were actually quite civilized in their attitude towards each other. But it was there all the time.'

This father-son war had not yet been declared when the newly reunited Proopses decided to visit Marje's ailing mother in Walton-on-Thames, where she had moved with Jo-jo, her husband David, their daughter Judith and Aunt Lilian. Young Robert, like any little fellow, was thrilled to be going on the steam train. Marje:

We got into one of those small carriages where you sit opposite each other, and Robert was leaping about and jumping backwards and forwards with excitement. I kept saying to him, 'Sit down, Robert. You'll fall over and hurt yourself. Just sit down and be quiet.' And his father said to me, 'I hope you haven't been bringing him up to be a namby-pamby mother's boy while I've been away.' I didn't want to argue with him in front of Robert but I suppose I must have glared, because he added, 'Better that he should break a leg than break his spirit!' Eventually we got to my mother's, where Robert's excitement knew no bounds, and we had tea, after which Robert was playing around outside. And then he suddenly ran up the long, narrow flight of stairs in the house, poised himself at the top of the staircase, and took a dive down to the bottom.

True to his father's word, Robert broke his leg. An ambulance was called, and Marje and Proopsie went with the child to Walton-on-Thames Hospital, where he was detained. Marje had to return to Golders Green with her husband, but spoke not one word to him, other than 'pass the salt', for a fortnight. 'I hated and detested him,' she says. 'And that was really the beginning of the disaster of our marriage.' Whether Marje was right to blame Robert's accident on his father's chance remark in the train is open to question. She certainly has authority on her side, though. Marje's confidant, psychiatrist Tom Kraft:

> It is perfectly possible that the little boy was breaking his leg to please his father, yes. 'My father will like me if I break my leg. He said so. He said, Better to break my leg than to break my spirit. So he's really saying that this is what I've got to do, and in this way I'm going to get favour with my father.' Robert wasn't the first child to be upset when his dad returned from the war, either, because suddenly a man had arrived whom he didn't know, and this man had taken his place in the household. Up until then, the child had been in that important position. Age five is just the Oedipal phase. That's the stage, in Freudian terms, when the child would like to marry his mother and kill his father!

At six, poor Robert caused another furore by waking up one morning covered in spots. He had a temperature, and Marje told Proopsie, 'I'm sure he's got measles.' Proopsie replied, 'Don't worry about it!' and proceeded not to worry about it. Marje says her husband was always very calm and reassuring. The couple normally left for work at the same time, Proopsie with his briefcase and Marje with a plastic bag. When the moment for departure came on this particular morning, Proopsie said, 'Now, I don't want you to worry. Just give me a ring at the office when the doctor's been.' And with that, Mr Proops picked up his briefcase and off he went. Marje, who merely had a newspaper column to go to, was immediately cast in the role of the wife and mother. Her hackles rose:

I was enraged. I got myself worked up into such a fury during the day, I couldn't speak! Robert had indeed got the measles, and I did what was expected. I stayed home. And when Proopsie came back that night, I turned on him like a virago. He was appalled at my outrage. He couldn't understand it. That was the only time that he let me down in that way, expecting the woman to play her correct role. In all other respects, he helped me with everything.

Marje, Robert and Proopsie had unknowingly embarked on 'two appalling years', during which Marje began to feel more and more distaste for her husband, both in and out of bed. She had not enjoyed sex with him before, when he was familiar, and she was altogether less fond of it with this army officer who had come back to her with one or two high-handed ways, having had rather a leisurely war. Marje thinks that had he risen through the ranks instead of going straight into the Royal Engineers as a second lieutenant, he might not have been 'so dictatorial'. During the war, he had seen two main areas of activity: one was building landing strips out of enemy range, and the other was running a radio station with David Jacobs in Ceylon. He was about to go on active service in Burma when peace broke out. So he had had the time to learn fluent Hindustani, and had grown accustomed to being shaved by his Indian batman while he slept.

Not Proopsie's fault, of course, but he had also developed diabetes (requiring a special diet), was covered in

boils, and had ulcers on his legs from wearing jungle
boots in sweltering heat – a condition which may well have
reminded Marje of her anguish over her father's accident.
But more important was the fact that Proopsie behaved
differently. He had crossed over to another culture. He
would dash up to passing Asians in the street and start
speaking to them in Hindustani, sometimes to their huge
embarrassment because they came from Birmingham. This
Proopsie looked different; he even smelt different. Marje
recalls:

He was dark-skinned from being in India and Ceylon
all that time, and he even smelt spicy in a funny kind
of way. I don't know whether that was my imagination
or not, but I believe that he did. And what with
Robert's hatred of his father for turfing him out of
my bedroom, and Proopsie's fury with the little boy
who had demonstrated his hatred – because children of
that age can't dissemble – Robert used to have terrible
tantrums, which he'd never had before. So we had two
very, very difficult, awful years, with a lot of quarrels,
a lot of arguments and shouting. And at the end of
that two years, I told Proops that I couldn't bear him
to touch me; that his touch made my skin creep.

I couldn't bear him to kiss me. I was revolted by him. I
lay in bed beside him quivering with horror. And in the
end I told him, 'I can't go on with this marriage. I've got
to leave you!' And his response was, 'Fine. OK. Leave
me. But you don't get the boy. I'll fight you for the boy,
and I will win. Because I shall have the divorce judge on
my side. I have been away for four years, longing the
whole time to get back to my wife and child, and what
do I find when I return but a wife who rejects me, who
won't sleep with me, who won't let me touch her? And
if you think that any divorce judge is going to listen to

all this and have sympathy for you, you are mistaken.'
So I then had a terrible, terrible dilemma. I didn't tell
anybody. I felt that I couldn't. There was nobody in
the whole world I could tell, that I couldn't sleep with
my husband. There was no Marjorie Proops around in
those days.

There was no Marjorie Proops around in King Solomon's
day, either, but when two women came before him
claiming to be the mother of the same child, Solomon's
response was to have a sword fetched, and to offer to cut
the boy in half for them. Whereupon one of the women
immediately withdrew her claim to save the child. And
Solomon, being a wise old duck, knew that this was
the real mother. What Marje eventually decided was to
suffer anything herself rather than have Robert made a
'tug-of-love' child. She says now:

In the end, the decision was not difficult: the most
important thing to me was that Robert was OK. I didn't
want his life divided; I didn't want there to be a fight
over him. I couldn't imagine what it would be like for
him if I were thrown out of the home and he were left in
his father's care without me. I had no doubt that I'd be
able to take care of myself. I was already earning money
and looking after myself, so I was pretty confident on
the working side of my life. But I said to Proops, 'OK,
I'll stay. But I have to tell you that I will never sleep
with you again.' And he accepted this. He then said
that he loved me; that he'd have me on any terms
rather than lose me. So after a very uneasy period of
adjustment to this new set-up, we settled down to live
what purported to be a happy family life.

Nobody knew. Neither Marje's family nor Proopsie's

parents were told for fear of upsetting them, not even when Proopsie's father came to live with them for a while. In fact it was the beginning of a deception that was to last for forty years until Proopsie's death. But because with biographies we have the benefit of hindsight, and can sit like gods in judgement on poor buggers struggling to live their lives on the hop, we can ask the grown-up Robert what he thinks about the matter. After all, the set-up was supposed to be for his benefit. Robert Proops:

My father came back from the war to find this was not a marriage made in heaven. This was a marriage that was a disaster at every level, with two people knocking cobs off each other in their different ways. My father did it in a way which is easy to criticize, because it's easy to say he was acting like a pig. He did act like a pig. My mother wound him up to act like a pig, with a dynamic that was equally reprehensible. But he wanted to be the devil and she wanted to be the angel, and they played devil-and-angel games all the time. That's the truth. With me as a football. And so this cosy little story of my father coming back from the war a changed man, and that circumstance giving my mother a lease to do whatever she felt like doing, is I think a fantasy.

The dynamic was much more complicated than my mother thinks it was. I think my mother organized her life in the way that suited her. My father didn't like that. My mother wished to keep her home environment going. She always swears that all she ever wanted to do was to leave, though I think that this is absolutely untrue. I think that all she ever wanted to do was to preserve the status quo. And if ever anyone was in a position in that day and age to leave her marriage, my mother was in that position, as ninety-nine per cent of women then were not. She had the choice, and she chose not to.

Her post-event logic was that my father threatened to take the child away. Well, actually, the law then was even tighter than it is now; if she had left, *he* would have been unable to hang on to me! And whereas she always said that she never left because she couldn't leave me behind, and he always said that he'd hang on to me, the truth of the matter is that that is a total blind. She was financially able to support herself, and she would legally not have been separated from me. And yes, I think there would have been an extremely embarrassing divorce case which she wouldn't have liked at all from a publicity point of view. And it wouldn't have suited her in all sorts of other ways too. No, they both had options which they decided not to take. And to some degree to my detriment, they both blamed me for the option that they did take.

But Robert, I said, what about the gangplank story?

The gangplank story would be typical, again. Both of them were concerned in an extreme way to be seen to be doing the right thing. 'I'm doing the right thing because you came back from the war not the man I married.' 'I'm doing the right thing because you're not behaving like a decent wife.' Everybody does this, yes, but they did it in spades! They did it internally and they did it for the outside world. And what my father was concerned about at Liverpool Docks was 'not playing the part right'. That's why she got waved away. Because he was concerned about playing the part as per his script, and she was playing the part as per her script, and the two scripts bore no relationship to each other!

Marje:

I have to argue with Robert's view of my relationship with his father at this period of his life – that is from when he was about five until he was about eight. He could not possibly have known at such an early age what my relationship with his father was like. In fact I think, with hindsight, that Proopsie and I did a good job of protecting Robert from knowing the truth.

Robert says his father didn't like the way I organized my life in the way that suited me, but in fact his father was very much party to the way my life was organized. Remember, Proopsie wanted me to work and pursue a career. He freely admitted that life was easier with two salaries than with one, and indeed he often remarked that this would be very helpful when we started paying school fees.

It is true that I was, as Robert says, in a position to leave and financially able to support myself and him if I had been able to take him with me, but what he hasn't taken into account was my very real terror of how both my family and Proopsie's parents would have reacted to a separation. I adored Proopsie's parents and would never have harmed them. A separation or divorce would have devastated them.

I also have to argue with Robert about his views on the gangplank story. At the point at which I first saw Proopsie on the ship after nearly four years of separation, I was an excited wife longing to be reunited with the husband she'd missed. At that point the marriage had not collapsed, although the seeds of collapse were, of course, there from the start.

When Robert was eight, Marje and Proopsie decided to send him away to boarding school. Looking back, Marje thinks he was too young, and if she had to make the decision now, she would have deferred it. But both parents were trying to protect Robert from the flying cobs. He went to prep school and then to public school as a boarder.

There are a few questions here. First, did Marje and Proopsie worry about the reputedly rampant boarding school homosexuality? Apparently not. Years later she told *Gay News*, 'I was perfectly aware when we sent him to public school that he would probably have homosexual relationships, and that they might well continue afterwards. I used to examine my feelings, and tell myself, and tell my husband, that if he did turn out to be gay, it wouldn't make any difference. As it happens he isn't gay.' Marje was glad, because she wanted to have grandchildren.

The second question is, since Robert was Jewish, why not send him to a Jewish school? After all, he was obliged to attend Church of England religious assemblies, and would come home chanting, 'Our Father, *chart* in heaven, forgive us our *Christmases* . . .' Marje: 'I wanted him to make up his own mind about religion, and to have the opportunity to be like the majority, rather than a minority.'

But the third question is the one on everyone's lips. Why would two *socialists* send their son to public school? 'Well, I didn't think it was right to subject my child to the strictures that I might put on myself when his future was at stake,' says Marje, without enumerating what these 'strictures' might be. 'I wanted him to have the best education I could afford. The state education even in those days was not up to much. As it turned out, Robert went to a state school too, but he's grown up a socialist despite his education.' A major factor, of course, was the need to get him away from the Home Front and 65 Dunstan

Road. Unfortunately, Robert's gratitude knew all sorts of bounds:

> Well, I ran the escape committee for the prep school I went to, in Westcote near Dorking. Eventually when I was nine or ten I ran away so seriously that my parents realized I wasn't going to stay put. I was finally picked up at the bottom of Box Hill in the middle of the night, waving down a car that was going in the direction of London. They took me to my parents, and I didn't go back to boarding school again until I was thirteen [he went as a day-boy instead to the local elementary]. And at thirteen I went to public school at Berkhamsted.
>
> At prep school my parents would come down from time to time and take me to the movies or something on a Saturday. But I hated school so much that I kept running away. I don't think I was particularly strong-willed, no, but I think I realized at quite an early age that to survive in this environment I was going to have to be self-sufficient, and to draw demarcation lines for myself.

Robert was already a tall, leggy boy, with a hair sprout on the crown of his head, and ears like open car doors. His main interests at seven were planes, coal-mines and cowboys and Indians, though he loved sport and the sea and could ride surf before most Americans. Marje's letters to her GI buddy Delmer reveal little portraits of 'a leggy, wild boy, keen on cricket and football and fighting; losing his teeth and tearing all his clothes. He's a nice little kid and still regards me as the most beautiful woman in the world.' At twelve, his voice began to break. He had joined the Scouts and was mad about building aircraft models. Marje wrote to Delmer, 'He's a nice kid, and fairly intelligent, though by no means a mastermind. He's got plenty of rough charm that will probably help him a lot. He plans to be an architect, and his father thinks he has the makings.'

When Robert was not away at school, or making escape bids, Proopsie was attempting to 'organize' him, as he had previously organized Robert's mother. Except that Proops Junior would not kowtow. 'Robert's much stronger than I am,' says Marje now, 'largely because he didn't have to live much with his father. And he defied his father, but I never could. And the interesting thing is that Robert is in many ways like Proopsie, and he orders me about now the way his father did. And I don't stand up to Robert either.'

In defence of father Proopsie's disciplinary measures, it must be remembered that Marje had been influenced by her journalistic contact with *laissez-faire* and Summerhill-style education. She had met A. S. Neill and been deeply impressed with his delinquent *Lord of the Flies*-type school, where the children would break windows and spit at each other without anyone lifting a finger to correct the little darlings. She was to say in an interview in the 1970s, 'Poor Robert was the victim of all this. I tried never to say a word to him, but every so often I used to get mad and lose my temper.' On these occasions Robert would get 'a good wallop'. He was inclined to wilfulness: even at six he had been found guilty of bullying at school, which had earned him the unfortunate title of 'Bossy Proops'. Nothing would induce him to eat strong-tasting food like cheese or onions. If put before him, these would cause volcanic eruptions.

No doubt Proops senior was sorely tested by these goings-on, having returned from the infernal regions with his leg ulcers and a grave desire to study his seed catalogues in silence. But we should not jump to conclusions about Proopsie's attitude towards the young stranger in his home. He wasn't a demonstrative person, and his feelings about children, as about everything else, ran deep. Rather like Princess Anne, he would no doubt have admitted to being unsentimental about kids, and then like her would take practical steps to help small waifs and strays. He had seen terrible poverty in India, and he cared very much about unwanted children in institutions back home, where people were supposed to be compassionate. We shall see shortly an example of Proopsie's humanity towards children, even wayward ones. Certainly, it would be wrong to assume he was hard-hearted. He simply thought that cuddling children was soppy, and spoiling them even worse. Marje:

> He really didn't understand children. He didn't understand how to cope with them. He was very detached and remote from them, and not responsive. He had no common ground. I love children, always have. When I go to the doctor's now, I sit in the waiting room watching the kids running about and playing, and within two minutes I'm playing with them, or reading to them, or shaking rattles. Now, Proopsie would never have done that. He would have sat in the waiting room reading *The Times*. I never saw him go up to a child and make a fuss of it. I don't remember him ever picking Robert up and hugging him. Ever. And yet the funny thing was that he was immensely kind. He would have done anything for anybody. But he wasn't demonstrative, like I am. I'm a great toucher and kisser!

What Marje chiefly regretted and resented was that Proopsie would never share any male pastimes with his son. He never played football with him in the park, or took him to a cricket match; the pair went their separate ways. Marje had hoped Proopsie would provide Robert

with a devoted dad, like other fathers. She would silently
accuse Proopsie of neglecting to do this, but never openly.
'I used to think that what a boy needs is a role model. I
was probably too frightened to say it, because Proopsie
was very good at putting me down, putting me in my
place, and showing his contempt. I think it was Proopsie's
attitude of superiority that made me so determined to have
a life outside of the marriage.' Ominous words, and ones
that will echo through future chapters.

Seeing that her dream marriage was over, Marje now
buried herself in her work. 'I devoted myself to my job,
I suppose to compensate for not having a man to whom
I could devote myself. Proops and I never had sex again.
I don't really blame him for any of this. I never did. I
blame myself. I feel that if I'd been the sort of wife who
could lie there under a man pretending to have orgasms,
thinking about somebody or something else, I could have
done what so many women do, and that is to endure sex.
I feel nothing but pity for Proopsie. I think that if he was
in any way at fault, it was in his lack of understanding of
Robert, and his bossiness towards us both. He was a very,
very stern father. He was the one who made all the family
decisions, even down to choosing the wallpaper.' Marje
doesn't agree with Robert's idea that a divorce settlement
would have given her custody either. 'The woman was
always at fault.'

They had a grand piano installed and Marje began
having lessons again, practising for hours in the evenings.
She would play her Chopin, badly but sadly, and Proopsie
would put his head round the door and then withdraw
to the far reaches of the house to listen to very loud
opera records. A small friend of Robert's, hearing the
piano music, wandered in and offered Marje his candid
opinion: 'You don't play very well, do you?'

She wrote to Delmer and Happy, congratulating them

on their new baby son, and said how she envied them. 'If I had another son, I think he'd be called David,' said Marje, knowing there would never be any more babies for her. At work she often thought and wrote about children. In early December 1950, following the screening of a Home Office film, she told her readers about the 20,000 children living in homes and institutions throughout Britain, 'who sleep in dormitories, eat in groups, live communal lives'. The government was seeking foster-parents for these kiddies, homes where they would enjoy family life whilst still remaining 'the responsibility of the state'. The foster-parents would be paid twenty-six shillings a week.

She followed this up with another piece just before Christmas 1950, thanking readers for the letters 'pouring in', offering Christmas holidays to these needy children. When she rejoined the *Mirror* in 1954, one of her earliest articles was about unwanted children like three-year-old Johnny Masterson, whose parents could not be traced. The little boy had just spent two years in hospital where he made up stories about a nonexistent father coming to visit him. Marje drew attention to the plight of thousands of other children like Johnny Masterson hidden away in homes, and said they needed something more than pity and the odd gift from well-wishers.

Proopsie, for all his stern reprimands to Robert, wanted to do something practical to help, and for once he and his wife were in total harmony, like they used to be before their marriage. The couple went along to the Fountain Hospital in Tooting, south London, and began taking home for Christmas holidays a little five-year-old boy. We shall call this child Sonny, to protect his identity. Sonny was small and scared. He thought Marje was another nurse, as he had only ever seen nurses, and he gripped her skirt with his podgy little fist. He had thick black hair and a slightly cherubic look. 'He had very

large, beautiful brown eyes. He was a good-looking little
boy, not like Robert. Robert had a kind of scruffy look. Of
course,' adds Marje, 'I would have had the lot if I could
have done.'

Sonny thought the Proopses' home was a fairytale castle,
with the kitchen a magic cave full of beautiful shiny jewels
called saucepans, which he had never seen before. The
Proopses had festooned the Christmas tree with presents
for Robert and Sonny, but saucepans were much more
important. Sonny could see himself in the base of every
one, and they made a pleasing clatter if you banged the
furniture.

Robert and Sonny shared a bedroom. Robert, after
an initial flush of jealousy, accepted the newcomer and
was glad of his company for the festive season. After
Christmas, sadly, Sonny was returned to the Home.
Marje told Delmer in her letters, 'He's a sweet little boy,
an orphan, adopted by the state. He calls us Mummy
and Daddy, and is very fond of Robert . . . We've found
it works very well generally and intend to continue to
be "Mummy and Daddy" to this small piece of human
flotsam. His real parents abandoned him when he was
an infant.'

The only unpleasant part was giving him back. Marje
remembers: 'At the end of the Christmas holidays I was
brokenhearted. So was Proopsie. We both said it was like
giving back a Christmas present, and to take this child
and return him to the Home – even now I can feel the
pain of it. This minute. That feeling of desolation. Because
when we took him back, we realized we were dealing
with a human being, not something off a Christmas tree.
It was like a blinding flash, this realization: the difference
between something you take off a Christmas tree and a
little human being who suffers and is being rejected. And
that was when we decided. We went back to the Home

and asked was there any way in which we could have
a relationship with him, and they suggested we become
his unofficial "aunt and uncle".'

Sonny's visits became more frequent. He would come
to the Proopses for other holidays, and during school
term-time they would write to him and send him little
presents. Everything looked rosy, and Proopsie, who
grew very fond of the boy, smiled with satisfaction to
see this experiment in benevolent socialism working in
his own household. True, there were still rows going
on between himself and Marje, and Sonny still had to
keep going back to the dormitory and community-living
in between his heady visits to where the Other Half lived,
but at least the Proopses were doing their best to give the
child a sense of belonging.

Then, suddenly, things started to go wrong. Sonny
began stealing. At first he stole money from Marje's
special housekeeping purse. Marje recalls, 'I thought, in
my kind of amateur psychology way, it was maybe because
he resented me for not actually being his mother, and it
was a sort of punishment. But Proopsie used to argue with
me and say, "Rubbish. He's just light-fingered." And I
would argue back, "Nobody's light-fingered naturally!" So
we would have these long arguments then about Sonny.
I always did my best to compensate Sonny for not being
his mother, and I probably overcompensated, the way you
do,' says Marje, hinting at more spoiling underway.

Sonny's expertise at stealing began to develop into an
art form. He began to pinch from other people, who could
not all be blamed for failure to be his natural mother.
Eventually, when he was fifteen and a half, his career of
crime attracted the eyeball of the law. Marje:

He was picked up – nicked. I can't remember what
remedial institution he was sent to, but it did no good

at all. He came out and went on stealing and nicking.
And eventually he ended up in prison. I don't know
whether he's still in the nick now, but we used to go
to visit him, and sit with all the other parents. It was
the most horrendous experience, to sit in the waiting
room and have your name called out – 'Proops!' – and
then to have to talk to him through the mesh. It became
increasingly difficult.

One day I had a call from the governor of the prison,
who said, 'You must dissociate yourself from this boy,
because he's using your name for his nefarious purposes. He's going round saying, "I'm Marjorie Proops's
son" and conning people. Not only for your sake but for
his, it would be sensible.' And Proopsie persuaded me
to break off the relationship, and I was terribly reluctant
to do it, and have always felt guilty ever since. But I
know that I'd have had a terrible time with him. The
governor said to me, 'One of these days, he'll end up
doing GBH – and who knows who the victim will be?'
Which was a clear warning. And I thought, well, the
chances are he'll come and hit me on the head.

The calamity upset Marje, but it left Proopsie shattered.
It was a deep disaster for him personally, because it
threatened his values and beliefs. Robert:

It was my father's greatest failure in life. I think that, like
my mother and myself to some extent, he had a naive
and cosy view of the world, and tried to make the world
in that image. I think he was saddened and embittered
by what happened to Sonny, because his rosy view of
the world and how wonderfully he could influence it
turned out not to be true. He'd had this splendid glass
picture of the world smashed in front of his eyes. There
was a large Victorian streak in my father and doing good

works was part of him. One could argue, and I'm not saying I would, that the way my parents handled Sonny could have precipitated what eventually happened.

They found this child and plucked him from the Home on an irregular basis, and brought him into a family which was well-off middle class, both parents working, earning good money, with the benefits of that going on around. He was brought into that environment for short periods, and then delivered back to the Home. And if you look at it through the wrong end of the telescope, you could say that what it may well have done is to distort Sonny's view of the world, by showing him the haves, and himself as one of the have-nots. One could easily argue that this blew up in my father's face. I'm not questioning my father's motives. He did it from good, avuncular motives. But when Sonny went wrong, this was a disaster for my father from which he never recovered. He never talked about it again.

Mercifully, the Proopses' longing to help solitary children was eventually rewarded by a curious turn of events in their neighbourhood. Two doors away from their Golders Green semi a group of Nigerians moved in – part of a more extended family. As Robert observes, 'Nigerians tend to have the biggest extended families on God's earth.' Being members of an ethnic minority themselves, the Proopses considered colour prejudice a kind of insolence against humanity. Marje: 'Before they'd unpacked, Proopsie was in there introducing himself and offering his assistance with everything. I dare say he did all the unpacking. And there was this little boy and two women who turned out to be his aunties. His mother and father were still in Lagos. He was an enchanting boy and Proopsie and I adored him from the moment we set eyes on him.'

This was a young student by the challenging title of
Olumade Okubadeju, or Made for short (which Marje
pronounces Mardi as in Mardi Gras). Made was shy
and quiet, an extremely conscientious boy, the son of a
lawyer and himself determined to be a doctor (he is now
a pathologist and director of the Public Health Laboratory
in Portsmouth). When he was a teenager, studying at
Norwich City College, the rest of the family had to return
to Nigeria and like a shot the Proopses offered Made a
place in their home. He and Robert were already close
friends. Robert: 'I had probably spent more time in their
house than in my own, and I became part of their extended
family. So when they left and Made got sort of left over,
he was not at all odd or strange to me. I regarded him
as a brother. Having him live with us was absolutely no
problem – in fact my only disappointment was that all the
others went!' Marje:

And that's how Made came to live with us. He was
like another son. He used to call me 'Mummy'. I'd
take Robert and Made on the bus and they'd argue
about who should pay the fare. Made would shout
from one end of the bus, 'Mummy – it's my turn!' and
all these toffee-nosed passengers would look at me and
clearly think I was having it off with a black American
GI or something. I just ignored the prejudice. I feel
sorry, always have, for prejudiced people. I think they
must be unhappier than the people they despise and
criticize. I myself was subjected to the pain of prejudice
and knew what it was like. So that made me all the
more determined that my son and Made should grow
up to regard all human beings as similar, fallible, happy
and unhappy, whatever their colour, religion, shape or
size. We are all the result of an accident at birth and
we don't choose to be what we are.'

What did Made himself make of the Proops household?

Although I was older than Robert, nevertheless we were both still young enough to communicate as young people. He and I would go out and enjoy ourselves, just talking, or roaming around the park with the dog. When we came back, Mr and Mrs Proops would still be at work, so we would make ourselves sandwiches and tea. She was always working. On Sundays she did her writing in bed, while Mr Proops organized all the menus for the week. They both worked in the evening as well.

Mr and Mrs Proops were like parental figures to me, *in loco parentis*, if you like. I looked to them as people I could trust and ask for advice. When I finished at Norwich, I came down to London to study medicine at King's College, and nearly every weekend I would visit them.

They took care of me, and gave me my meals, and they would take me out, to the Proms, for example. Mr Proops used to talk to me a lot about music. He told me he had seen *The Mikado* seven times, and the whole of Gilbert and Sullivan. I couldn't understand that! But they did teach me to appreciate concert conductors. I can remember once, when we were coming home from a concert at the Royal Albert Hall and I was full of the atmosphere, Mrs Proops said she thought the conductor wasn't very good. And Mr Proops agreed. When I asked them why, she said, 'The orchestra ran away from the conductor!' [Gales of laughter from Made.] So then it dawned on me that you have to watch the two together, conductor and orchestra, to appreciate them well. That has stayed with me ever since. I still think of it when I'm at concerts with my wife.

I called Mrs Proops 'Mum'. I was always impressed by

her intellectual powers, although she keeps on saying that it's nothing. She always had a very active mind, and another way in which I'm sure they both helped my development was that they helped me to think. We always listened to *The Brains Trust* on a Sunday and we would have discussions afterwards. I enjoyed that. I always felt comfortable with them. I didn't encounter a lot of prejudice during those years because the Proopses took me as one of their own people, and it didn't really occur to me that I wasn't. I suppose I was sheltered. I just felt at home. They made me stable.

By a strange irony, Marje was once accused of racial prejudice. When Made grew up and married a white schoolteacher, Fay, Marje wrote rejoicing in her column that she had 'beautiful coffee-skinned grandchildren'. And what did she get for her song of praise? A lot of enraged letters from the race-relations lobby.

7

Mirror Mirror Off the Wall

*I*f Marje ever had a god, Hugh Cudlipp was he. She once described him as 'a life force' and said she always knew instinctively whether or not he was in the building. When the Welsh Dragon beckoned her back to the *Mirror* from the *Daily Herald* in June 1954, she was drawn like a ship to a lighthouse. Percy Cudlipp had been kind and courteous, 'but Hugh was different, the sort of man who would take you over. If Hugh said, "I want you to do this," you did it. I obeyed him. I loved him – not in any kind of sexual way, because I don't think he even touched my hand – but I so admired him. I thought I was terribly terribly lucky that such a brilliant man should even bother to think I was worthwhile bringing back to the paper.' Cudlipp may not have touched her hand, but a photo of a merry press lunch in the 1960s shows Marje standing up making a speech, with the great editorial director, in high spirits, holding his svelte journalist by the hips.

She returned as columnist, and was to be sent all over the world nosing out material for her humorous, highly personal off-the-wall articles. 'The whole thing was enormously flattering and I felt very important,' says Marje. She was inspired by Cudlipp, frightened by Cudlipp, and given star treatment by Cudlipp, from which she rose to renown.

It never went to her head. She once came away from the fishmongers to find her smelly purchase had been wrapped in the *Daily Mirror* – 'And there was my face around the stinking wet fish. I thought to myself, "That's just about what it's worth, so don't get any ideas about yourself. Don't think you're ever going to be Mrs Shakespeare."' Lord Cudlipp:

A significant aspect of the Proops phenomenon is that her fame never sullied her modesty or professional integrity. There were never any tantrums or airs and graces, no threats of resignation or peevish complaints about the order of the 'billing' or the typographical size of her name in relation to that of other writers in the same newspaper. God knows, that sort of megalomania is not as common in the publishing world as in the theatre, but it is not unknown . . . Marje's prominence over the decades in what, in my time, was the popular newspaper with the world's largest circulation, made her as well known and instantly recognizable by the public in her own country as any Hollywood film star, Liz Taylor included. Walking with me along the corridors of a couple of carriages on the London to Glasgow express, she was stopped eight times for her autograph. Then in the restaurant car she said to me, without the slightest affectation, 'isn't it fun?'

Why did Cudlipp want her back, particularly?

She has, *par excellence*, the gift of mass communication, talking *with* and not talking *down*.

Mirror Group ex-chairman, Ernie Burrington:

She was a natural to join the *Mirror*. It was quite clear

that here was a writer with a great touch for a popular newspaper and she could have been recruited by damn nearly any one of them, including the middle market. But she was utterly natural for the *Mirror*, and no doubt shared the same feelings and attitudes to people that were then being reflected best in the *Daily Mirror*.

The *Mirror's* former industrial editor, Geoffrey Goodman:

Her pulling power was enormous. The *Mirror* formula as it developed through the fifties and sixties was uniquely geared to the mood of the country, orchestrated by the genius of Cudlipp and brilliantly executed by his journalists. And Marje fitted into that package with her supreme pulling power. She's the World's Woman.

Former *Mirror* columnist and assistant editor, John Knight:

Cudlipp always saw her as one of the few women journalists with a truly popular touch. I think she's probably right when she says Cudlipp 'invented' her: he was a brilliant newspaper impresario – a bit of a bully but he had this incredible flair. He knew that a successful newspaper had to have 'stars'. Marjorie became one of the Cudlipp All-Stars. He knew how to project people and she was given the gun, but equally she was a performer, and a star performer over many many years.

Felicity Green, former *Mirror* colleague and the first woman journalist ever appointed to the board of a newspaper:

Marje is a great communicator, which after all is what journalism is about. To watch Marje work is really the most eye-opening experience. She writes everything in

longhand, and her pen is an extension of her hand. She
writes almost without hesitation: it just pours out of her
like liquid gold. Many writers suffer about what to put
next, and can't think of the first paragraph. Marje is just
the opposite. She's the most uninhibited communicator
I have ever come across. She knows what she wants
to say and she knows how she wants to say it. She
can't help writing with style. It isn't something that
she strives to do. It's just there, and her language is
equally well-defined, totally her own, and as acceptable
to somebody almost illiterate as to readers of *The Times* or
the *Telegraph*. She pitches herself straight in the middle
so that she doesn't write above the heads of one lot and
condescend to the other lot. She is a classless writer. And
she never sounds like anybody else.

On Marje's first day, Cudlipp took the nervous columnist to
meet the editor. There he sat, resplendent, in a large leather
chair behind his mega-desk, suave and dapper with his
white hair and his posh suit. He looked to Marje more like
a cabinet minister than a journalist. Marje: 'Hugh Cudlipp
said to this well-groomed gent, "This is Marje Proops, your
new columnist." And then he turned to me and said: "This
is Jack Nener, editor of the *Daily Mirror*." And this very
elegant, good-looking man stood up from his leather chair
and shook me by the hand. "Fucking glad to meet you!"
he said.'

Mrs Jack Nener, journalist Audrey Whiting: 'Jack would
never have said such a thing.'

Marje: 'He did! I was there! I don't think perhaps Audrey
had any idea what he was like in the office. He used
to walk up and down the newsroom, as any of the
journalists who were there at the time will tell you,
calling them all arseholes. That was his favourite word.
"Fucking arseholes" he used to call them. And when I

first arrived back at the *Mirror* I used to wander round the newsroom having kittens at Jack's vocabulary. I was horrified because I'd never heard language like it, other than from the meat porters in Smithfield.'

Driven on by Nener's expletives and Cudlipp's charisma, Marje and the others would hit their straps. It was a witty and wise newspaper, often in bad odour with the government but always maintaining an intimate link with the masses through readers' letters and polls. (The year before Marje rejoined the team, Cudlipp had caused yet another furore by polling readers on whether or not Princess Margaret should marry Group Captain Peter Townsend – they reckoned she should.) Just how great the *Mirror* was at the time Marje rejoined it is explained by one of its writers in the 1950s and 1960s, one for whom Marje helped to drum up popular support when he stood for the first time for Parliament. Ex-Shadow Foreign Minister Gerald Kaufman:

The *Mirror* was the single strongest political force for any political party in the country over a considerable period. It was a brilliant newspaper, probably the most brilliant there has ever been in British journalistic history. It was very, very serious, but at the same time extremely popular. So it managed, unlike today's tabloids which look for circulation by lowering standards, to hold an increased circulation by setting very high standards, both of political comment and factual accuracy. I was proud to work on the *Daily Mirror*.

Woodrow Wyatt, former Under-Secretary of State in the Labour War Office, praised the *Mirror* in 1955, saying it outdid 'in clarity and depth of thought anything which appears in its more pompous rivals'. And Marjorie Proops's own contribution to this newspaper during its heyday,

despite her modesty about fishmonger's wrappings, was
to prove considerable.

Marje's 1950s page was billed as 'The sparkling new
column for every woman' and 'The woman's column with a
sparkle'. Just between ourselves, Marje has never approved
of separate sections in the paper for women (despite *Mirror*
Woman'), and it soon becomes clear that whatever the
editor intended, she is talking to men as well ('Men, pin
back your ears'; 'Am I right, boys?'). As if to emphasize
the fact, she highlights points from her postbag that have
been sent in by male readers, such as 'a group of Liverpool
gents'.

Furthermore, anyone reading these old cuttings is struck
by the way she flirtingly curries favour with men ('I love
sailors'; 'I'm sold on boxing', etc.) and occasionally lets
slip anti-female sentiments ('Let it be *young* glamour . . .
For there's nothing more embarrassing than a woman who
doesn't know when the moment has come to stop kidding
herself'; 'We women have got ourselves a fine reputation
as clanger-droppers, and I am sorry to say we deserve
it', etc., etc.). When a group of servicemen write in to
say they don't like women dumping their high heels for
health, Marje replies, lamely, 'Well, women were born to
suffer . . . So we'll suffer to please you.'

The column was always accompanied by a caricature,
similar to the one she had used in her latter days at the
Herald, with a squiggle for hair, a dash for a nose, and
a couple of flourishes to suggest specs, lips and cigarette
holder. Amusing, but why not simply use a photograph?
A *Herald* reader had once asked this question, urging her
to abandon that 'awful insignia of lipstick and glasses'.
Marje replied, 'Sorry, no go. I haven't the kind of face
photographers love. That insignia hides homely features
I'd rather you never knew about'. She was not entrusting
her unorthodox looks to the tender mercies of *Mirror*

readers either. But there was a difference in the artwork: whereas the *Herald* cartoon had been full-face, the *Mirror* ones are in profile, and have a curious mixture of smiling lips and hawkish brows and specs, as if to say, 'I'm a humorous gal, but don't mess with me.'

A competition offering five guineas to readers who could complete the caricature lines to look like the real Marje brought in 10,000 entries. No one got a close likeness, but all the published winners were by men. She assured readers, 'No, I am not an aged spinster living in a Victorian mansion with cats. Nor am I thirty and a sophisticated jazz fan. And I am definitely not a gentleman – nor a male of any sort – despite your unkind suspicions. No photographs are available. You will just have to make do with the caricature, drawn with the specific purpose of leaving out all the bits like crooked teeth and too much nose which the camera never fails to emphasize'. She gives her 'vital statistics' as: 'Age, over 20, under 50. Height, 5'7". Weight, 9 stone 4 pounds. Bust, 37" [a slight enhancement], hips ditto, waist 25".' And her full-length caricatures emphasized these sexy bits. Marje: 'My self-portrait was probably a very glorified version of me as I got on a bit, but I did have a pretty good shape in those days. Somewhere knocking about I've got some pictures of myself in a swimsuit and I don't look a bad shape at all.'

The columnist's signature, 'Marjorie Proops', looped the loop under the headline, and the contents skated about in a lively ice dance over subjects amusing to women and saucily provocative to men, without keeping any of them up nights worrying their heads. Soon Marje would start to rattle a few cages, but her job in the early days was to be, like Austen's ladies, 'light and bright and sparkling'. *And* sexy. Percy Cudlipp had told her off about this at the chaste *Herald*, saying there were no frilly knickers in the Labour Party, and that 'You've got to watch it, Marjorie – you are a

sexy writer'. Well, at the *Mirror* the Welsh Dragon and Jack
Nener didn't seem to mind.

One of her first pieces was an interview with a bra
manufacturer about the size of cups. Another is a trip
to Hamburg's Reeperbahn ('Phew . . . the night life!').
Another is 'a date with my dream man'. The dreamboat
in question, or rather dream dinghy, turns out to be
David Nixon, bald but sincere, 'good-looking enough
without being maddeningly handsome' (maddening to
male readers, perhaps). She also likes Jack Hawkins, 'on
the wrong side of forty' with 'a homely, rugged mug'. Some
women like these hunky fellows. 'Me, I like them middle
aged, homely and cosy. A man's got to have a few grey
hairs – or even practically no hair at all – before my pulse
begins to quicken.'

She really lusts after Cary Grant and Gregory Peck as
well, but the dream dinghies give welcome reassurance to
all those ordinary men 'out there' who read her column –
which tells you something about Marje Proops's attitude
to her readers. Pity the millions of plain and pear-shaped
ladies, out there as well, who don't get their egos cos-
seted in newspapers by some equally compassionate male
journalist. Only a Marje Proops remembers their feelings.
When she hit back at the beauty business and did a piece
in 1957 saying she was sick of 'The Big Bust Cult', she
was flooded with mail from like-minded women readers.
'I was horrified that a girl with a 33" measurement regarded
herself in this day and age as a freak – a social failure. And
you are with me.' Marje adds, without intending any *double
entendre*, 'Never have I had such overwhelming support.'

In another article, 'Battling Marje Proops' announces,
'It is very clear to me that women are getting more and
more fed up with other women's vital statistics.' Sabrina's
forty-one-inch chest was being thrust up women's noses
at the time, and other Booby Girls, clad in swimwear,

began to jut forth from the *Mirror* as well. Marje, evidently fighting a rearguard action, called for fair dos and for male hunky pin-ups to be printed too. As a matter of fact she held a photo competition, and 2,000 snaps poured through the post revealing 140 tons of glorious beefcake. American feminists had been up in arms about such double standards for quite some time, but Marje was still nervous about tackling men on the real issues. 'I have reached the conclusion that equality is not worth fighting for,' she says. 'We women are better off without it.'

As usual with Marje, we get little glimpses of her home life, talcumed slightly for public consumption. She gives her impression of two marrieds having a meal, perhaps our Proopses:

He (Swallowing dinner with one eye on the paper): Bit overdone, these chops. Any news today?

She: No. Tea's up again. (Ten minutes' silence.) Any news at the office?

He: No. Busy day today. Bill's away.

She: Who's Bill?

He: Chap at the office.

She: Oh.

Elsewhere, Proopsie (always referred to as 'my spouse') has asked Marje 'six times' to sew a button on for him and eventually has to do it himself. His pipe and his pork-chop fingers get in the way, he starts swearing and ends up with large loops of cotton hanging from his work. Poor Proopsie is also seen tending his garden, chasing Marje with a spade to defend his daffs, and 'perking up' at the sight of the television cancan girls, the Toppers. When their TV set conks out, Marje rejoices. 'It's wonderful to have the heir to the Proops overdraft doing his homework and agreeing to go to bed without the everlasting battle to stay up to look in for just five minutes more. It's wonderful to be able to watch my spouse weeding the garden uninterrupted by filmed parlour games.' She attacks the BBC for showing women's programmes on kitchen-and-wardrobe subjects. 'Me, I'd much rather watch boxing than be told how to make an omelette.' ('Do you like boxing then, Marje?' I asked. 'No I don't. I hate it.')

Marje's personal struggle against Proopsie's dominance at home is also shared with readers. Marje wants to go blonde. Proopsie says, 'If you do, I shall walk right out of the house.' Marje responds, 'Boy, fetch the peroxide!' And she later tells her readers that she has gone and done it, having had blonde streaks put in by a chappie in Paris. Sometimes, even in these early days, there is a note of downright feminism. She tells women, 'Let him do some of the understanding for a change and see how he likes it.' 'Why do men always assume that anything bad in entertainment is good enough for women? And anything good, witty or intelligent is far beyond the limits of our fluffy, empty little heads?' She tells husbands off for withholding cuddles. 'It's your fault, husbands, if your wives regard you with amazement when you show them a bit of affection. They're simply not used to it. Ever wondered why your better half likes reading heart-throb novels and seeing romantic pictures? It's because they supply the romance and glamour you fail to provide.'

To keep things equitable, the paper tigress also has a go at the little woman: 'I am *sick* of the way housewives regard themselves as a downtrodden class – a kind of female race apart, with grey faces and grey lives. I'm *tired* of the timid voice of the woman behind the stove who thinks she's an inferior being. I'm *enraged* with the mother who, elbow deep in soap suds, sighs, "Life holds nothing more for me than drudgery . . . I'm only a housewife." It is high time such a housewife snapped out of her depression and realized how well off she is.' Marje thinks the housewife has chosen her lot, and should stop moaning. She can always put her feet up and listen to the radio, which is more than a career girl can do. A readers' poll on whether mums should go out to work, though, came down very heavily on the 'no' side. 'And that goes for you too, Proops,' added some, unkindly.

Having no help with her private hell at home, Marje preserved her sanity by using her column from time to time as a kind of psychiatrist's couch, to work out her feelings on hurtful events in her life. One of these was delivering Robert to boarding school. Prince Charles had just been deposited at a small-boy institution in Cheam, and Marje confided the details of her own trauma: how she had misgivings sewing the name-tags on Robert's clothes, how it gave her a catch in her throat to see the boy in his school cap, how she worried about him: 'Will he be lonely? Will he like his food? Will he miss us? Will he weep softly into his pillow after lights-out?'

She tells her readers, 'I remember how I steeled myself to be gay and to smile happily and not pass on any of the fears and anxieties to the boy. I remember my spouse's nonchalance and the stiff-upper-lip look on his face when the three of us had lunch together before we left for school. I remember him muttering, "Don't, for heaven's sake, kiss him goodbye in front of any of the other boys."' We see the naked Marje and the unvarnished Proopsie here, and this was not the stuff of which journalism was normally made in the 1950s. It created a very personal bond between Marje and the *Daily Mirror* readers. Perhaps, in a way, she was crying on their shoulders.

There are occasional 'in at the deep end' pieces, with

Marje spending the day as an usherette, salesgirl, or hairdresser's assistant. There are interviews with stars like Ingrid Bergman (Marje compares Ingrid's perfect nose with her own 'businesslike snitch'). There are tours of the provinces, tea parties with Welsh housewives, an excursion to Jersey with fifteen honeymoon couples, society bashes, such as Princess Alexandra's first grown-up ball. But the high points of Marje's column in the 1950s are the trips abroad. Cecil King, the new *Mirror* chairman (who had recently got rid of his rough-hewn predecessor, 'Bart'), urged Hugh Cudlipp to send Marje on these trips 'to freshen her up' – whatever that meant. Marje says they were intended to broaden her mind. As you will see, they succeeded.

There were regular excursions with woman's editor Ailsa Garland and fashion editor Felicity Green to Paris, with comic relief from Marje at her own expense. She is seen sitting outside a Paris restaurant with a pot of basil the restaurateur has given her 'to keep the flies off'. Other women get orchids. Felicity Green remembers how Marje was writing her amusing articles for 'the woman in the street':

By the time Marje and I went to Paris, I was covering the fashion and she was doing the human interest stories. We would go to the collections together but Marje was looking much more at the audience and the characters, and she took a very askance view and could always see the funny side of everything. If the skirts went down to ankle length and they were very tight, Marje would write a story about how we were all going to fall flat on our faces in the gutter in these silly skirts, and why didn't the men designers think more about flesh-and-blood women instead of dolls their mothers gave them?

She was the greatest possible fun to travel with. One

particular year we were in Paris, and waists were in and bosoms were bursting out all over, and what you needed was an embonpoint – you needed a bottom like two peaches, and the shops were full of gimmicks to round up your bottom. And Marje and I were staying in a lovely hotel with a courtyard, and we had bought something in the local pharmacy which was guaranteed to improve the shape of your derrière. It looked like a land mine. It was a ball with a lot of spikes all over and the idea was that you put it on the floor and sat on it, and rolled about on the thing. So in our room one morning I was rolling round on this spiked medicine ball, in my bra and pants, and Marje was standing there sketching me for her humorous article, and our windows were wide open because of the heat. And when I looked up, there across the courtyard were about three windows agape, with absolutely gobsmacked men looking out at the two of us performing this most extraordinary feat in our room.

On another trip, covering ski-wear, we were staying in the very picturesque little French village of Megève, where Bardot and Yves Montand had houses. At the centre of the village was a sort of bed-and-breakfast hotel-cum-nightclub, and we'd got ourselves transferred there from a boring Bournemouth-style place on top of the hill, as Marje was looking for an *après-ski* story. We came down to dinner and this very distinguished-looking grey-haired manager showed us to our table and hoped that the *mesdames* from the amazing *Daily Mirror de Londres* would have a lovely evening, and we had a whisky bebe or whatever the drink was that year, and ordered dinner. Suddenly I noticed something peculiar, and leaned towards Marje.

'Have you noticed anything odd about all the people in this restaurant?' Marje looked round.

'Yes – they're all women, and no men.'

'Have another look.' Marje did.

'They're all women,' she repeated.

'They're all *men*, actually!'

We'd got ourselves into the main transvestite place in the whole of Megève, and all these terribly elegant, sequinned, false-eyelashed ladies had hands like boxers! They were all men dressed as women. And when the cabaret came on, the leading act, a Danny La Rue-type figure, turned out to be the very elegant manager of the hotel.

Marje was still doing a few fashion sketches, sometimes too accurately for the designers' liking. She had already been expelled from Heim's salons for putting in too many vivid details, and on one occasion actually got the *Mirror* withdrawn from sale in Paris after she had sketched a Dior gown – not from the catwalk, but from a description given to her by Ailsa Garland who had been to the show alone. When Marje's sketch was wired to London and appeared in the *Mirror*, all hell broke loose in Paris because Dior thought Marje had given all his design secrets away. She hadn't even seen the bloody dress.

Other – non-fashion-related – trips followed, always with Marje flying out and sailing back: Australia (her slow boat back took twenty-three days, with editors running frantic), Scandinavia, Moscow, Canada, Hong Kong, Italy. Sometimes there was a focus for going, such as a conference, but a lot of the venues came off the top of Cudlipp's head. 'Hugh would say, "Good idea if you went to this conference in Melbourne. While you're there, drift around and see what else you can pick up." In those days we had offices in almost all the major capital cities, and I used to make the *Mirror* bureau, or the British embassy, my first port of call, to find out what was happening. And then I'd drift off on my travels, staying away for as long as I needed to pick up some good material; sometimes ten days, sometimes two or three weeks. It was left to me.'

In Rome, Marje was at the *Mirror* office when she received a strange, hush-hush assignment. They had a horoscope-writer called Francesco Waldner, who was supposed to deliver his copy to the Rome office and hadn't done it. The editor was pacing up and down yelling, 'Where's this fucking Waldner?' and foretelling what sort of fate the stargazer might enjoy if he didn't reveal himself shortly. At last, the Rome editor noticed Marje, and an evil light glinted in his eyes. 'Marje!' he exclaimed, '*You* write the copy!' So Marje gave all the signs excellent predictions and said they were going to have 'wonderful riches and marriages and travel'. It went down well, and readers never noticed the hiccup. 'After that, I had no belief in the stars at all,' says Marje. 'Nobody knew but the Rome editor and myself.'

In Moscow, where in those days Western visitors were welcomed with open firearms, Marje got into difficulties with the street signs, as she had just about mastered '*niet*' in Russian. The only landmark she recognized was an onion-shaped cathedral, which she tried to keep always in view. 'All I had was the name of the bloody street I wanted on this piece of paper, which I was thrusting at dozens of passers-by. I could have been knifed or strangled because I was totally unaware of danger of any kind. It never entered my head that I could be in peril just by talking to people. After all, that was my job as a journalist.' She ended up being driven round in a Rolls Royce – a provocative sight in Communist Russia – and visiting a state laundry, where she helped to wash Khrushchev's linen – perhaps the great leader's smalls.

In Las Vegas, however, trusting Marje came unstuck. She had been sent on an extended trip to America by Cudlipp and was using her own initiative to sniff out interesting stories, talking to anyone and everyone as usual. She had been to New York ('sinister'), to Washington and the White House (Bobby Kennedy was fanciable) and to Hollywood, where she got into a tangle on a dance floor with Groucho Marx, interviewed Marlon Brando about antique jewellery and saw Robert Mitchum fast asleep in a bar. She had heard there were quickie divorce shops in Vegas, and she thought there might be a story there. Marje:

One of the reasons why I used to get on well on these trips was that I have two qualities essential to journalists – curiosity, and an anxiety to talk to people and get to know them. I think that because of my youthful insecurity about the way I looked, and this certainty I had that no man would ever want me, or love me, all my life I've gone out of my way to be friendly, and to try to get people to like me. I think I've really gone over the top with this craving to have people liking me. Looking back, I see now that I was unbelievably naive.

On this particular occasion in Las Vegas I was hot and dishevelled and feeling revolting, and I was wandering round looking for these little supermarket-style places where you could get a divorce and get married to somebody else straight away. And a man came up to me and said I seemed lost. He was dark-haired and rather swarthy, and he asked if I was looking for something. I answered, 'Yes, I am actually'. 'Oh, you're English!' said the American. I told him that I was, and what I was looking for, and he assured me it was 'No problem' and that he would take me there. [Marje wrote twenty years ago that she had seen this man already in the hotel complex, and that he had told her he was an archery instructor, teaching actors and actresses to look good with a bow and arrow on film sets.]

He drove me over to the divorce shops in his car, and then he wandered about with me and bought me cold drinks, and I thought how very nice and kind and helpful he was. Eventually, when I decided to go back to my hotel, he said, 'All right – I'll drive you.' I got in his car again, trusting him, and when we arrived at my hotel I said, 'Would you like to come into the bar and have a drink?' because he had been so kind. And he answered, 'Well gee, I'd love to.'

I noticed that his eyes were rather red, and I began to wonder how much he'd had to drink, because whenever we'd stopped for refreshments he had knocked back quite a lot of strong booze, and I'm pretty sure he'd been drinking before he came to my aid. And he said, 'Well, why don't we go to your room, where it'll be cool and quiet?' and I said all right. [Marje seemed to think this reasonable enough, because she was actually staying in a studio cottage across the lawn from the main hotel complex, which was infested with noisy one-armed bandits, even in the loos.] In my room I called room service and he ordered two double brandies and a ginger ale – I said I only wanted a ginger ale. He said he'd run out of cash, so I had to sign the waiter's bill. And he waited for room service to arrive and leave, so that he wouldn't be interrupted, and then he pushed me onto the studio couch.

He started tearing my clothes. I was being quite badly knocked about. He didn't say anything. It was an awful, silent attack. He was so determined to rape me. And I don't know how I found the strength – well, I do know how I found it, because I was sober. I hadn't had a drink, anything at all. I was a strong young woman, and I used my knee and got him in the groin. And because he'd been drinking, he fell over. I grabbed him by the hair I think, and I dragged him to the door of the room and pushed him out, shoving him with my feet and kicking him as savagely as I could.

I slammed the door and bolted it. I was in a very bad state. My head was bleeding, I was bruised and battered, my eyes were black, and I had bruises all over my arms. It was only because I was stronger than him, and sober, that I won the fight. I didn't know what to do next. I felt I should ring somebody, but it was no good ringing up the police or the hotel manager, because I knew what they would say. 'Well, hell, you invited him in – what do you expect?' So I rang our Los Angeles office – we had one in those days – and the editor told me to stay where I was and clean myself up, and not to move but just to get whatever I needed from room service, and he'd be there as soon as he could get a plane to Las Vegas.

I don't know how long it took him – it might have been the next day before he got there. I didn't leave the room. When he arrived he was pretty horrified to see what I looked like, and the bruises I had. He took me back to Los Angeles, where I stayed for long enough to recover and for some of the bruises to disappear. And then I came back to London. But I was very, very shaken by the experience, largely because my faith had been undermined. I knew very little about sexuality despite being married, and 'rape' wasn't exactly on the tip of everyone's tongue in those days. I just hadn't thought about the danger. It was like the air raids during the war: I didn't consider anything untoward would happen to me. If I were young now, I'd be the sort of girl that goes mooching across Australia with a backpack. And girls like that are very vulnerable.

Perhaps the worst thing about the whole attack was the silence of it. Marje found that despite her fear and fury she couldn't scream, and this has given her an insight into rape cases where the victim, choking with shock, has been unable to call for help.

Men were behaving badly back at the *Mirror*, too. They were just more subtle there. Women were a rarity in Fleet Street, and some preferred to keep it that way. In the *Daily Mirror* itself, as in other newspapers, female readers were to be kept in purdah by means of a separate women's section.

Marje says now, 'I don't agree with having an exclusive women's section. Nobody's asked me, but if I had my way there wouldn't be a *"Mirror* Woman" now. I'd like it all to be part of the paper. There's not a separate sports section, though ninety per cent of the people who read about sport are men. I don't see why there can't be three pages in the *Mirror* devoted mainly to women's interests, like sport is devoted to men's interests. But why we have to have a separate pull-out, as if women were a depressed section of society, I don't know. I think it's akin to putting women in a ghetto.'

When 'Woman's *Sunday Mirror*' was launched as a newspaper for women on 13 February 1955, it announced a 'sparkling new' column by Marje. Sparkles were few. The formula was for the page to contain half a dozen bagatelle female items on fashion, travel and gossip, such as 'Husband Hunters – That's Us!' and 'Proops Answers a Moaning Wife' ('Her husband doesn't understand her. She's so lonely. She's so bored'). The whiff of anti-feminism is faintly detectable, consistent with the idea of keeping women in their place in the paper. Indeed Marje, the future placard-wielding feminist, at times appears to come across as a sort of Auntie Tom, propping up the old boy network: 'I've wondered if the women who shout so loud for the right to their careers aren't perhaps those who have tried to find a man and failed. Could it be that their aggressive denials cover up a sad lack of feminine allure?' And so on.

('Woman's *Sunday Mirror*' was later re-launched as *Woman's Mirror*, a weekly photogravure magazine and eventually absorbed into *Woman*. Marje wrote for all these publications.)

What was going on? Felicity Green (once dubbed 'Ferocity Spleen' for her sad lack of feminine submissiveness):

> For every woman that succeeds in newspapers, a hundred bite the dust on the way up. It's still a totally male-dominated, very very harsh, punishing world. I've seen women get promoted – it happened to me when I was at the *Mirror*, and I've promoted promising, talented young women myself – and they get to a level and say, 'It's too nasty, it's too rough, I don't want this, I have a family, I'll look after my children.' Let's not fool ourselves. Newspapers are run by men. There are wonderful exceptions, but they are laughably in the minority. All the decisions are made by men, and when they have to choose between a girl in a bikini and an elderly lady knitting a sweater, they don't see much choice.

Marje, a lover of men all her life, agrees about the macho business: 'I think you have to be a pretty tough character to survive. Women remain on a kind of lower plateau.' She says that she has been unusually lucky in having kind men to protect and promote her. She never advanced with intent on the editor's chair, or indeed anyone else's. 'I have never been particularly ambitious. Only ambitious to do my job to the best of my ability.' Her close friend Felicity remembers the little male newspaper tricks that might have grounded lesser birds:

> A certain Fleet Street genius came to work on the *Mirror* – I won't tell you his name. He was full of wonderful

ideas and he worked mostly with the women on the paper. One day he sent for me and said, 'I've got a brilliant brainwave for this women's feature and you are the only person in Fleet Street who has the talent to do it justice.' He outlined his idea to me and said, 'I'm going to put this all over the centre spread! Only you can make it work!'

I went back to my office walking on air and vanity, and I suddenly thought, 'Why is he asking me to do this, when he's got Marje, and knows she'll do it better than I will? It's much more up her street than mine.' And a little black thought came into my mind. So I went round to see Marje and told her about this man's idea. Marje said, 'He's just said exactly the same thing to me! He said I was the only person on the paper who could handle it.' I told Marje, who didn't know him like I did, that this was so typical of this man – his sole *modus operandum* was to get women on the paper at each other's throats. And I said to Marje, 'Come with me!' And we marched to his office, walked in and shut the door. We said, 'What are you playing at?' 'Oh my goodness!' he replied. 'Did I do that? How amazing. That really was an oversight on my part! No, no, of course I wanted you to do *this*.'

Such ruses, apparently, abounded. How was it, then, that Marje – in her own reckoning not ambitious, in her own admission submissive to every man she ever worked for – went from strength to strength in this hard-swearing, hard-swilling, male-dominated press world? How did Marje charm the men of the *Mirror*, with their love of Booby Girls and their constant publication of beautiful faces? For it is quite clear that she *did* charm them, or mentors like Cudlipp would not have groomed her, and even if they had, ruffled male colleagues would have seen to it that she did not survive. Well, according to observers, Marjorie Proops had a brand of glamour all her own. Geoffrey Goodman:

> She exuded enormous personal warmth and charm and *élan*. It's a kind of irresistible attraction, a magnetism that she has. It's not glamour in the conventionally accepted sense of Hollywood beauty and sexual attraction. It's her personality which is so evocative. It transmits. You feel the transmission of understanding and warmth and generosity. It's glamour of a kind that very very few people have.

Felicity Green:

> Marje per square inch has more sex appeal than many beautiful women. She has tremendous sexual impact. She likes men enormously and I have seen her flirt outrageously in a way that would become the most gorgeous film star. Now Marje would be the first to admit she is no beauty. But she has always had an absolutely splendid figure, and when this well-set-up figure of a woman decided to turn on the sex appeal, it was pretty potent stuff. I don't think I've ever actually seen Marje meet a man with whom she wasn't prepared to flirt, except for one homosexual cookery writer who didn't fancy her. Most men who meet Marje find her highly fanciable, because her sex appeal is infinitely more powerful than a pretty face.

Brian McConnell:

> The old *Mirror* building was a slum, and Marje wasn't normally seen on the editorial floor but on this occasion I remember she was going out to dine, perhaps with the executives. And she was dressed in a long, black,

flowing evening gown with some sort of decoration on it. And as she wafted through the office some wag at the back let out a loud wolf whistle. And Marje turned and gave him such a deep, dramatic curtsey that everybody started clapping. And all these foul-mouthed sub-editors stood staring at this amazing sight gliding across the editorial floor.

Clearly, a Cudlipp All-Star was born.

8

'Passion Put to Use'

O nce a ceasefire had been declared in the Proops household, Marje and her husband had gradually settled down to a quiet companionship that was to survive, despite some flaming rows later on, till death did them part. But there were no dreams, no fond embraces, no heightened senses, no looks of love, no sex. Marje still kept Elizabeth Barrett Browning's poem 'How do I love thee?' in her handbag, but without any object in mind.

She was now into middle age and still not pretty, despite her glamourous vibes. No doubt mutual love, that most desirable and needful of all human experiences, had passed her by. It passed a lot of people by, as she knew from her journalistic work. There was really no 'happy ever after' for many lonely individuals. They just grew up and found out. With Robert and Made away at school and college (Robert was at Berkhamsted), Proopsie concentrated on his career with the building firm Bovis, where he was now a director. Marje's life as a *Mirror* columnist, which took her round the globe and away from home for long periods, meant that she could burn off a lot of her passion in print. A lot, but not all.

The Golders Green semi kept its dark secret from the

world. Such warmth as there was came from the central heating and various animal companions – a series of precious dogs and cats, budgerigars, tortoises, goldfish and a duck, plus caterpillars and frogs in season when Robert was small – all looked after by 'the help' while the family were absent. The dogs in particular became a lifeline. They welcomed otherwise unwanted cuddles and gave unquestioning love in return, especially to Marje, who thought it cruel to spoil anything insufficiently.

Her parents had loved wire-haired terriers, and Marje had one of those, as well as jolly Jock the black mongrel. And the family had several cocker spaniels, including Dushka, who was a gorgeous redhead, and a series of Humphs, all named after Humphrey Bogart. When she actually saw Bogart in Hollywood she was struck by the resemblance. These crafty, humorous, rumple-faced Humph dogs became celebrities in their owner's *Mirror* column; they had their adventures and cartoons published regularly, and received fan mail. Marje also fell deeply in love with a certain party called William.

'I was having dinner one night with some friends I didn't know very well, and there was this wonderful dog named William, a schnauzer. And this William and I took an immediate shine to each other. He sat beside me the whole time and we had a good conversation together, William and I. It was love at first sight. And the next day I was still so crazy about this dog that I nagged Proopsie to let me have a schnauzer. My first was a little girl, Sophie. They have beards and fluffy legs,' adds Marje, admiringly. White, shapeless Sophie would be photographed occasionally in the *Mirror* in connection with various stories. When the issue was 'Voting Yes' in the Common Market referendum, she sat with her back to the camera, no doubt fearing rabies as a consequence.

Marje's private life, covered with an enormous Band-Aid

at work, was hurting her more than usual at home. She had no one to tell her troubles to. Her mother, Martha, huddled indoors at Jo-jo's new family household in Hendon, had not outlived her husband for very long. This poor, fastidious, proud little lady had died of a heart attack in the toilet in 1955. She had never escaped from her agoraphobic prison, and Marje and Jo were not really surprised by her death. She had said, after their father's funeral, 'I've nothing left now,' and wouldn't be comforted.

Marje had not been well herself since the operation to correct her retroverted womb, but she was afraid, as many women are, of having a hysterectomy, with all the implications it held for womanhood, motherhood and ageing. So she had put up with a lot of pain and embarrassment for years, once haemorrhaging on the carpet at work but managing to conceal the evidence. One mild spring afternoon she was walking through a leafy square in London when suddenly she felt herself fainting with nausea and pain, and went down with a smack on the pavement. A wave of fear came over her when she realized she was haemorrhaging again, this time much too severely to help herself. A passing taxi-driver stopped and took her to her own doctor's surgery nearby.

Her sense of failure and despair about undergoing the inevitable hysterectomy was assuaged at the hospital by an unusually sensitive gynaecologist, who took the trouble to talk to her about it and to explain that she would still be, in every sense, a woman. Marje admitted to him that she had been frightened half to death about this, and she only wished other women in the same position could have the benefit of such a pep-talk. After a few days' manageable discomfort she was on the mend, and a few weeks later she was fitter than she had been for a very long time.

In 1959 she became the proud possessor of a great big, gleaming, red Ford Zodiac, which was, she told

Mirror readers in an attempt to avoid arousing envy and heartache, 'the result of robbing the housekeeping for some years'. In fact it was a perk from Hugh Cudlipp, and the only parts she could operate on it as yet were the radio and the windows. She took lessons with a 'dishy' but sarcastic instructor from a well-known school with which somebody was supposed to pass every few seconds. He told her never to lose her temper, and to say to herself at the wheel, 'I must keep calm.' With him, this was a struggle. He would plunge her into London traffic, bark orders and then sneer at her motoring efforts. Among other things he thought her hand signals too languid, and would ask if she was trying to dry her nail polish.

Demoralized, she wobbled through her first driving test, but managed to pass second time round. She was then licensed to kill, and took revenge for the nail-polish remarks on insolent male road-users everywhere, honking them up and showing them some wellie. Her next car would be an MG BGT, but for now she would make do with this Zodiac as her Boadicean chariot. She was interviewed at the time for an Italian magazine, who sent her a very literal translation of their article. In it, Marje is seen driving their journalist ferociously round London and finally parking her 'fire'. When her young son Robert acquired his own jalopy, Marje reversed into his pride and joy in the drive, completely writing it off. Robert went into paroxysms and tore his mother's driving licence to bits, saying she was a danger on the roads, but this didn't stop her. 'It was an old licence,' says Marje, grinning toothily.

Her *Mirror* column reflected all her pent-up passions. She says of male-chauvinist-pig drivers, 'I marvel at their villainy!' and lambasts them right and left. A male dinner guest remarks that a rich man can have any woman he wants. Marje, inflamed, offered her readers half a

dozen five-guinea bottles of perfume for the best post-
card replies to this geezer (men who were not 'dishes'
were either 'blokes' or 'geezers' during this Wild Woman
of Borneo phase). Several thousand cards flooded in,
most of them saying that Marje was right. An exhibition
of work by abstract painter Keila Hurst included a very
fearsome-looking, cubist Marje, with an enormous head-
piece and fag-holder thrusting forth, not unlike one of
Tony Hancock's daubs in *The Rebel*.

There were the usual foreign trips, with Marje mighty
angry in Tokyo seeing the wife of her host having to kneel
on the floor in the corner. She nominates Marlon Brando,
Jimmy Greaves and 'Bertrand ban-the-bomb Russell' as
bores of the year, and unleashes such an onslaught
against actresses Vanessa Redgrave and Leslie Caron
that one wonders how fur failed to fly. Redgrave and
Caron had been 'spreading alarm and despondency' by
voicing CND claims, following recent nuclear testing in the
atmosphere, of unacceptable strontium-90 levels in meat
and milk. Marje says, 'Now, for the benefit of the two
talkative actresses, I will give you the *facts*,' and proceeds to
quote the *Mirror* science editor and government ministers
to the effect that the explosions (which included one of
50-megatons) were perfectly harmless to farm produce.
More 'facts' followed, including news that three Harwell
scientists had lived for a month on a strontium-laced diet.
(Marje did not say whether important bits had fallen off
the geezers.)

Things were moving so fast and furiously in Marje's column that even *laissez-faire* education came under scrutiny
(Robert had, you may recall, been brought up along these
lines). 'Today's Mum has been drilled by all those child
guidance bods to lay off the rod and give the child a loving
kiss instead.' Before, they would have got 'a slosh'. Now
there were so many 'wayward, undisciplined teenagers'

with illegitimate children of their own and no respect for
anybody, that Marje questioned the wisdom of all those
experts. 'Maybe, then, the answer is: back to Victorian
discipline, church on Sundays, respect, obedience – and
a good slap when it isn't forthcoming.'

She crossly reviews one or two displeasing sex manuals
('Pre-marital intercourse is impracticable and idiotic'), rails
against abolitionists like doctor and former MP Lady
Summerskill calling for a ban on boxing ('What do they
want to do – ban boxing and encourage young Englishmen
to simper "Who's for tennis?"') and waxes incandescent
over recent divorce proceedings in which a man set his
wife seven conditions for a reconciliation: 'If any man
tried to lay down conditions to me, I'd see him straight
to hell.'

But her deadliest rage is reserved for the so-called
human being who, in the summer of 1962, tied his
Alsatian bitch to a railway line. The pitiful creature died
of her injuries, including severed legs, and Marje is ready
to do bloody murder to avenge her. 'I'm assuming it's a
man,' she says, and asks for information leading to his
capture, whereupon he should be 'horsewhipped'. 'My
fury is cold and hard and unforgiving. The monster has
made me hate again . . . the way I always do when I
hear of bestial cruelty – whether it is to animals or human
beings.'

The searing passion of Marje's article and the barbarity
of the crime itself touched a nerve with many thousands
of *Mirror* readers. One of those who wrote in was Dame
Edith Sitwell, as great an animal-lover as she was a poet
and author. She congratulated Marje on her fine piece
of journalism and invited her to her Hampstead flat,
which was to be the setting for a rare and remarkable
interview. When Marje arrived with her photographer,
Doreen Spooner, the great woman was sitting up in bed

in an extraordinary Medusan headscarf, tied in a mass of
bronze and black lamé sausages round her venerable head.
She told Marje in a 'high, sweet voice' like a teenager's,
that the two of them had much in common. They both
loathed cruelty, both loved animals, both believed women
were human beings deserving to be treated as such, and
both fearlessly expressed what they thought and felt.
Marje was immensely flattered, but added, 'Dame Edith
is a genius.'

The poet, never married but 'never lonely', had slipped
two discs and been ordered to stay in bed. She advised
Marje, 'All women should spend one day a week in
bed. Tell the husbands.' Marje did. The conversation,
interrupted by Dame Edith's Siamese cats stalking about
the quilt, ranged over passionately important subjects
such as ageing. Marje said: 'Seventy-five is a good age
to reach. Do you mind being seventy-five?' Dame Edith:
'I don't think about age. You need never grow old except
in your body. The trick, of course, is to think of other
people and other things besides yourself. The people who
grow old are the ones who are completely self-centred.'
Dame Edith believed it was important not to worry over
trivialities. She waved a bejewelled hand at Marje and
urged, 'Don't you worry about things like the laundry
and you won't be old at seventy-five either.'

Following this interview, the two female individualists
became very close. Tiny, frail Dame Edith would refer to
tall Marje as 'my little friend', and the pair would sit for
hours chatting over sherry, whereupon Marje would go
home and tell Proopsie how funny the old lady was, and
how much she loved her. When the dame was the subject
of *This Is Your Life* shortly before her death, Marje was the
first celebrity guest on the show. Backstage, Proopsie told
the poet, 'Madam, if you were a man, I would sue you for
alienation of my wife's affections!' Dame Edith crinkled

her gorgeously ugly face and gave a girlish laugh. 'Sir, if I were a man,' she answered, 'I would not contest the action.'

Proopsie was once asked (by Kirsten Cubitt of *The Times* in June 1971) if he was ever jealous of Marje's success. He replied, puffing his pipe carefully, 'I've been expecting this question, and I've been doing some soul-searching. I can't think . . . this may sound phoney . . . I don't know whether I've got a mental block over it and won't admit it . . . but really I don't seem to feel jealous at all.' You will see the significance of this reply, and the pain the question may have caused to Proopsie, later on. He could certainly be forgiven for jealousy over some of Marje's journalistic endeavours during the late fifties and early sixties. For example, there was a series of special lunches with 'dishes' of Marje's choice – and she wasn't referring to the menu.

Half a dozen chaps, including cricketer Ted Dexter, gardener Harry Wheatcroft and crooner Yves Montand, are wined and dined by Marje for weekly articles (so she says), with the interviewer having her hair done specially for the occasion and wearing false eyelashes. Marje tells me that during the Yves Montand nosh-up, one lot of eyelashes, evidently worn out from too much fluttering, fell off and landed on the pink tablecloth. Yves Montand stared at it with his heavy-lidded eyes for some moments, wondering if it were a caterpillar.

Some of the conversations during these lunches were what we might call warm-blooded – and these were the printable parts. Yves' eyes are the same colour as Marje's brown chiffon scarf. They gaze at one another, pulses quickening. Marje asks if he is interested in food, and he breathes, 'Food is not a great passion with me. There are far more important things than food.' They discuss nudity, striptease shows they've seen in Tokyo, and what turns Yves on ('One button casually left undone is more alluring than deep cleavage') and so forth. The familiar Proopsian humour and banter, the mock 'thickie female' pose that she would often adopt when interviewing men, are balanced here on a steak-knife edge, and the *Mirror* reader is left wondering what time Marje got back to the office, if at all. (She did go back – her copy was always on time, and always professionally polished.)

One night she slept with the Duke of Bedford. Well, at least in one of his vast bedrooms at Woburn Abbey while his Grace was in residence (he pronounces it 'Woo-burn' Abbey, by the way). She had a good look round her accommodation and found two large brass beds, seven satin-damask armchairs, 'whatsits and whatnots' and eleven oil paintings. Marje had spent a droll day going over the building, smoking her fags and calling the duke 'Ian', which was what his friends called him. She was about to shake the butler warmly by the hand when she twigged that damn it all, this was going a bit far.

His Grace liked to do his own ironing and had twenty-two pairs of socks. After dinner the duke and the journalist strolled in his Grace's moonlit park and came back around midnight. Marje was gasping for a cup of tea, but the nineteen servants had gone to bed and the Duke didn't know where the deuce the tea was kept. 'We'll just have to explore!' Ian exclaimed. His grandmama had hated the place because every time she wanted a sandwich she had to phone the footman, who would phone the butler, who would phone the chef, who would make the sandwich. Marje didn't think much of the drawing room herself. It was 'about as intimate as Victoria station'.

Proopsie and home were a welcome relief from all this splendour, says Marje. But an interview with Yul Brynner *did* cause Proopsie some concern. She admitted afterwards that she had gone 'overboard for his ridiculous nude bonce' and 'nearly drove my old man to drink'. During the interview, Marje comes close – or pretends she does – to losing her journalistic poise. 'It was very difficult,' she confesses in the piece, 'to concentrate on the job in hand.' Brynner was as usual so laid back as to be almost horizontal, but having flattered the Bald One quite shamelessly and turned up her vibes to maximum kilohertz Marje concludes, 'I left Yul Brynner convinced that he, like most other men, warms to a woman's appreciation.' Also, 'I can tell you that he is a dreamboat who cancels out all past dreamboats – with or without hair.'

This was an arrant lie, of course. He didn't cancel out Marje's most enduring screen idol. Robert arrived back at Dunstan Road from his educational establishment one day to find a strange man sitting on his mother's bed (she was ill with hepatitis at the time). This immaculate, grey-suited personage had gun-metal hair and all the trappings of spondulicks about him (his Rolls was parked outside). He had evidently brought Mother a huge bouquet, and Mother was laughing and giggling, and saying what lovely yellow flowers they were, thoughtfully chosen to match her skintone. And when the man turned round, it was – Cary Grant. Marje:

He was sitting on the bed with this enormous bouquet of yellow flowers and me to match. He even stood on his head at one point, to demonstrate how he avoided illness by doing yoga, and my daily came in with a tray of drinks and dropped the lot. But that was the sort of jokey relationship we had. I was so different from these gorgeous women he used to have to beat off in his life, so he could relax and have an amusing time with me. I used occasionally to go to the Ritz with him, but he liked a salt beef restaurant in Berwick Street, so we used to go there. He'd sometimes ring from the States and say,

'Book a table for two in Berwick Street, Marje,' and we'd
go and have salt beef, pickled cucumber and lemon tea.
Once his Rolls was parked opposite, and when we came
out the car had been scratched all along the side with 'I
love Cary'. I was distraught, but he just laughed. I said,
'And I suppose you want me to say I love you too.' He
wanted everyone to say that.

We shouldn't read too much into this, of course, despite
the undoubted warm friendship between them. Marje
was a highly professional columnist and usually had a
photographer with her on outings with her magical males.
One was certainly present for the bedroom scene in
Golders Green. Marje's picture would appear in the paper
the next day, her face always shyly averted so that you can
just see the hair, the smile angled away, and the trademark
cigarette-holder. Sometimes her face was actually cropped
from the photograph – this happened, for instance, with
George Sanders. Only later was she fully revealed to the
goggling masses. But photographed or not, when Marje
appears most shamelessly to be flirting, she has nothing
to hide. It was when she was *not* flirting that something
happened of which she was forever guilty. Forever glad,
but forever guilty.

What you are about to read has never before been
disclosed. The secret has been kept by Marje, not only
from the *Mirror* and the general public, but from most of
the people who think they know her well. For more than
thirty years she has told no one, other than her son, her
psychiatrist confidant Tom Kraft, and one or two of her
intimate friends. Marje, the nation's most eminent agony
aunt, agonized for a very long time indeed about allowing
these extraordinary revelations to be made in this book, but
finally decided that if it were indeed to be her biography,
then whatever anyone thought of her afterwards, it could

not possibly answer that description unless the hidden heart of her life were included in it. Apologies to all those who think institutions like Marje should keep their dignity and keep their traps shut. It would be all the same if she were the Queen.

Besides, Marje feels she owes it to her millions of readers, who believe in her and trust her advice on their heartaches, to tell the truth about her own, and to explain how such a thing could happen to a woman like her – one who has tried all her life to study other people's feelings and give them a high priority, and one who happens to believe marriage to be the buckling girder holding our society in place. When she poured out the story to me, gripping her hanky and her emotions in her fist, I wondered what all those readers would make of it, and whether any of them would be reminded of that old David Lean film, *Brief Encounter* – the one where two awfully nice, awfully jolly middle-class people, played by Celia Johnson and Trevor Howard, are swept out of their depth to the accompaniment of Rachmaninov's Second Piano Concerto. Proopsie is dead now, so the revelations can't hurt him. But towards the end of their life together, Marje would scream at her husband and beat her fists against his chest in her anguish, because she couldn't tell him what she is about to tell you.

The *Daily Mirror*, like all modern newspapers, found it necessary to keep a team of lawyers at hand around the clock, to scrutinize copy for potential libels. These lawyers were exalted men, forbidding and formidable, who largely kept apart from the rough press persons with their pencils behind one ear and their fag-ends behind the other. Hugh Corrie, one of the heads of the *Mirror* legal department in those days, explains, 'The lawyers were rather a class apart: in fact when I took over the office, one of the things that I tried to break down was this idea, held by the journalists, that the lawyers were some sort of foreign body foisted on them. There was undoubtedly a "them and us" atmosphere.'

One of the most aloof of the senior lawyers was an Oxford-accented, Jewish-Australian barrister who went by the title of H. Phillip Levy MA LLM BCL (Oxon) of Gray's Inn. The 'H' stood for Herman, but anyone addressing him as Herman, much less 'Phil', would immediately have been impaled on the point of his umbrella, along with anyone else showing him a document bearing his name without the double 'l' in Phillip. Levy was a bachelor, and far from gay. He was a prominent, prominent-nosed, per-nickety, frightening member of the wig-and-gown profes-sion, self-confident and extremely fussy about his clothes. He was better-dressed than most judges and beakier than most magistrates. He had been brought down by the *Mirror* from Manchester in 1955 to get to know the ropes before taking over the London office. Put up in a small hotel in Lexham Gardens near Cromwell Road, Kensington, for a fortnight, he remained there for years.

Now in his fifties, he was something of a celebrity in his own right, quite apart from being the *Mirror*'s principal legal adviser in the 1960s. Author of *The Press Council, History, Procedure and Cases* – then the lawyers' bible on press freedom, press ethics and press litigation – Levy had also played an important part in postwar immigrant labour negotiations between the British and Italian governments. He was not to be trifled with, but Marje, because she treats everyone, on principle, like a close chum from school, trifled with him quite a lot, despite secretly trembling in his presence. He would question her beakily over potential legal problems with her copy, often ringing her at home. His abrupt voice over the telephone was apt to frighten Marje's secretaries; what Proopsie thought of it, we do not know. What were Marje's earliest impressions of him?

Phillip was a strong, highly disciplined man. I never saw him in his wig and gown. That would have knocked me out. But he was not one of your florid courtroom-star-type barristers. He was much more the sort who deals with company law. Very meticulous. He had quite sparse hair, and it receded more and more over the years that I knew him. But unlike many of the men who write to me for advice about their baldness, he was such a self-confident man that it would never have disturbed him. Ever. It never occurred to him to question his appearance. He had quite a nose, but he never worried about that either. He would have brushed such matters aside. He had an air of authority, and he had a wonderful withering glance. One wither, and they would shrivel away, partly because he was so tall and distinguished-looking. I didn't just respect authority – I was frightened of it. I always seemed to end up with men that I was scared of . . .

Marje has an autographed copy of Levy's book. The inscription says:

> Marjorie –
> to a greatly admired writer
> from a very undistinguished one.
> Phillip, November 1967

She had known him for several years by then, but the greeting is formal, the handwriting correct and meticulous. The book might be left lying around, and someone other than Marjorie might have chanced to open it. There is a photograph of the author on the flyleaf. It is the only picture of him that Marje has ever owned, though the two of them were passionately in love for twenty years. And all that time, says Marje, 'Nobody knew him except

me.' This was the lover Marje had longed for as a lonely,
plain teenager, the lover Proopsie turned out not to be,
and Elizabeth Barrett Browning's poem, 'How do I love
thee?', which for so many years Marje had kept in her
handbag, would now refer to this man, and no other, for
the rest of her life. How did it all happen?

I can't remember exactly when I met him – I think it was
in 1958 – but I do remember the first time I realized that
he was more than just an amiable colleague. I was about
to drive home in my red Zodiac and he came out of the
Mirror building just as I was pulling away. I asked which
way he was heading, and offered him a lift. He was
going to Hyde Park Corner for some reason. And when
he got out of the car in Park Lane, with all the traffic
roaring round us – he never understood newfangled
things like cars or traffic and had never driven in his
life – he thanked me for the lift, and then he put his
head through the open window of the passenger seat
and kissed me.

It was not a little friendly, conning kiss that I get from
all these characters you see around the place kissing me,
but quite a different kind. The kind of searching kiss that
asks a plain question. And the answer from me was yes.
I drove home and thought about him, and that was the
beginning of a relationship which was incredibly like a
marriage, and it lasted twenty years.

He was very fussy about his appearance. I used to
have to go with him to his tailors in Savile Row, and
sit there while he had his fittings. His handmade shoes
came from Lobb in St James's, where I think the Prince
of Wales and the Duke of Edinburgh and all the nobs
get their shoes from. All this was terribly important to
him, that he should be correctly dressed. It amazes me
that he ever took his trousers down. We slept together

whenever we could. I became brilliant at finding excuses to get away, so that I could be with him. He didn't have to make excuses to anybody – he wasn't married. He had no commitments. He lived in this small hotel off the Cromwell Road. Typically of him, it was very modest, and he had a very modest room, which I got to know well. I used to try and leave the office early, so that we could creep off to his hotel. He didn't have to look over his shoulder, but I had to look over mine. Because there was always, at the back of my mind, the fear of being found out by Proops, and being divorced by Proops.

When the idea of this book was first put to me, I had to make a decision, whether it was going to be an honest account of my life, or whether I was going to conceal Phillip's existence. And I decided I couldn't do that, because he was so much a part of my life. I loved him so desperately and deeply, and without him I wouldn't be the person I am. He gave me so much – quite apart from sexual fulfilment, which was part of it, and a very exciting and wonderful part because he taught me so much about sex, and I think that's one of the reasons why I'm able to write about it now – but apart from that, there was the confidence that he gave me. Nobody, but nobody, had ever given me confidence before in my life the way he did. He taught me to value myself as a person. Apart from my son Robert, he was the pivot of my life. I couldn't leave him out of it.'

Early on in the relationship, Marje talked to Phillip about her marital troubles and asked him, as a barrister, whether Proopsie had been right about the threatened consequences of a divorce. Had there really been a risk that Proopsie would be awarded custody of Robert? Phillip told her that there was certainly a risk; that if Marje didn't want to gamble over losing Robert, she was right not to chance

divorce proceedings. However, since Robert would have
been seventeen by the time Marje met Phillip, fear of a
custody battle was not the issue now.

Worries about losing her comfy companionship with her
husband, dread of breaking up her marriage when she
firmly believed in marriage, terror of a divorce scandal
and the possible effect on her career – these, you would
surmise, were the issues now. Levy's former colleague
Hugh Corrie: 'I think that, at one stage, if it had come
out that they were carrying on, she might have had to
leave the *Mirror*. After all, she was very much the symbol
of respectability to the readers, and she was always writing
about Proopsie in her articles.' A sidelight on this comes
from Marje's column back in May 1977. In a humorous
piece on keeping a diary, she writes:

> A chance remark of my mother's, many years ago,
> warned me of the dangers of putting anything in
> writing. She was recounting how an aunt of ours
> wrote, 'Dined with S. J. at the usual place' – and
> added a colourful account of what happened after
> dinner. Uncle, it appears, found Auntie's diary hidden
> in the breadbin (where else?) and all hell was let loose.
> It all turned into the great family scandal, with talk of
> horsewhipping and even, shame, shame, divorce.

My own view is that Marje's darkest dread was not any
of these things. She was profoundly insecure about her
personal attractiveness, and for a woman so desperately
dependent on men for her self-esteem and happiness – and
even her sanity, as we shall see later on – being unwanted
by them was an abyss down which it was always possible
to fall. I suggest this was the *real* reason why she was afraid
of leaving Proopsie during the 'two years of hell', and not
the threat of a custody battle at all. As her mother would

have said, at least she had a husband, and 'a bird in the hand is worth two in the bush'.

Now, though, she seemed to *have* two in the bush. She had two men. But Proopsie clearly didn't love her in the way that Phillip did, and as perhaps every woman dreams of being loved. Proopsie's love was more like that of a bossy father than her other half. So she couldn't possibly give up her relationship with Phillip. On the other hand, supposing she had divorced Proopsie: Phillip may have changed, or changed his mind. Perhaps, after so long living alone, he was a natural bachelor. Like many a mistress, she might not have seemed so desirable if available. So I would suggest that she feared being stranded between two men, and left like the lonely Guinness Girls in her father's pub. And to Marje, there was no more terrible fate than that.

There was something else to haunt her, too. Of all Marje's relationships, the one with her loving readers has in fact been the longest and the closest. I think Marje was very afraid that if her readers knew, in the days before extramarital love was viewed with compassion, perhaps they would not like her any more, or need her, or listen to her advice. Perhaps, though Marje has never judged anyone else's morals in her agony column, they would write in and say that Marjorie Proops was immoral, and a hypocrite, not qualified to understand their problems, and that she should get out of journalism, or go to hell. They may still say that, though one hopes they won't. Because such judgement from her readers would be far too terrible for Marje to bear.

If all this speculation is right, then Marje had no option but to keep her options open. She had to maintain two husbands, and be mistress of two households. And this is precisely what she did.

Marje's double life went on under the noses of the

beady-eyed *Daily Mirror* journalists and legal eagles. Marje
likes to think that nobody in the office knew. The high
points of their available time together were their trips
abroad. Marje:

Whenever I was going on a foreign assignment – apart
from Moscow because he didn't like the cold weather
– Phillip would try to join me. He came with me
to America – I can't remember which trip it was.
He certainly came with me several times to Paris.
Wherever I went, if it were feasible for him to travel
and he could get away from the office, he came with
me. If not, wherever I was he rang me every day.

Once, I went on a trip to Australia, and he had to
stay behind. Phillip came from Melbourne, which is
the Australian equivalent of Bath, very middle class
and respectable. Melburnians look down on other
Australians, and Sydney in particular they regard as
a roughneck area. When I arrived in Sydney, I found
this huge bouquet of red roses waiting for me – from
Phillip. He was a very reserved man. He found it very
difficult to express his feelings. He used to break my
heart when he wouldn't say 'I love you.' Proopsie did,
but for Phillip to say 'I love you' was a rare and absolutely
marvellous treat for me. And on this one occasion in
Australia, there were these roses, with a little note from
Phillip that said, 'I miss you – I love you.'

Our trips abroad had to be arranged very carefully
indeed. He used to plan his holidays around various
trips of mine. We used to travel separately, and only
very occasionally together. Very often we would go by
boat, because I wouldn't fly anywhere if I could help
it. And we would meet up at the hotel. It was very
fraught, trying to set things up, yes, but on the other
hand, it added to the excitement of it. I think that a

lot of illicit love affairs gain a sort of *frisson* from all these tense arrangements. If it's much more difficult to organize, when you finally get into bed together, it is wonderful! The gratification then goes even beyond the sexual gratification.

It's quite different. The first time I found sex enjoyable and unforgettable was with Phillip. You're on a level of heady excitement. With the added tension and fear of being found out. Probably, if I had been able to marry or live with Phillip, I'd have been bored out of my skull with him, and he with me. But you have to remember that our times together were so limited, so stolen, that we didn't sit there having long conversations about his work, or my work either. We were there holding each other.

Although the lovers remained blissfully ignorant of it – and Marje still did not know when we did the interviews for this book – Phillip's colleagues had in fact registered that something was going on, and it is probably fortunate for Marje and Phillip that the lawyers *were* a race apart from the *Mirror* journalists, and by nature more secretive. Hugh Corrie: 'They both went to the West Indies, and this was how it really came to light as far as the legal department was concerned. Phillip had got a holiday and had booked his passage out, and the travel agents rang up with a message to please tell either Mr Levy or Mrs Proops that unfortunately they were not able to get them adjoining cabins on the boat.' After this, there was talk. There was also, one Friday evening, very nearly a scene in the office, precipitated by Marje herself. She explains:

We did have rows. We were both jealous. Very jealous. And this is another aspect of this sort of relationship. You find it's very difficult to trust each other. Because

you can't help wondering if he's fancying somebody
else the way he fancies and wants you. And why should
he be loyal to you, and faithful to you, when you're
always away? Well, Phillip loved Brighton. He used
to go down to Brighton a lot, because he had friends
there. And I was terribly jealous of these visits. Because
I used to have to go home to Proopsie at weekends,
and Phillip would go sloping off to Brighton. I was
always suspicious that he was going sloping off to
meet some female there, with whom he would sleep.
And despite his protestations that he never did, I was
always suspicious and really behaved very badly –
because I would seldom be able to get away from
home at weekends anyway, and yet I expected him
to go to his room in that crummy hotel and sit there
on his own. And when I look back now he was quite
right to go to Brighton. But I used to be insane with
jealous rage and have terrible rows with him about it.

And I remember one particular evening he told me
he was going to be leaving the office early: he was
going down to the coast. I walked out of my door and I
saw him leaving his office with his rolled umbrella – he
always had this umbrella – and wearing his overcoat and
looking very lawyer-like. And when I saw him, knowing
where he was going, I had this surge of outrage and
jealousy and agony, and I had to stop myself running
down the newsroom after him, and stopping him from
leaving.

I used to flirt with other men in the hope that I
would inflame him. But looking back from my present
perspective, he wasn't that sort of man anyway. He was
really very honourable. And although it may sound like
he was a dishonourable man because he was sleeping
with another man's wife, he wasn't dishonourable. He
was loyal to me, of that I'm sure. In the same way that

I'm sure Proops was. And I really don't deserve the loyalty that these two men gave me. Because I cheated on them both. Well, I didn't cheat on Phillip, but I didn't behave too well. I did try to wind him up. He didn't have the sort of peace and tranquillity that his nature demanded, because he really wanted a quiet life, with me there to share it with him. He didn't want all these scenes with this raging woman.

But you felt everything, whatever the emotion was – whether it was jealousy or anger or love or whatever it was – you felt it ten times more passionately and deeply than if you'd had a legal married relationship. You were always missing each other, and never believing. I could never, ever, believe that he really loved me. I could never understand why he should. I always used to think he was a very good-looking man, very appealing and attractive in every way, and I felt he could get any woman he wanted. Why should he pick on a plain, ordinary-looking one like me? I never felt myself to be – worthy's not quite the word – I had a very poor self-image.

Poor Proopsie. I asked Marje if she thought he knew. 'It's very difficult for me to say. Sometimes I think he did. Sometimes I think he couldn't have done, because he couldn't have gone on living with me the way he did. I mean, he was good-natured, kind, good-humoured. Oh, we quarrelled a lot, it's true. But probably that was my fault. I probably quarrelled with him more than he quarrelled with me, if you see what I mean. But whether or not Proopsie knew, I honestly don't know. If he did know, he certainly was very clever at concealing it.' I suggested that perhaps he didn't want to know. 'Yup. Yes. In fact he was the sort of man who wouldn't have wanted to know.' The lovers were quite professional in their deceptions. 'One of the excuses that Phillip used to make to ring me at home, if Proopsie answered the telephone, was to say to Proops, "I want to have a word with her about her copy." And he would pretend he'd got a legal query on my column.'

If we cast our minds back to that interview Proopsie gave to *The Times*, you will recall that he seemed to have what he called 'a mental block' about jealousy. Judging from what his son says now, this was deliberate. Robert:

I knew what was going on. When Mother told me in a fit of emotional outburst about two years ago, I'd known for *years*. Of course I had. And I am in no doubt that my father knew as well. I was realistic about the situation. I had a very unhappy childhood as a result of all this, though at the time I didn't know why. It was only in my teens that I began to step back and realize my parents had feet of clay, and that I wasn't blameworthy. It wasn't a case of 'working it out'. That isn't the way people give clues in life. People who, on the surface, seem determined that whatever they are doing should remain secret, leave whopping great clues around almost on purpose. The realization didn't come in a flash of lightning. It was a sort of creeping additional knowledge, that they were playing games into which I was being woven unwillingly. And I had to blow the whistle on these games, and say 'I will kick up shit if you try to use me to play these games.'

Robert didn't in fact 'kick up shit'. He said nothing.

Absolutely not, no. What was the point? But I think that my father was an embittered man, and although my mother thinks he didn't know, I am almost certain he did know. And I think he was very bitter and difficult as a result. He was a very difficult man anyway, but he then became very embittered. I think that he blamed me. It was my fault. 'Take it out on the dog.' You know, kick the dog. I think I got kicked an enormous amount by my father. If you ask me to theorize, I suspect that my father felt that my being born was the cause of the rift. And also that he blamed the affair on what had happened during that earlier time.

Marje would spend much of the rest of her life as a journalist trying to help solve other people's problems. Strangers' problems. She found that more rewarding, and less devastating, than trying to solve her own.

— 9 —

Aunt Misbehaving

*I*n this chapter we shall be finding out how Hugh
   Cudlipp launched Marje Proops on her career as the
   'World's Greatest Advice Columnist' – the 'Dear Marje'
of the *Daily Mirror*. It didn't happen overnight. Marje at
the start of the Swinging Sixties was still first and foremost
a columnist and humorist who, as we shall see, began
answering a few readers' letters in an entertaining way.
She wasn't a maternal, moral voice offering homespun
advice, but a vibrant, gutsy, witty journalist with a hidden
life, who happened to have an ongoing correspondence
with her readers – not so much 'agony aunt' as 'aunt
misbehaving'. Through the cuttings, though, it is possible
to see a gradual shift of emphasis from wit to wisdom, from
frivolity to fiery social commentating, and last of all, from
the liberal crusader to the compassionate correspondent,
writing directly to, and for, the people who needed her
most. Why the transformation?

Marje's friend, then industrial editor, Geoffrey Goodman:

> If you go back thirty or forty years, counselling was fairly
> new territory in popular journalism when Marje came
> into it and the *Mirror* did develop it extremely well. But

I'm puzzled why she allowed herself to be converted into doing agony aunting and becoming everybody's mother. The cruel explanation is that it embodied her own problems. She was a woman of immense social wisdom and commitment but throughout all that she had within herself emotional turmoil all the time. I don't think Proopsie fully understood it. I think it was this search for somebody to 'understand' that drew her into counselling. The professional involvement developed from the personal need. *She* needed an agony aunt. So she became the caring mother, the Yiddish momma. It's almost tangible. You can sense that she really does care. Any member of staff could go and sit with her in the privacy of her office and discuss his personal troubles, and she would somehow invest herself with the other person's problems. She would do that, even though she had problems herself.

Problems weren't uppermost in Marje's mind at the moment. In July 1960, she had amused her readers by telling them that she had opted to sell the Golders Green semi without consulting Proopsie. This was Marje's little joke but the new, neo-Georgian residence in Hamilton Terrace, St John's Wood, was unlikely to amuse many socialists. Marje, who by all accounts was receiving a cabinet minister's salary at the time, resented comments thereon. 'The implication was that the house was the size of Buckingham Palace. It was only a five-bedroomed house, with two bathrooms. It certainly had five lavatories, which I often had to clean. I think it was built at a time when people had servants. We'd taken out a huge mortgage and we were deeply and heavily in dept all the time we lived there because that house was Proopsie's dream. He used to drive past it, longing to live in it, and one day he rang me, very excited, and said, "It's on the market!"'

The furniture also cost 'a hell of a lot' because their old stuff, apart from the grand piano, wouldn't do. Jesus would have needed to perform a miracle similar to the one with the loaves and the fishes to eke it round the rooms. So they bought lots of antiques, including a big Georgian dining table, two Sheraton chairs, and six fair copies to match. Marje couldn't tell the difference and Benjie, the 'punk' cat they acquired later, couldn't have cared less and clawed the lot. They also had some Georgian silver, old porcelain, and contemporary Swedish and French glass. Marje says she never felt comfortable in the place. 'It was altogether too big and grand for me. I never felt it was my home. I just lived in it.'

One Christmas while they were living in this pomp and circumstance Mike Molloy, the *Mirror* cartoonist who later graduated to *Mirror* editor, was trying to think of a suitable gift for La Proops. Mike Molloy:

> I said to her over lunch, 'What would you like, Marje?' and she said, 'Do you know, Mike, I've always fancied one of those mynah birds!' So I sent my PA off to Harrods and we presented Marje with this bird in a cage, saying 'For the woman with everything!' And months went by, and she never mentioned it again, so I thought, 'Something's happened with that bird.' Eventually I said, 'By the way, Marje – how are things with that mynah bird?' And she looked a bit furtive. She said, 'Well, they're strange creatures, aren't they. It miaowed at Benjie and Benjie hid under the table and wouldn't come out.'

In truth, there were other difficulties. Marje:

> I'd taken this wonderful-looking bird home and stood him in his posh cage on top of the telly and tried to teach him to talk. And I started by saying 'Hallo', and the bird

just stared at me resentfully. And from then on I went mad trying to teach this mynah bird to talk, and so did Proopsie. We spent hours in front of that cage, saying 'Hallo, my name is Marje, and this is Proopsie. Say "hallo Proopsie".' And anyone walking into the house would have thought, these poor things ought to be locked up. Anyway, in the end we gave up. We thought, well that's it – he's not going to talk but he's lovely to look at.

Proopsie was then very active in his job, and this meant that I had to do a lot of entertaining because he had lots of contacts – architects, surveyors and so on – and I would rush home from the office and set up these bloody great dinner parties which drove me potty. And this very big dining table at Hamilton Terrace had leaves, and I think at a pinch it could seat twelve. And I used to sit there with these boring people with whom I had absolutely nothing in common, being the gracious hostess and trying to understand what they were talking about. One evening we had one of these parties going on, with architects and their wives seated round the table, when suddenly there was a lull in the conversation and this mynah bird shouted out, 'I can't 'ang around 'ere all day – I've got to get to the fucking airport!' – in a real cockney voice. The bird looked so malevolent! My guests couldn't believe what they'd heard, so he repeated it in case they didn't catch it the first time. And do you know, he never said anything else. Proopsie blamed me. He said, 'It's your language. He's obviously heard you shouting out how you've got to get to the airport.'

The *Daily Mirror*, in 1961, had also grown very grand, despite its sworn opposition to the Tory government telling everybody 'You've never had it so good'. Editorial director Hugh Cudlipp and chairman Cecil King now presided over the world's largest publishing enterprise, and the newspaper with the UK's largest daily sale, in an £11 million, eleven-storey building in Holborn Circus, EC1. It had what Cudlipp called 'an orchestra of rotary presses at subterranean level' which gave one 'the eerie feeling of being in a technological cathedral'. Marje's office was then on the third floor amid the features department. When she gradually shifted shape from columnist to agony aunt, she would move upstairs with her team of secretaries and assistants. *Mirror* colleague George Thaw, then the paper's youngest sub-editor:

At that stage what she basically had was a secretary and a PA, sometimes just a secretary. But she had a much greater editorial function then, writing her topical column and major features. She was very trenchant in her opinions at editorial conferences, and very much a part of the team. When I joined in 1964, I subbed her stuff, which was very good copy, always clean and straightforward. In those days you wrote to a length, like a craftsman. You didn't write it and then saw bits off to make it fit. Marje always wrote to a length. She had this ability to produce quality stuff. There were only six features subs then, and no layout artists before Mike Molloy came along. Marje had a good eye for a page, and could look at it and decide where things would go. There were times when she'd say, 'Don't worry – I'll do a little illustration.'

There was considerable cachet at the time in working for the *Mirror*, but if you didn't deliver, it was goodbye. Marje could deliver. People think of her now in terms of holding the hand of an anonymous pregnant girl. They don't realize she was a hard-working, extremely professional journalist. She covered everything, and she had a lot of intelligent women readers. In its heyday the *Mirror* was *the* women's newspaper. Thinking women read the *Mirror*. And Marje stood in her own right as a

woman with common sense, someone you listened to.
It was only later that she was, in a sense, diminished by
becoming an agony aunt. To a certain extent Hugh side-
tracked her. Because Marje understands newspapers,
and the *Mirror* in particular, and was never afraid to
make decisions. She was technically good enough to
do it, and would have made a good editor, probably a
better editor than Lee Howard, who in 1961 had actually
succeeded Nener.

Celebrity heart-to-hearts were still Marje's stock in trade.
She would go anywhere, interview anybody. She talked to
Diana Dors and Sophia Loren about having babies and the
pain of miscarriages. Sophia looked like Orphan Annie and
had just fainted on the set. She was beautiful, shapely, rich,
talented and successful, but she didn't yet have a son. Marje
had a son. 'I envy you!' said Sophia, pouting sorrowfully.
Marje replied that this was 'a funny deal'. Marje went to
see Dr Michael Ramsey, Archbishop of Canterbury, and
beheld him standing at the top of the stairs at Lambeth
Palace, brows beetling. Marje, being Jewish and none too
sure where she stood in the religious debate, noticed the
Archbishop's arms were spread out in beatific greeting. So
she ran into them and gave him a cuddle. She talked to
Spike Milligan about a joint writing project and found him,
beneath the goonish grin, deeply depressed. She suggested
they write about children, and Spike said he knew a child
called Carrington Briggs, who wouldn't mind being dead.
Sad Spike produced a poem on the spot:

> Carrington Briggs cared not two figs
> Whether he lived or died.
> But when he was dead
> He lay on his bed and he
> Cried and cried and cried.

She attended a big *Daily Mirror* lunch with a well-known, very raucous sixties rock star who turned to her, half pissed, and rasped, 'Fancy a snort of coke?' Marje, not an easy woman to phase, smiled winsomely. 'Oh but dear,' she said, 'I gave that up in the 1920s.' She followed this up with an amusing article on a rocker romance, giving a glossary of 'rock speak'. 'Once upon a time a Hot Rocker was pegging a magic sort. "Marvellous barnet," he said to himself. "That's no cracking tapper. I could have a panic with her."' [Cracking tapper = girl on the cadge.] He asks her to dance ('Let's struggle') but is turned down. 'Split the scene,' the sort mutters to the Hot Rocker, 'Swallow it.' 'Whereupon our hero realized he had crumpled his cooker [missed his chance].'

La Proops was getting very political lately. Despite her comfy lifestyle she had always espoused the socialist struggle and had started being wheeled out with other *Mirror* icons at the TUC and Labour Party conferences and being hailed as royalty by the members. They would swarm for Marje's autograph and several fairly famous observers, trampled in the crush, have told me, 'It was like being out with the Queen Mum.' Of course she supported Labour and had marched beside Nye Bevan in her youth, but she was not above flirting with Jo Grimond ('He's a wow!'), or even a Tory MP if he took her fancy. She urged other women to get off their bums and start stirring things up in the constituencies. Did they want equal pay and creches or didn't they?

She had a lot of clout with Labour supporters and would throw her weight behind Labour candidates to considerable effect, joining debates and 'shoving leaflets through people's letterboxes'. Of course she whooped it up with the *Mirror* over Harold Wilson's 1964 election victory. 'It was even better than Chelsea winning,' says Marje (one of several ardent Chelsea supporters). She related to the common man, and the common woman, in a way that was quite unscripted, thoroughly genuine and probably, when all the electoral head-banging was over, apolitical. She was everybody's mate before she was everybody's agony aunt. When Cassandra died in 1967 and Marje was leaving his memorial service, a woman crept up to her in tears outside St Paul's Cathedral and said, 'You're the only voice we'll have to speak for us, now that he's gone.'

Sent to interview Labour's flame-haired transport minister Barbara Castle in 1967, Marje was not one of the churlish ones who complained that the woman couldn't drive a car. She had another idea. Dame Barbara Castle:

> Everybody warmed to Marje, and I used to meet her through Labour contacts and at the Party conferences, though I never knew her in the early days when I worked on the *Mirror* myself. In 1967, Ted and I were on holiday in Ireland, and Marje rang me to say that some opinion poll had put me 'top of the pops' as she called it, in the ministerial ratings. And she was going to write a piece on me and wanted to send out a *Mirror* photographer. As it happened, Ted and I were just going out pony-trekking. So next day, there in the *Mirror* was Marje's article with this hilarious picture of the Minister of Transport. Never one of life's horsewomen, there I was, precariously balanced on the back of this pony.

Marje did an in-depth interview on another occasion and found this Yorkshire housewife was a fusspot for spring-cleaning. The minister confided to the columnist, 'I like to *bottom* the dirt.'

Marje made herself at home with the Wilsons. She regarded Harold as a distinguished and 'cuddly' PM and grew very fond of him, despite the notorious baggy golf cardigans which she felt bound to criticize. She found he had a memory like an elephant, gnawed his pipe stems, and snoozed in the afternoons in their 'untidy' flat above Number Ten, leaving his slippers outside the door. Mary, who wore Chanel Number 5 and described herself as 'a dreamer', would creep about so as not to disturb him, but would sometimes get out of her armchair and recite one of her poems for Marje's benefit. Only later was the rug pulled from under Marje in her cosy relationship with cuddly Harold.

Marje was still 'a sexy writer'. In 1967 this brought her under the scrutiny of the Press Council. Her secret lover Phillip may have been the author of the standard work on that subject, but he was not himself a member of the Council and could therefore have had no direct influence over the eventual outcome. Marje had produced a piece on what women find attractive about men. In it, she betrays her personal leanings. She writes: 'Although women claim they seek men who are steadfast and rocklike and devoted, they secretly yearn for men who are likely to bring them much suffering and heartache.' Fair enough, thought Mrs Hilda Myers, of Altrincham, Cheshire. But Marje presses dangerously on: 'Nine out of ten women would rather have a man who would surreptitiously caress their thigh under a nightclub table than a good rugged chap who'll slap them heartily on the back at a Saturday football game – even though they suspect that their nighclubber will be caressing another girl tomorrow and the good rugged chap would never look at any other girl.' It is difficult not to poke our noses in and cast Proopsie and Phillip as the two sporty chaps described, though Mrs Hilda Myers was not to know of Marje's split decision there. Hilda's complaint to the Press Council was that something should be done to prevent publication of such suggestive views in a popular newspaper, which might give 'the wrong impression' to young readers.

The *Mirror* editor, Lee Howard, stood foursquare behind his sexy columnist. He replied that 'Mrs Proops, a journalist of wide experience and high repute, was writing in what was considered to be the idiom of the readers of the *Daily Mirror*' which, he believed, had more young readers than any other newspaper. 'We think it is our job,' submitted Howard gravely, 'to talk to these readers in terms that they accept and in terms that they believe and understand. In talking to them, we must address them so that they know we are alive to how they think and how they talk and not in terms which try to tell them that this is the way they should think and talk.' This is a little like saying, 'Our readers are young and like a bit of the other, so we shall give it to them.' But the Press Council accepted the editor's discretion and rejected the complaint.

Racy Marje was now racing about in her MG BGT, always trying to be first away at the lights. She had had a bit of a prang in her Zodiac when something hit her up the backside, and it is quite possible that the slight injury she sustained to her back then was the cause of future disc problems. She suffered from these periodically, and in the sixties she was forced to wear a steel corset and even, for a brief period, to go to work in a wheelchair – a foretaste of what arthritis would do to her in years to come.

She was always off to faraway places with strange-sounding names like Oahu, Noumea and Niuafo'ou, either vacationing or working, either with Phillip or alone. She would sometimes wake up in a hotel a thousand miles from home and wonder what the blazes she was doing there, but she would pull herself together and say, 'You've got a job to do – get on with it.' Once a waiter entered her single room in a New York hotel to find her talking to herself, and wrongly supposed she had a man stashed in the wardrobe (Phillip would have been far too tall for that caper). In 1968 she gave a resumé of some of her little trips:

I have drunk questionable beer in Bugis-street in Singapore
at 4 a.m., driven round Moscow in a Rolls Royce,
spent a wild weekend with four wild Aussies in New
South Wales [we'll come back to that], admired the
sarong-skirted policemen in Fiji, danced the High Life
in Trinidad and collected coral off the beach in Barbados.
I've argued with a talking bird named Jack in Honolulu
(honest), learned a few tricks of the trade from a geisha
in Kyoto, Japan, and attended a mass wedding there on
a propitious day for nuptials. I have eaten man-sized
steaks with man-sized men in the log forests of Canada,
had cinnamon toast for tea at Rumpelmayer's in New
York, fallen over Groucho Marx in Hollywood, watched
nude ladies and gentlemen sunbathing in Stockholm,
strolled in the Tivoli Gardens in Copenhagen. I have
fished for trout in the Laurentians in Quebec, window-
shopped in Hamburg's Reeperbahn, quarrelled with
taxi-drivers all over France, and put on a stone in a
week in Holland (pickled herrings make you so thirsty
and so for that matter does curry in New Delhi). I could
go on . . .

When Marje writes of her travels she is conscious of the
dangers of a) boring the backsides off her readers and
b) arousing envy and enmity. But the Australian trip at
the end of 1964 was particularly unusual. It combined
unseemly luxury on board the SS *Monterey*, cruising the
South Sea Islands, with the rigours of the outback. The
luxury cruise inspired a piece by Marje entitled, 'The
loneliness of the long-distance voyagers'. Anyone wishing
to understand Marje's seemingly selfish dilemma over
Proopsie and Phillip, and her deep black terror of being
manless, need look no further than this article.

In it she tells us about the 'sad cargo of people', mostly
rich middle-aged and elderly women, 'with that terrible

haunted hungry look of the desperately lonely. This was a cargo of people seeking and searching, their eager eyes raking among the other passengers or around the crew of dishy officers. This was a cargo of people on the prowl, looking for companionship or for love or for another marriage.' These 'pathetic' women would spend hours in the beauty shop, and tog themselves up for dinner in their sequins only to sit for hours watching other people dance. The officers referred to them as 'L.O.L.s'. Marje was chilled by the discovery that this meant 'Lonely Old Ladies'. They never met romance, and would toddle alone down the gangplank at the end of the cruise with their souvenirs and picture postcards.

Having sunbathed on Bondi Beach over Christmas, Marje advances into the bush with a group of rugged Aussies, one of whom is actually called Bruce. They take her out to a small hot town called Deniliquin, two hundred miles from Melbourne, to visit their farmer mate, Greg. They travel light, with fifty cans of grog and a set of Aussie male priorities. These are: One, grog. Two, the racing page. Three, food. Four, Sheilas. 'What about work?' asks Marje. 'Put work four,' says Bruce, 'and make women fifth.' They belt and bounce along dirt roads, the sun frying the paint off the truck.

Greg's homestead, in the middle of nowhere, has a gigantic fridge and a washing machine. That's about it. They have fried bangers and more grog, which finally upsets Marje's tum. They give her a dose of cure-all and call her a bloody good sport. Then they all go out, still swilling, to look for kangaroos and 'Joe Blakes' (snakes). An eagle with a six-foot wingspan banks overhead; wild ducks and parrots flutter up out of the green paddy fields. An eighty-year-old cattle rancher they call 'Pa' bellows at them (actually at Marje) to 'Git back in the bloody car you bloody idiots! Dangerous bloody bulls here.' Marje learns a lot of Strine and later ends up in Alice Springs, a collection of bungalows with corrogated roofs, and flies – 'Loving, friendly flies that cling to you adoringly the moment you step off the train.' She is upset by the plight of the Aborigines, 'gentle and dignified', living in hideous settlements on the edge of town. The Aussies despise them almost as much as bloody Poms.

In Adelaide, she is met by a cable from Proopsie. 'Guess what?' it says. 'We have a prospective daughter-in-law!' Robert, now twenty-three, had become engaged to his girlfriend Olivia. Marje was 'stunned and delighted', if a little piqued that Robert hadn't even hinted at her impending mother-in-lawhood. But then Robert often behaved impulsively. He had, for instance, dropped out of the Architectural Association and abandoned architecture for a career in management. Robert, Olivia and Proopsie were waiting for Marje at the airport on her return. Olivia was slender, brunette and beautiful. She reminded Marje of a ballet dancer, and this was what she was. She had been a member of the Royal Ballet, and was adored by Robert for her fragile loveliness. As Marje well knew, men consider it sufficient for such a woman to be, rather than do.

Robert and Olivia had a white wedding (the womenfolk, already hand in glove, insisted on this) and went to live in Birmingham, near Robert's new job. Olivia hated Birmingham. Before long they were back at Hamilton Terrace, living in Robert's old room while the happy hubby looked for a new job and a new house. They were there for ten months, having rows. Marje tried not to fall into the stereotype mother-in-law mould, and determined not to interfere. Olivia called her new mum 'Dolly' and told her not to worry; they were simply getting things off their chests. At last they found a place of their own, in Barnes. Olivia wept, leaving Hamilton Terrace. She had

Marje and Jo-jo, aged about ten and eight, with their father and teddy bears.

Marje and Jo-jo as bridesmaids, aged eleven and nine.

Beach belle Marje (third from left) in Bournemouth, 1932.

Proopsie in 1941, a newly commissioned officer with the Royal Engineers.

Miss Scarborough 1964? (*Daily Mirror*)

Phillip Levy, love of Marje's life, 1967.

Robert Proops, aged five, in Trafalgar Square.

Robert as a happy teenager.

Dr Olumade Okubadeju with his wife Fay and children.

Marje and Proopsie in November 1972. (*Daily Mirror*)

The caricature that launched a thousand columns. (*Daily Mirror*)

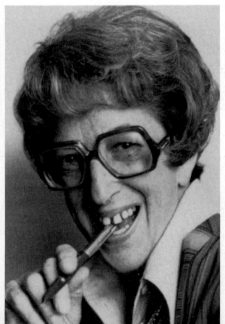

The *Daily Mirror*'s agony aunt as the readers see her every day. (*Daily Mirror*)

Marje receiving the Woman of the Year Award from Dickie
Henderson, 1984. (*Daily Mirror*)

Left to right: Lady Cudlipp, Lord Cudlipp, Marje and
Daily Mirror editor Mike Molloy. (*Daily Mirror*)

Emma, Marje's invaluable treasure, and her boss
having a laugh on the job, 1992. (*Daily Mirror*)

Marje with her constant
companion Fred, in her
garden in Barnes, 1992.
(*Daily Mirror*)

enjoyed both her neo-mother-in-law and the neo-Georgian comforts.

Marje's column was beginning to change. There were more serious, punchy pieces, more unpalatable subjects, more home truths creeping in. Marje could still be brisk and bright, but she was also capable of stirring up a manure storm. She would gladly go along to the daft Dunmow Flitch trials in Essex and adjudicate in a gown and wig on couples claiming never to have quarrelled and hoping thereby to win a flitch of bacon. But in 1964 she hauled two real high court judges over the coals for awarding car crash widows less money if they were pretty on the grounds that they would remarry. Who were these bewigged goons to judge a woman's remarriage prospects? She took a dislike to writer Colin Wilson over his book *Sex and the Intelligent Teenager*, in which he pleasantly suggests that the male sex drive is impersonal and that in the future sex will become usual among kids of twelve and thirteen. Marje retorts, 'Have you ever, Mr Wilson, come upon the agony and terror of pregnant teenage girls? Have you had any little chats recently with girls tormented by the dilemma of whether or not to keep the offspring?'

Marje had been having such 'chats'. She had begun to receive a lot of mail from *Daily Mirror* readers in response to campaigning 'social' articles on the generation gap, on the illegitimate birth rate (one baby out of every fourteen in the UK in 1967), on the demoralizing effect upon women of 'dolly bird' pictures, on David Steel's Bill to reform the Abortion Law, on the Pill, on sex, on colour-prejudice, on drug-addiction, on the neglect of the elderly, on incest. Much of the mail was supportive. Some was 'vicious' (as for example when Marje wrote about teenagers who thought their parents were 'past it', 'drips' and 'bigheads', and received a quarter of a million letters in reply). Some of the mail asked for guidance and help. Some was desperate, like a note from a thirteen-year-old girl who told Marje she was pregnant by a married man of twenty-seven. All of these letter-writers thought raunchy journalist Marje Proops a suitable person to give them advice.

Former secretary Penny Vincenzi recalls: 'I was taken on in 1962, pregnant with my first baby, and Marje was like a mother to me and really got my writing career going because I moved over to helping her with the features. And although she wasn't doing her advice column in the *Daily Mirror* in those days, what happened was that a letter would spark off an idea for her regular column.'

One example was a note from a girl which read, 'I am sixteen, fat and ugly.' Marje asked the young lady in 'for a cuppa' and was told, 'Other people laugh at me.' Marje knew exactly what she meant but said, 'So what? People have been laughing at my comical face for years.' 'Boys don't like me,' said the girl. Marje: 'I'm not surprised. You look so mournful. And I bet you don't look at them either, do you? Start looking. Gaze in wonderment at the miracle put on earth to make life worth living for us females – men!' A widow wrote in to say she had been trying to make contact with men in the laundrette by asking for help with the machine, but wasn't having much luck. Marje tells her, 'Don't be discouraged, Mrs X. Keep trying. Remember there are lots of things a washing machine can't do for a fellow.'

Marje asks doctors to shut up giving bloody descriptions of abortions and foetuses that go on kicking, because women having abortions were sufficiently reluctant and terrified and anguished and ashamed about their terminations already. She weighs in on the Divorce Reform debate, giving her readers the pros and cons and asking for humane new legislation. She writes compassionately about mental illness, reveals the 'staggering, shattering statistics' that one in nine women and one in fourteen men will spend some time in a mental hospital, and runs a series of pieces on psychiatry, offering herself as a guinea pig for analysis on somebody's couch. She writes an open letter to her son Robert, asking him to remember her in her old age, since so many elderly lonely pensioners end up freezing or starving to death unnoticed in their homes (one desperate woman victim had tried to stay alive by eating cardboard). There is nothing arch or clever-clever about Marje's style, which weeps and swears and beats its fists on the doors of authority. And Marje's readers, shocked and aroused, could hardly refrain from writing in to tell her their own private experiences of such things.

Hugh Cudlipp was not slow to observe what was happening to one of his All-Stars. Clearly, Marje was being 'adopted' by the *Mirror* readers as a sort of spokesperson. The alchemy was there for the making of gold. He had always firmly believed in the vitality a newspaper could derive from readers' input, and had keenly encouraged readers' mail. There were surveys on love and sex. There was even a column in the 1940s called 'Truth', offering prizes for readers' confessions. Cudlipp wrote, in *Publish and Be Damned* in 1953, 'The relationship between reader and newspaper became more intimate, and tantalizing problems of the heart were much in favour . . . We were setting out to prove that the experiences of ordinary men and women could make exciting reading, and it was not the meagre prize of 10/6 which attracted them; here at last was a national newspaper dealing sensibly, sympathetically and understandingly with their own problems and which published their own views.'

To this end he had employed a widow and former welfare officer, Mary Brown, to do a small but regular 'One Minute Problem' feature, with the question and advice outlined in a little box, intended to reflect her 'Christian approach to the shaping of the world'. There were also the 'Old Codgers',

'Live Letter Box', and 'Viewpoint', all dispensing snippets of information, and a *Daily Mirror* Readers' Service, which was to run for many years. In *Walking on the Water* Cudlipp explains: '. . . My principle contribution [in the 1930s] was to humanize the feature pages and enjoy myself thinking up wacky and controversial ideas. I amassed a team of psychologists, soothsayers, doctors, pet experts and scribbling priests whose services were at my command by merely picking up a phone and later dispatching a cheque . . . Cassandra called the whole thing "Cudlipp's Circus".'

This circus was about to get its high-wire woman. At Cudlipp's behest, and without a great deal of fanfare, Marje had begun writing, in 1959 in the colour magazine *Woman's Mirror*, a light-hearted advice page called 'Dear Marje'. The letters were short and sweet, and signed, 'Shorty', 'Doubtful', 'Worried Wife', and 'Mrs Falsie'. The replies were juicy, pithy and sometimes tart. The principle purpose was to amuse. The first page appeared on 3 April 1959, announcing, 'Now Proops launches a help-you column that is the wisest and wittiest of them all.' The reader is titillated: 'It's always fascinating to read other people's letters . . . so take a peek over my shoulder and read mine. If you feel like it, write to me – names and addresses strictly confidential.' There is a large cartoon by Marje of Marje reading the juicy bits. An item in May suggests that readers should write in 'for advice or a rocket', and promises that they will receive a guinea if their letters are published. Marje told a reporter, 'It is not the function of a journalist to analyse these problems in depth,' and some of the first ones printed appear to be either spiced up or cooked up.

Dear Marje,
I'm an attractive young woman of thirty-four going around with a man of thirty-nine. We have been going

together for nearly four years but he refuses to fix a date for the wedding. What should I do?

Impatient

Dear Impatient,
Do you want to go to the altar a silver-haired old lady? Reading between the lines of your letter, I suspect you're too easy with this reluctant swine – sorry, swain. He's found you're a cosy number, dear. Like this, he'll keep stalling till he's forty-five – and then change you for someone younger. Stop being nice to him. Give him the runaround. And if this doesn't work, give him the air and cast around for a more enthusiastic prospect.

Dear Marje,
Can you tell me why middle-aged women with false teeth look so down in the mouth? I feel so droopy and depressed because of my dentures.

Mrs Falsie

Dear Mrs Falsie,
Take your falsies back to the dentist and give him some lip. No reason why false teeth these days should get you down in the mouth. Don't be depressed. Grit your teeth – take 'em back and give that dentist a drilling till he improves your dentures and gives you the confidence to grin and bear them.

Dear Marje,
My boss has started making advances towards me. I suspect that if I refuse to co-operate I'll lose my well-paid job. What should I do?

Undecided

Dear Undecided,
Sorry, dear, but there's really only one thing you can do, isn't there? Find another job – fast!

Dear Marje,
Every Saturday evening my husband goes out with the
boys until after midnight and is out again on Sunday
afternoons. Then he comes home for a sleep and goes
out till midnight once more. When I object he tells me a
woman's place is in the home. I have a young baby and
feel so helpless. What would you do?

                                                    Livid

Dear Livid,
Slosh him, like as not – but I'm not advising you to do the
same. Find a reputable baby-sitter one Saturday night,
then clear out and be sure you're still out when he rolls
in at midnight. That'll teach him a woman's place is *not*
next to the sink seven days a week.

And so on. The page was gradually refined, with tech-
nicolour artwork from 1960, but continued in the same
breezy, light-hearted vein. At one point under the editorship of Jodi Hyland, later Cudlipp's wife, *Woman's Mirror*
achieved an 800,000 circulation, but insuffient advertising
revenue. Bowing to economic reality it was at last absorbed
into *Woman* magazine, where Marje continued to do her
stuff, with a team of six assistants, from 11 February 1967.

Marje's inconsequential little 'Dear Marje' had been running for five years in *Woman's Mirror* when, in 1964, Hugh
Cudlipp had another brainwave. He would send Marje on
an extended tour of the United States to do a series on 'The
American Way of Life', and on this tour she could meet
the American advice columnist Abigail van Buren, 'Dear
Abby' of the *Courier-Express*. An American (*Buffalo Courier*)
journalist wrote at the time that Marje's page in 'the London
Women's Mirror' [sic] was 'not nearly so flip' as the column
of 'Dear Abby', but the American agony aunt was very
popular, and in any case Marje had a former secretary,

Mary Hawke, living in Buffalo, from whose home she could do reconnaissance on the van Buren phenomenon (if there was one). Marje could also visit Ann Arbor, Michigan, where her old GI buddy from the war days, Delmer Wright, lived with his wife Happy and family. So off Marje went to the States, having her hair done by Jackie Kennedy's New York hairdresser, Kenneth Battell, who was very surly and wouldn't chat ('I'm a hairdresser, not a psychiatrist').

Marje spent a week in the mid-West town of Ann Arbor with Happy and Del – whom Marje hadn't seen for twenty years and who now had a grizzled moustache, a careworn expression and five children. The couple worked all the hours that God sent, said grace before meals, and belonged to every local association going, including a Bible group, a dance chaperon group and a swim-and-trim club. The kids were disciplined at home but Marje was taken aback by the degree of freedom in the local co-ed school, where students chewed gum, snogged in the classrooms and slept together whenever possible – if necessary in the nearby woods. They didn't see themselves as immoral. Marje was welcomed as a buddy everywhere and was offered a job at the University of Michigan as a lecturer in their school of journalism, which she turned down. She was impressed by the whizz-bang intimacy of all-Americans. A woman she had only just met told her all about her husband. 'Marje, he is so wunnerful and so good. Why only the other night when we were having innercourse, he said to me, "Doll, this is what makes me believe in Gard."'

American advice columnists had to cater for this market, and Marje was deeply impressed by Abby van Buren. The woman wasn't 'flip' at all. She was acerbic and wise, though sometimes short with her inquirers. One of her most celebrated replies was the one about the nine-pound baby. A mother-in-law, suspicious about whether a nine-pound

baby could really have arrived 'prematurely' is told, 'The
baby was on time. The wedding was late. Forget it.' It was
the sort of iconoclastic, punchy style that appealed to Marje,
who was already committed to it in her own little magazine
column. At lunch the two women chewed the fat over their
readers' letters. Marje asked Abby if she made any of hers
up. Abby 'got mad'. She was very dedicated to her poor
souls, but she laced her advice with some tart humour and
common sense. It seemed Abby and Dorothy Dix were a
touch less moralizing and less maternal than their olde
worlde British equivalents like Evelyn Home. Marje:

> I was knocked out by 'Dear Abby'. I thought she was
> wonderful. She and her sister had kind of cornered the
> American advice market, and I found her inspiring to talk
> to. When I came back to London I told Hugh all about her
> and he said, 'How would you like to be the Dear Abby of
> the *Daily Mirror*? I think it would be a cracking page!' I
> declined. I said that I didn't want to copy 'Dear Abby'
> or anybody else: that if I were going to write anything,
> it had to be me.

Marje had reservations. If she were to shift her light-
hearted column up a gear from the *Woman's Mirror* to the
huge-circulation *Daily Mirror*, it would mean a lot more
responsibility, a lot more work. It would mean dealing with
hundreds of serious problems, perhaps thousands, if not in
print, then at least in private correspondence, publishing
the more entertaining ones. It would require more trained
staff, and a team of experts, though these would not be hard
to come by. Marje still had her network of contacts from
her 'Mary Marshall' days, including psychologist Eustace
Chesser, and Hugh had his 'circus' of professional advisers
on hand, or on the phone. But Marje liked the idea that, in
the *Daily Mirror*, she would get letters from *men*. It might

take a few months, or a few years, to evolve the system. The pair mulled it over. They could do it. They would do it.

Marje's page in *Woman's Mirror* magazine was attracting international acclaim for its pithy style and amusing frankness. It made such a change from the dreary, commonplace morality of Victorian and post-Victorian advice doshed out in other British publications. Marje didn't moralize. She didn't consider herself qualified to judge anyone else's morals because of her own private life – aunt misbehaving. Her implied 'moral code' in any case was a fairly simple one: 'Don't be a stinker. Don't let anyone be a stinker to you. Show a little common sense.' She wasn't a judge and jury. She couldn't very well be a 'sexy writer' on one hand and Aunt Maud on the other. All she wanted to do was to give people a bit of comfort, a slap on the back, a realistic quip, a fresh insight: 'Look at it like *this*.' She was shrewd enough to know that her readers, once they had had their cells illuminated by light from the outside world, had to solve their own problems anyway.

The trickle of letters to *Woman's Mirror* in 1959 turned gradually into a steady stream of some 400 a week, already requiring three assistants (at *Woman* she would have a further half-dozen). The more complex or serious problems, for example on suicide, were answered privately. 'The primary purpose of "Dear Marje" is to entertain,' 'Marje told reporters. 'The problems are carefully chosen because they are not too deep, and in many cases will provide a laugh or two.' Not quite a send-up of agony columns, but not a mile away. She added, 'I try not to preach. After all, I'm only giving my opinion and goodness knows, I'm not infallible.'

The page always bore a lively cartoon sketch of Marje in pyjamas, or tennis shorts, or poring over her mail from 'Troubled', 'Skinny' and 'Depressed' (she made up the jokey signatures herself). She never answered medical

questions ('strictly for the professionals'), and referred
those wanting a shrink or a plastic surgeon to their GPs. She
was trumpeted in Milan's *La Stampa* as 'the highly qualified
godmother', both because of her magazine advice and her
stirring, reader-inspired journalism in the *Daily Mirror*: 'No
one, perhaps, knows better than she the aspirations of the
little typists, the troubles of the masses.' The German *Neue
Blatt* proclaimed that she received '*Tausande von Briefen die
Frauen*' (thousands of letters from women) and that they
trusted and respected her.

The advice given, especially on sex, was raising a few
eyebrows. No Victorian morality here. Marje had been
impressed by a 1963 BBC TV *Meeting Point* discussion
by a Quaker group who thought that 'Many instances of
extramarital intercourse do not lead to divorce or obvious
harm' and that 'sex experience before marriage tends to
make people better-adjusted partners'. Marje said amen
to that, and she was all in favour of contraception. She
told an interviewer, 'I once wrote a piece saying that boys
should take their contraceptives to a party, and that created
a terrible furore. And I only wrote it because I used to insist
that my own sixteen-year-old son took contraceptives to a
party. I didn't want him causing distress to sixteen-year-old
girls or the mothers of sixteen-year-old girls.' What's more,
she admitted to hoping this teenage son would experiment
with sex before marriage, so that he didn't prove a complete
duffer on his honeymoon.

In 1969 Marje told the *Sunday Times* magazine: 'I remember in the early days I got a letter from a spinster – not
young – who had established a stable relationship with
a divorced man. It was the first real love of her life and
they were going to get married. But she wasn't sure about
sleeping together before that. Having saved up her all for
so long, she couldn't bring herself to give it to him. So I
wrote and said, "Go ahead, dear, and good luck to you."

The next week I got summoned to see [*Mirror* chairman] Cecil King. He had my column in front of him. "Do you sincerely mean this?" he asked. "Yes", I said. "Fine, Proops," he said, "That's all I wanted to know." And I have never had my copy altered – before or since. I wouldn't want to be a journalist if I couldn't stand or fall by what I write.'

Marje: 'According to Hugh Cudlipp I was the first journalist ever to mention "masturbation" in print – in the *Mirror*. I asked if he minded and he laughed and said, "No, I think it's great."' Her son Robert believes the key to Marje's success has been her professionally informed, modern-minded approach: 'She started to answer readers in a professional way because she was consulting professional advisers. And she started giving *true* answers to questions rather than the non-real, moralizing, hearts-and-flowers advice offered in previous columns. And what happened was that this struck an immediate chord. People realized that she was writing in relation to the real world, and that this wasn't the sort of advice they had been getting before.'

There were attacks. Not everyone liked Marje's freestyle swimming in public morality. The Salvation Army's publication, *War Cry*, fired off a salvo in November 1965: 'Just how competent is Proops? She says she has no moral code herself; indeed, she confesses to a frivolous attitude to life, yet many of the letters that reach her desk are concerned with moral problems. To the ever-recurring question "Is it wise to have an extra- (or pre-) marital sexual relationship?" she can only point out the risks and tell the inquirers they must make up their own minds. Now that advice is not good enough!' And the banner headline bellowed: 'NOT GOOD ENOUGH, MISS PROOPS!'

In 1966, Marje became embroiled in a row with a doctor's wife from Essex, who accused Marje of telling troubled

readers to take what she described as 'trivial problems'
to their family doctor. The set-to ended up in the *Lancet*.
'Do you really think,' wrote the smouldering spouse, 'that
a doctor should be involved in petty domestic quarrels?'
Marje did really think he should, as they often weren't
'petty'. The furious *frau* argued that doctors' surgeries were
bunged up with patients sent there by people like Proops to
discuss 'minor emotional upsets'. Marje, with a well-timed
jab, replied that if anyone had cared to help them in the first
place, they wouldn't have needed to write to a journalist.
And she rounded off with a taste of her boot: 'I expect
a doctor's wife to be compassionate. Maybe I expect too
much.'

She was becoming used to such hazards at work. She was
already doing radio advice programmes, and in September
1966 a tentative stab was made at an 'agony aunt' television
show called *Ask Proops*, starring Marje in all her vigour. This
ill-conceived show gave such uproarious pleasure to the
Financial Times guest reviewer, Francis King, that he nearly
soiled himself. And since this book shall be warts-'n'-all,
here, to round off our chapter, is one of Marje's most harsh
detractors in his pomp.

King was 'astounded that this talented comedienne – a
cross between a younger Hermione Baddeley and an older
Roy Hudd – should not have a greater following . . . Why
is she never the star of *Sunday Night at the London Palladium*?
The World of Proops – as I like to think of it – is the world
of Nathaniel West's Miss Lonelyhearts and of William
Trevor's Lady Dolores Bourhardie. What more brilliant
device could be found to satirize, week after week, the
pretensions, snobberies, timidities and tribal customs of the
British than to take off the advice column of a newspaper?
. . . Not that Marje is lacking in sympathy. "Poor love",
"Yes, I do see the problem", and "Try and carry on" are
phrases often on her lips. "Watch it", however, is her

excellent advice to the couple who wonder if it is wise to spend their holidays apart.'

'Equally brilliant,' says King, were the mirth-giving experts Marje summoned for advice, including a clergyman figure, a man-about-town and a 'Molly Dumont type'. 'Such for me was the risible World of Proops: one to cherish beside the World of Frankie Howerd or the World of Tony Hancock.' Sadly for us all, the *FT* reviewer then goes to his local railway station and picks up a battered copy of *Woman's Mirror* magazine. Oh dear me, Marje is real. She *'actually exists*. At any moment now I expect to make the same kind of unpalatable discovery about some other folk heroine of mine. Ena Sharples, Modesty Blaise, Auntie Mame – where will it end?'

10

First Lady

Women are catty and competitive, or so men say. When Jean Rook of the *Daily Express* was dying of cancer in 1989, Marje wrote to send her love and to say, 'You are, indeed, the First Lady of Fleet Street.' Jean Rook wrote back immediately: 'You were, are, and always will be, the greatest, and the person who liberated us all to show what women could do in journalism.'

Marje has gone a little short of gongs considering her services to the British public, but she received two in 1969, when she was made an OBE and Woman Journalist of the Year. The citation on the former was 'for services to journalism'. The latter was one of the International Publishing Corporation's national press awards, retrospectively for 1968, and came with a special tribute from the judges. 'Not only does she cover so-called women's interests with wide knowledge, gaiety and dash, but she has the power to write about emotionally disturbing issues with a disarming common sense. She never moralizes, but is always on the side of tolerance and humanity.' Marje says, of the 'never moralizing', 'With my private life, that would have been a very hypocritical stance, wouldn't it?' – though her compassion would in any case have discouraged her from moral tutoring ('Well, I hope so!').

Marje was still hammering bumble-headed judges and statesmen who refused to demonstrate any signs of life. One Lord Chancellor had sent her a lot of patronizing letters. Marje wrote back, 'What the hell are you doing sitting on your woolsack?' She fiercely defended BBC disc jockey John Peel for revealing on the air that he had been treated for VD. She said he had behaved responsibly, and she despaired of the dim-witted protestors who had jammed the switchboards: 'The fools. The silly, ostrich-like fools, who cannot – or will not – see that if there is one subject which is overdue for frank and honest public appraisal, it is the subject of this awful, scourging disease.' VD was then Britain's squalid little secret. Reported cases had recently risen from 78,487 to 119,545, with thousands more keeping quiet through ignorance or fear.

Domestic violence was another malodorous subject Marje was determined to air. Baby-bashing, child-beating and savagery towards wives were on the increase, and a major 'shock issue' feature from Marje took a look at brutal Britain. Parents giving their kiddies a little smack was one thing. Unleashed sadism was quite another. 'Don't get me wrong – I'm not advocating an approving pat on the head from the parents of young offenders. But it's the actual laying on of belts – and of savage hands – which can set the pattern of a child's life and make certain he grows up to believe that violence is as much a part of it as eating.' Children were seeing their mothers punched and kicked black and blue in front of them. 'It is horrifyingly commonplace for me to get letters from women telling me how their husbands have come home from the boozer, bellies full of beer and unexplained anger, and hit out at their wives. "I am terrified of him," women write, "and so are the children."' The cycle was very vicious indeed. Many of the kids would themselves overcome their anxiety by growing into hard-hitting thugs.

Marje was fast becoming the nation's confidante, and she received some extraordinary mail, including a letter from someone called Tony Crofts which said, 'I am on bail awaiting trial on a charge of murdering our three-and-a-half-year-old, near-blind, totally physically helpless daughter. Whom I dearly loved . . .' In one of the most moving pieces of correspondence even Marje had ever received, the thirty-three-year-old father told her the story of his spastic little blue-eyed toddler Naomi; how the doctors had despaired of her condition and how she couldn't sit up or see. If he took her out of their poky flat in her pushchair she would stamp and kick and arch backwards, sliding out of the seat as though trying to hide herself. She slept four hours a night and suffered from spasms.

One day he had become so deeply despairing that he decided to put her out of what he felt was her misery. 'I was feeding her and the sun was shining through her hair. She looked so angelic. I gave her two sleeping tablets. She went into a peaceful sleep while I sang. I put a plastic bag on her head while she slept.' Crofts, a studious Quaker, was found guilty of manslaughter on the grounds of diminished responsibility, and sentenced to three years' probation. Marje talked to him and his wife, Helen, who said, 'At first, I felt neither relief nor tremendous grief. I felt quite blank. It was like being in an accident where you know you are hurt but do not feel it.'

Another extremely moving item in Marje's postbag came from a widower who wrote in, 'Thank you very much for a few years of heaven. I had been married for twenty-nine years when my wife died last month. Some years ago you wrote an article in which you said a woman should be told every day "I love you". After reading this, I tried it. I am afraid I always took my wife for granted. The response after a week or two was marvellous. Ours changed from an ordinary marriage into a wonderful one . . . When she became desperately ill, she knew she was not going to live long, but she never lost her sense of humour and her spirit, and her last words to me were, "I love you, Dad." So thanks again for your article and for the years of happiness you gave us both.'

Marje was still campaigning hard for more liberal attitudes towards abortion and divorce, though she was finding lesbianism more of a challenge and gave an uncomfortable review of the controversial film *The Killing of Sister George*. 'I, like most other heterosexual women, prefer not to think about lesbianism,' wrote Marje, who was nevertheless wholly sympathetic towards gay men. The piece brought in a mixed mailbag, much of it critical of male-adoring Marje's double standards. Two years later, suitably chastised, she produced a caring article on a 'sad gay girl', pleading for 'a deeper understanding' of lesbianism.

Her Adoration of the Male was causing her some qualms, too, about women's liberation – the real thing, rather than the amusing flourish of female spleen Britain had seen in the 1960s. She argued vociferously for things like equal pay and the new Sex Discrimination Act, and rejoiced over the shackle-smashing Pill – calling for it to be made available on the NHS and for doctors to prescribe it for young girls without telling their parents. But she drew the line at the more unpalatable feminist claims about men, despite having herself been nauseated by the sight of *Playboy* mogul Hugh Hefner sitting in a chair shaped like a woman's body. She was quite taken aback during a radio debate with radical US feminist Nanette Rainone, who made worrying suggestions about housewifery and penile servitude. Marje admitted, 'I have spent the best years of my life going on about a fair deal for women. I have always regarded myself as a champion of our rights, but compared to Miss R. I am but a beginner. I have only just got around to being pleased we're more or less emancipated, but it seems I am old hat. It's liberation we've got to go for now.'

Marje's reaction was 'Whoa! Most women enjoy being women . . . In spite of all its disadvantages, they'd rather be married and enslaved than free and lonely' – a statement not only sweeping but hoovering and polishing as well. She is worried, she says, that the American form of liberation 'could infect us here' – a surprising turn of phrase from a self-proclaimed feminist. She also dismissed her hero Harold Wilson's prediction, in a televised David Frost interview, that Britain would see a woman Prime Minister in their lifetime. This was 'a lovely dream'. Why so, Marje? Because men don't like female go-getters, and 'Women don't really trust other women or admire them very much. They think a woman who gets ahead is a bit of an oddball, besmirching the warm, wife-lover-mother image,' said La Proops, forecasting her future enmity, perhaps, towards Margaret Thatcher.

Marje was still giving *Mirror* readers the lowdown on sex in all its forms, with major features on sex myths, male impotence in the face of female sexual demands, and wives' nightly feigning of orgasms. But she was not a fan of hedonism or misery-making promiscuity, and she hoped and predicted that the permissive society was on its way out rather than in. *Oh Calcutta!*, the birthday-suited stage hit of 1970, peed Marje off. She counted 'five sets of dangling male genitals' and thought the ladies underfed and insuffiently busty. There was a series of 'immensely unfunny sketches' about masturbation and wife-swapping, and Marje had the impression that half the audience were keeping their eyes open by means of matchsticks. After an interval in the pub, 'we all trudged back and there was the cast again, hopping about and exhibiting their dangling genitals and sparse bosoms defiantly and saying, with equal defiance, all the four-letter words most citizens have seen at some time or other scrawled on lavatory walls.'

There was also a Boob War going on in Fleet Street. Hugh Cudlipp had suffered a terrible blow to his ego when the old *Daily Herald* broadsheet, relaunched and renamed *The Sun* under his patronage, had starved to death in the circulation battle. The corpse had been bought in 1969 by one Rupert Murdoch who, instead of decently going under as expected, had turned the paper into a tabloid and filled it with tits. As the mammaries inflated, so did the *Sun*'s circulation – at the *Mirror*'s expense. It was a depressing spectacle for Cudlipp to watch. After his retirement at the end of 1972 the *Mirror* for a time toyed with a few bristols itself in the hope of luring back some of its lost male readership. Globetrotting Marje would phone over her copy from Australia or Mexico and next day her article would appear – illustrated, regardless of subject matter, with a girl in an inadequate bikini. Even Marje's serious features on contraception or promiscuity would be accompanied by a Booby Girl. Who was responsible? George Thaw: 'Oh, the men.'

At first Marje didn't object: she was never a spoilsport and considered a few boobs brightened a man's day. But even the most liberal-minded of women can get a bit fed up with a diet of newsprint knockers. Felicity Green, appointed to the board of directors in 1973: 'I used to think that pictures of girls bursting out of bikinis were charming and gave a little bit of joy. But you have to ask yourself, in the end, if you are not helping to create an atmosphere that is detrimental to women. The other day I was walking past three ten- or eleven-year-old boys sitting on a wall, and what they were calling out was not a compliment. It was an absolutely horrific sexual taunt. And I can't help feeling that the attitude of those kids has been coloured by all the images put in front of them.' Marje:

Editors know that pictures of pretty, nubile girls with
big boobs and pouting mouths sell more papers than
pictures of plain ones. But I find it demoralizing. I find
it boring, and it makes a lot of women angry. Years
ago I used to get quite a lot of angry letters from
women readers complaining about the boobs, and I was
responsible for stopping the *Daily Mirror* from following
the line of the *Sun*. It was during the time when there
was a real struggle with our circulation, and the *Sun* was
leaping ahead. It was suggested that we ought to run
page three pictures like the *Sun*'s page three – boobies!
I did everything in my power to stop it, and succeeded,
in fact. I persuaded the editor that we'd lose far more
readers than we'd gain. And I don't know whether I
was right or wrong, but I fought against having those
bare breasts on page three.

I remember saying that women feel sick opening their
Daily Mirror and eating their bacon and egg with those
bare breasts in front of their noses. The men argued
with me, saying, 'The *Sun* does all right!' but I argued
back, 'Well, the *Sun*'s got more male readers than we
have. It's the men who buy the *Sun* for the bare breasts,
not the women. And we've got a very strong female
readership.' We've always laid great emphasis on our
women readers. So to me it was very important that
we shouldn't offend them by publishing those boobs,
and I also found it personally offensive. I hated it. I
hated the whole idea of using women in this way. It
was against all my principles, and all the fights I've had
all through the years for equality, marching up and down
Downing Street and pushing petitions through doors. I
was so deeply offended by that business that I could
have resigned over it. But I got them to agree.

Marje had recently succeeded Lady Georgina Coleridge as

president of the Writers and Press Club, formed originally in 1943 to give women journalists the chance to meet and recruit, and now sadly defunct. Her duties took her around the world to international conferences of female 'newsmen'. Author and journalist Mary Stott was part of the British delegation to Washington DC in 1971, and met Marje for the first time at the gathering. The pair were strikingly similar in appearance and struck up a firm friendship.

Ms Stott wrote of the conference in the *Guardian*: 'This odd, unrepresentative, uncoordinated gaggle of females set itself to reach conclusions about the journalist's responsibility in the fields of traffic of drugs, world hunger, the population explosion, and the status of women – across formidable linguistic and cultural barriers. What a hope, you might say!' At breakfast the Brits were fishing in their handbags, not for their shorthand notes but for their family snaps of the grandchildren. Marje had recently made an attempt to give up smoking fifty a day by switching to a few 'pongy' cigars, and she felt, as she gazed at her chubby Daniel and Anya, a sense of wellbeing and immortality.

The 1970 election saw Marje busier than ever on behalf of the Labour Party. Felicity Green: 'She was a very, very powerful political voice talking to them [the readers] in terms that no one could misunderstand or mistake for party political dogma. This came from somebody's heart.' She had earlier attacked Bernadette Devlin, MP for Mid-Ulster, for failing after an 'entrancing maiden speech' to take her Commons duties seriously (if at all). In an open letter which caused some unpleasantness among Marje's Irish readers, she came as near as La Proops ever comes to moralizing about the unmarried young Catholic woman getting pregnant and going AWOL from the House.

Marje, a prominent figure in the *Mirror*'s 'Mrs Britain' and later 'Bride of the Year' contests, wasn't a stickler for

marriage certificates: indeed she told an interviewer in 1972,
'I don't think it matters whether people get married or not.
I think the thing that matters is stability of relationships.
The actual marriage certificate is fairly worthless. But I just
happen to think that until someone thinks up a better way
of maintaining a family unit, we might just as well go along
with marriage as a viable way of bringing up children.'
What Marje objected to in Ms Devlin's case was dereliction
of duty.

Mrs Proops herself made her maiden speech from a
political platform in support of Labour candidate David
(now Lord) Ennals. Richard Crossman commented that he
was glad Marje had lost her virginity at last. Ennals was a
reformer of the kind Marje admired. As Labour health minister he had praised a major feature of hers highlighting the
plight of widows like Mary Stocker, her own housekeeper,
who because she was aged between forty and fifty had
fallen through some DHSS loophole and was living in
thirty-bob-a-week penury. Ennals immediately pledged to
raise the benefits of widows like Mary in the new Pensions
Bill, and was as good as his word. Marje also supported
another Labour candidate. Gerald Kaufman:

> When I was standing for the first time in my constitu-
> ency, in which I was elected in 1970, Marje, whom I'd
> known for years because we'd both been on the staff of
> the *Daily Mirror*, came and spent the eve of poll with me
> and spoke at my eve-of-poll meeting – and of course got
> me a *huge* audience because she was so well-known and
> so popular. And she helped me through my first election
> to Parliament. I've always been extremely fond of her
> in any case, but I was naturally very grateful to her for
> doing that.

When the Heath administration got in, Marje was wounded,

but determined not to abandon the cause of the hard-done-by. In August 1971 this brought about a confusing bun-fight in Parliament, with Marje's honour being defended in the blue corner instead of the red.

She had been helping to advertise on television the new Family Income Supplement for low-income families, which had so far failed to sell (the Government admitted that only 23 per cent of those eligible had taken up the offer). Marje volunteered her services for the advert, but there was a question in Parliament from a Labour MP – Arthur Lewis – about whether she had received a fat fee. The man who sprang to her defence was none other than the Conservative Secretary for Social Services, Sir Keith Joseph (who declined to be interviewed for this book, although Proopsie once worked with him). Sir Keith, who seemed angrier about this suggestion than about the low take-up of FIS, stormed, 'Since that question seeks to impugn an individual, Mrs Proops had every right to ask for a fee for her advertisement. She voluntarily forewent her fee and is doing the service for nothing!' Followed by Conservative cheers and shouts of 'Withdraw!'

More reversals: when *Mirror* columnist Keith Waterhouse, successor to Cassandra, let fly at the new Tory administration, he got an unexpected rejoinder, not from the Tories but from his colleague Marje. Keith Waterhouse: 'It was an attack on the Government, and I'd used the form of the agony aunt page: "I am the Foreign Secretary and my problem is that I find it very difficult to make friends" – that kind of thing. And I dealt with various members of the Government. But Marje, who of course takes her job as agony aunt very very seriously indeed, took it as a send-up of agony aunts. She was quite upset about it!' Marje replied in her column with a heavy-breathing, open love letter to Keith Waterhouse, saying, 'It did make me wonder whether, after all, I'd made a mistake in setting you

up as my secret love. It is true that advice columnists are
the subject of much ridicule and the butt of comics . . . We
really do not mind because we're not pompous, and most
of us have a sense of humour along with compassion for the
very real anguish of those with no one to turn to, who seek
our help for their desperate and difficult problems.' Hang
your head, young Waterhouse!

The election year, 1970, was significant in other ways
for Marje. Her secret lover Phillip retired from the *Mirror*,
unwillingly and in bad odour with his colleague Hugh
Corrie: 'I liked him actually much better after he left, and
I used to have lunch with him. But he'd played a very
nasty trick on me while he was there and fudged his age,
which meant that he should have retired very much earlier
than he did. He was caught out by the introduction of the
now notorious *Mirror* pension scheme, because people over
sixty weren't allowed to join. You had to show that you
were under sixty, and of course he wasn't able to do that.
Nobody quite knew how old he was, in fact, but I think
that he was very nearly seventy when he retired.'

Worse things were coming out of the woodwork. IPC
chairman Cecil King had been bundled out of office in
1968. His successor as chairman of the Mirror Group of
newspapers and magazines was Hugh Cudlipp, but the
Welsh Dragon was a firm believer in youth and a man who
had, in the past, called for various doddering politicians to
be put down or put out to graze. True to his own principles,
Cudlipp announced in 1971 that he would retire at sixty (the
following year).

In 1970 the *Mirror* had been merged with the Reed Group
who, among other things, manufactured wallpaper. The
new firm of Reed International was now being steered by
commercial interests. When Cudlipp, like his old guard,
took the unfashionable view that wallpaper was rather different from newspaper, and decided to call it a day, Marje

was devastated. Without Cudlipp, the *Mirror* would be Hamlet without the Prince. Before his departure, however, Marje's great mentor did two things that would ensure her job security and fame for years to come. He put her on a special payroll, so that she would not need to retire at the statutory age, and he launched her as the *Daily Mirror*'s very own godmother.

On Thursday, 20 May 1971, after several years of agony aunting for other publications, Marje Proops became the much-heralded advice columnist of the *Daily Mirror*. Cudlipp himself planned the pre-publicity and the layout, and Marje's glamorous, smiling photograph was seven inches by five. The new page was called (as it had been in *Woman's Mirror*) 'Dear Marje' and the headline proclaimed: 'You write and the *Mirror*'s own Proops answers.' Marje hit the ground running. She was already an experienced social affairs journalist and counsellor, ready to shoot from the hip as well as from the heart, and she had professional advisers and a team of personal assistants cranked up and ready to go. The first letter was from a man, K. R. of Essex, who complained that his wife had lost her beautiful figure after childbirth, and that 'It is becoming more and more difficult to pretend a show of passion in bed. The lack of sexual satisfaction is already showing in her in fits of violent temper.'

Marje, not yet lauded in the *Mirror* as 'the World's Greatest Advice Columnist' ('I was so hot with embarrassment when I saw that, I could have put ice cubes on my head'), replies: 'I can see why you are so upset and why your wife is beginning to show signs of desperation and frustration.' She urges the husband to show compassion, help with the chores, and be patient, as it may take a year for his wife to recover her lovely shape. In the meantime he should 'cheat a little bit' and pretend she is Raquel Welch. 'You'd be surprised how many men think of Raquel Welch while they're making love to their wives and even more surprised at how many women think of their favourite pin-up man while their husbands are caressing them . . . And it's my bet that it won't be long before you can't keep your hands off the real girl you love.'

There were letters from a mother shocked at finding her little boy reading pornography at school, from a woman worried about her son looking after himself in a bedsit, and from a fourteen-year-old girl from Bucks who wanted to know 'how far you go in lovemaking before you actually lose your virginity'. But inevitably, since adultery was on the up-and-up as a popular British pastime, there were always going to be letters that bore some relation to Marje's secret life, inviting odious comparisons. And so it was with Marje's very first *Daily Mirror* page.

The problem concerned a perpetually philandering husband with a lot of promises to reform on his lips and condoms in his pockets. Marje tells the distressed wife who wrote in, 'It's astonishing how many women go on loving men who treat them like dogs; incredible that a wife can go on forgiving infidelity, knowing it's a pattern that will be repeated again and again. That's women for you.' And then, after an elaborate discussion of the problem, she says, 'You've either got to get really tough with him – or leave him, I think.' She says it's one thing for women to put up with men who lose their heads after a few drinks and sleep with the nearest girl, and quite another to suffer a man whose affairs are 'a way of life'. One might interject, 'Marje's affair was a way of life', but at least she deeply loved both her men and wasn't being promiscuous. I leave it to the readers of this book to decide what they think of such advice in relation to her Great Secret. Those not without sin, and those in glass houses, will hopefully save their stones to make a rockery.

I showed Marje a photocopy of her 1971 page, and she

says she wouldn't answer the letters any differently now. 'But I hope that the writing would be tighter. I think it would be: I think my writing today is more positive because I've got more confidence in what I'm saying now than I had then. And not only would I give the same advice, but the letters – any of these letters – I would still be getting today. The one about the wife who's discovered condoms in her husband's pockets: I did one like that last week, and the advice I gave to the wife last week was very similar to this. But certainly the writing would be better. I mean, if I had the chance to do this again, I'd cross out half of it, including a few clichés.'

The *Daily Mirror*'s new 'agony aunt' and 'sob sister' – the job descriptions originally tripped off the tongues of indignant male journalists – wasn't letting on about her anguished double life. *Mirror* colleague George Thaw thinks this was wise. 'It's very sensible, especially if you think of the sort of gang who always run newspapers. It's better that you never expose any weakness. They might well help you privately, but professionally they'd either bollock you or mock you. It's a hard life. "We've got to produce this newspaper. Bloody well say something or piss off. Don't try and battle through because all you're doing is holding me up." If you consider working in that environment for a long time, the last thing you'll admit to is weakness. Marje most of all – because she's a tough lady.'

Mrs Proops wasn't showing a soft underbelly – not even in the course of helping other people's problems, as would increasingly be the case from now on. You might say this was self-preservation. After all, if Marje's readers had known that she had insoluble problems of her own, wouldn't that have reduced her authority? Might they not have thought, 'If she can't sort out her own blasted life, how the hell can she help me with mine?' Novelist and agony aunt Claire Rayner: 'I couldn't disagree more. The whole thing about Marje is that she is a woman just like the rest of us. We are all doing a job to the best of our ability. There's no magic about it.' Indeed, buried pain might even be one of the qualifications for the job. Psychiatrist Tom Kraft:

> I think she is getting as close as she can to being a psychiatrist. No, she didn't have medical training, no, she didn't have psychiatric training, but she is doing the nearest that she's able to do in that direction. And if you look at the whole of the caring professions, whether you're talking about social workers, psychologists, psychotherapists, psychoanalysts or whatever, there has to be some seed in the person's background to account for why they want to spend their lives helping other people. If you asked an engineer or a physicist, they would not be able to sit day after day in a consulting room seeing patients. Day in, day out, Marje is dealing with people's distress, and if you have no distress yourself, you cannot do this.

Marje:

> One of the great difficulties about being a counsellor or an agony aunt is that if somebody asks your advice, there's a tendency to tell them about your problems. You relate your own problems to theirs, and their lives to yours. If they've got a husband who knocks them about, you may not have that but you may have a husband who is cruel in some other way, so your instinct is to tell them about this. Well, that would be the worst thing that you could possibly do. Nobody wants to hear about your troubles. Everybody thinks that their troubles are unique to them, and they are unique people. Not one of the hundreds [and over the years millions] of people

who have written to me every week even considers that
there's anybody else with a problem. Let alone that I
might have one! So I think that you develop this side
of your personality. But the fellow feeling has to be
there in the first place, otherwise you couldn't become
a counsellor. Ever. You relate to other people, and it
gives you a little understanding of the way they feel.
You don't sit in judgement, but you understand, and
you're available. And you don't burden anybody else.

Marje has often told reporters that, had she not been a
journalist, she might have gone into politics. Not true: the
hours would have mucked up her domestic life (*both* her
domestic lives). What she would *really* have liked, more
than anything, was to become a psychiatrist. 'Had I had
a proper education and the chance to go to university and
take a medical degree, I'm quite sure I would have become
a psychiatrist. Because I've always been fascinated, ever
since I was a girl, by what motivates people: why they do
the things they do to each other, why they cause each other
such pain, and why they can't give each other happiness.'

What were Marje's other qualifications as a sob sister – or
was she simply an unqualified success? A most interesting
insight comes from Dame Barbara Cartland:

I get thirty thousand letters a year, mostly on health since
I formed the National Association of Health, but Marjorie
started long before me. People don't go to a priest or a
vicar nowadays if they have problems, because we have
no religion in this country, and schoolchildren are not
taught about God in schools any more. And people can't
go to the doctor either because he's usually too busy.
So these people write to me, or they write to Marjorie.
And she cares. She's warm and loving and she minds.
She knows that to get love you have got to give love.

You've got to give yourself. And she has given herself,
and given her love and warmth to everybody that has
written to her. That's why when I'm on the air I quote
her as a good example – not like another problem-page
person I could mention who shall remain nameless.

Of course, Dame Barbara won't know of Marje Proops's
secret life until she reads about it in this book, and she
may well be very shocked. But what does the Queen of
Purity say of the need for morality in a counsellor (let
alone an internationally best-selling novelist)? 'I do not
allow my heroine to go to bed with the hero until after
they're married. My characters are ladies and gentlemen,
and the point about being ladies and gentlemen is that
they have good manners. A man can sweep the street
but if he has good manners he is a gentleman. People are
not behaving like ladies and gentlemen at the moment.
Marjorie has put this in her letters for years. With good
manners they can go away and live a better life.' Perhaps
that sums it up, really.

Marje continued until July doing her advice page in
Woman (which had absorbed the now defunct *Woman's
Mirror*), and wrote features there as well. Her magazine
column had matured since the frivolous early days and was
now just as thoughtful as the one in the *Mirror*, with long
questions and answers – though Marje often seemed to be
straining at the leash writing for a purely female audience.
Subjects included homosexual love, the generation gap
and sexual brutality. There was a series on 'Male Mail',
looking at problems sent in by chaps who evidently read
the old girl's magazine while she wasn't looking, and even
a series based on the intriguing idea of printing a reply to
the letter-writer's partner – the one, very often, causing
all the problems and the one most in need of help.

Marje explains her idea to her *Woman* readers: 'Every

time I read a letter from a wife whose husband is driving her to distraction, I write back to the wife of course, but the one I really long to write to is the husband. When a mother-in-law tells me about the selfishness of her son's wife, I yearn to write a strong letter to the girl . . . Like there are two sides to a coin, there are two sides to every human situation and dilemma. Like the coin, one side can be observed, the other remains hidden from view unless you turn it over. I now propose to turn over a few coins, to write open letters to the *subjects* of complaints, starting today with a letter from Mrs Madeleine R., who wrote to me about her husband Richard.'

She tells rotten Richard, 'Your unfortunate wife has got herself tied for life (if you're lucky) to a man who committed a nasty crime by marrying her. You are a married bachelor.' No woman deserves a husband, says Marje, who regards marriage as a prison himself and gets out as often as he can, but who likes to see the little woman doing chores. There is also an anguished letter from a woman professional whose salary outstrips her husband's, and whose spouse is beginning to get revenge in bed. Marje therefore addresses her remarks to 'Dear John J.', and advises him to stop his nasty and vicious sexual practices and show a little kindness to his desperate wife – 'Yours must be the healing hand.'

Talking turkey to the culprit like this was a fascinating idea, but one not without its dangers. Marje was aware of the need to protect her letter-writers and would later abandon the practice of identifying them by first names, initials or anything else, for fear that the very partner complained of might take it all amiss and take it out on the missus. Even the facts of the case are now carefully edited and disguised on Marje's page so that the published reply doesn't get the complainant into trouble. The private reply is of course personal.

Marje regards herself as a journalist rather than a 'writer' (though anyone who has produced as many millions of evocative words as she has surely merits the description before pap fictionists), and she describes the hermit profession of the writer as 'the loneliest job in the world, because you simply have to go away by yourself and do it all. I think that's why it's lonely.' She has a way of working on her mail which reminds one of a novelist dreaming up her characters:

> I hear it in my head! I hear the sound of it. And when I'm doing my letters and people are writing to me, in some curious way I hear the sound of their voices. And I think about who they are, and what kind of lives they lead, and I look for clues like the postmark and the handwriting, and whether the writing looks like it's from somebody in trouble and anguish or whether it's confident writing, bossy writing. And after years and years of looking, you get a feeling about what people are like, simply from the letters they write. And when I'm reading them, and hearing their voices in my head, I hear accents, believe it or not.
>
> I hear Scottish voices or Irish voices or north of England voices. In other words, the letter-writers take on a very definite character. It's probably all wrong because clearly I'm only guessing, but when I'm responding to them I have this feeling that I'm addressing them directly and having this conversation with them. So that when I'm actually writing the reply, although I don't do it deliberately, I feel that I'm writing to a real person. And I don't think, 'Ah, this is a cocky car salesman so I'm going to write back in a cocky way' or anything like that, but nevertheless there is a sort of characterization.

Marje and Proopsie had decided to move house in 1970. Marje was finding Hamilton Terrace too roomy now that

Robert and Olivia had gone, and they wanted something
more cosy, away from the hurly-burly of the Lord's test
match parking problems in St John's Wood. Barnes was
eventually chosen for several reasons. First, Robert and
Olivia lived there ('Why don't you come and live in Barnes?'
Robert said. 'It's lovely!'). Second, Hugh Cudlipp lived
there (near the duck pond). And third, Proopsie had
reconnoitred the area: 'Whenever he saw building work
going on, he always interfered and told them how to do it.'
And Proopsie discovered, from questioning a site foreman,
that ten little houses were under construction in a tranquil
close near Putney Common, convenient for dog walkies
and watching village cricket. He had his eye on the largest
of the ten, going for £15,000, but Marje talked him out of
this and they settled for one of the small £10,000 jobs –
with one sitting room, two and a half bedrooms and a
secluded garden – later described by one journalist as a
'carpeted dog kennel'.

In fact they are extremely pretty little homes and Marje
lives in hers still. Like Marie Antoinette she prefers a
Petit Trianon to a Palace of Versailles. 'Much more my
style of house,' she says. 'It's very rural and pretty. The
boat race goes right along there, and when I had decent
hips I used to walk down to the river with Sophie, our
last dog. The whole thing is very villagey. Mums bring
their kids to feed the ducks and old people sit around
the pond saying 'Aahh!' Marvellous cheese shop, and one
little help-yourself supermarket. Lots of theatre people –
I've got two actors living right next door to me – and plenty
of lawyers. The place is bristling with judges. There's at
least one who goes to work on a bicycle with his wig in a
pannier. Ten minutes from Hammersmith Broadway, yet
we're surrounded by fields. I love it. I do love it.'

The couple would put a welcoming note through the
letterbox of any newer neighbours and Proopsie soon took

charge of the close, organizing everybody's gardening
affairs including 'common parts'. He was very security-
conscious, and up went a garden gate, and concertina
lattice bars at the french windows. Marje described it as
'Wormwood Scrubs with curtains', but she is eternally
grateful. She has always realized how vulnerable she is,
being well-known and doing such a sensitive job. All sorts
of highly unusual characters pop out of her postbag, and
one or two might long to crack her skull.

By this time she thanked her lucky stars for Proopsie, and
still mentioned him frequently in her articles – if less than
flatteringly. Readers were told that he rustled the paper in
bed when Marje was trying to get off to sleep. Suggesting
names for men's toiletries such as 'Eau de Stale Tobacco',
'Whisky Whiff' and 'Old Spouse', she would add, 'Just send
my loved one a sample. Any would suit him fine.' Proopsie
took it all on the chin and puffed his pipe. His wife's career
broadened his own horizons, as well as helping with the
housekeeping. 'He was happy,' says Marje. 'The only thing
he missed was sexual intercourse.' And according to his
wife, that wasn't a high priority. He would glance at her
in her curlers in the bath and say she resembled a lovable
pixie. They had achieved a happy marriage by a strange
and circuitous route. As Marje wrote in the *Mirror*, 'Those
who can yawn together have got it made. Women can be so
idiotic complaining of being taken for granted. It seems to
me it ought to be every woman's (and man's) ambition.'

Marje's close friend Felicity Green:

They had become good companions, though they had
a very unsatisfactory emotional bonding. Proopsie was
an unsympathetic man. He was Mr Know-All and fairly
boorish. But as they grew older together they established some kind of mutual companionship. They were
together for a long, long time, and in her passing years he

supported her, emotionally and physically, and Marje, because she is a kind, good-hearted woman, supported him. And this is not an unknown situation – when you stop yearning for sex and romance you settle for good companionship and I think they very much settled for that. She stopped resenting all the things about him that she had resented, and he stopped being competitive and jealous of Marje's fame and celebrity. Because he was a very jealous man. One part of him was proud, but the other resented that he was not the centre of her universe.

In March 1971, Marje was urged to have her hair done for the evening editorial meeting, 'as it was being filmed for a television documentary'. This would explain the cameras, thought Marje, who never doubts the sincerity of friends and colleagues. Mirror Group ex-chairman Ernie Burrington was at the time night-editing: 'I went into the conference in the editor's room and there was a funny sort of air about. We knew the Queen wasn't dead or war about to be declared but there was an expectant hush about the place, and lots of tittering and whispering. In fact most of us knew that there was going to be a bit of a surprise. We all settled down, and Dan Ferrari, the old news editor with a bristling moustache, began to pipe out his song about what were the best stories of the day, when the door opened and in burst Eamonn Andrews.'

Eamonn announced, 'Sorry about the interruption but I've got a news flash. Marjorie Proops, star journalist and confidante to millions, THIS IS YOUR LIFE!' Marje let out a squeal and threatened new *Mirror* editor Anthony Miles: 'I'll see you later, Tony!' Eamonn was quite shocked when he set eyes on Marje's lookalike sister Jo-jo at the studios, and asked if she was often mistaken for Marje (the two had grown more and more alike as they got older). Jo replied that she was, and that the fishmonger charged her double.

Proopsie had also acted as mole for the programme researchers. He himself was asked which person in all the world he would like to have on the show, and replied that he would like best to see Made, their black 'son'. So Made was the final guest, with Marje quite overcome at the sight of him, giggling and howling at the same time. Danny La Rue did a Marje impersonation, MP Leo Abse said Marje was worth 'a hundred MPs' and one of Marje's long-standing letter-writers, a little dumpy pensioner called Vicki Childs, came out to say what it had meant to her life to have Marje as a pen-pal for years and years (they had long since forgotten what her original problem was). Best of all, there were Marje's grandchildren, Daniel and Anya ('We saw Anya actually walk for the first time on that programme'), and Hugh Cudlipp paid Marje a startling tribute. He had always said that if by some misfortune Marje should be snapped in half like a stick of Blackpool rock, you would see the word 'genuine' printed all the way through. He told the twenty million viewers, 'People feel, I guess, that they can warm their hands on her heart.'

11

Caring Thatcher, Cuddly Wilson

M ale critics who have dismissed Marje Proops as 'merely an agony aunt' may be surprised to learn that successive Governments have sought her advice. During the seventies she served on two important Government committees. The first, appointed by the then Secretary of State for Social Services Richard Crossman and chaired by Sir Morris Finer QC, took four and a half years (from November 1969 until 1974) to report by Command of Her Majesty at a cost of £206,332. This was the Committee on One-Parent Families. The second was the Royal Commission on Gambling, chaired by Lord Rothschild, GBE, GM, Sc.D., Ph.D., F.I.Biol., LLD, FRS. This took a mere two and a half years (from 1976 to 1978) but cost £589,312, as gambling eats up the small change.

She was chosen for the first honour because of her wide journalistic contact with social affairs and the fact that she was a Member of the National Council for One-Parent Families (formerly the Council for the Unmarried Mother and Her Child). And she was selected for the second because she had acted as comforter to unseen but distraught droves of gamblers, unable, unlike her jovial father, to treat those two imposters – winning and losing – just the same. The work involved taking

home enormous Acts of Parliament, studying dry tomes
and statistics 'instead of relaxing and watching telly', and
spending many hours, and a good many weekends away
from home, attending endless meetings and listening to
evidence from literally hundreds of organizations.

Marje added a disarming sense of humour to all the
proceedings, which, when they were not warlike (as
the One-Parent Families discussions often were) could
sometimes be snail-slow, lead-weighty and ditchwater-
dull. Forwarding the provisional Report on Gambling to
'Dear Marje', Lord Rothschild said it 'might be of some
slight interest to you' and added, 'To turn to more serious
matters, as the actress said to the bishop, *ça passe sans
commentaire.*' Marje wrote back that it was intriguing to
note how many of their recommendations had not been
accepted by the Home Office, and how many they were
still 'brooding' about. 'But, as that same bishop said
to that same actress, you can't expect miracles.' Royal
Commissioner Marje was named in the Royal Warrant as
'Our Trusty and Well-Beloved Marjorie Proops, Officer of
Our Most Excellent Order of the British Empire', with a
lot of 'know ye's and 'whereas's. She was known about
her office as a 'Commissionaire'.

The Gambling Commission, whose members included
sports broadcaster David Coleman, studied everything
from bingo and greyhound racing to illegal gaming,
blackjack and the suspiciously named craps, and recommended, among other things, that the Government
should set up a 'Gambling Research Unit' to monitor the
psychology and popularity of having a flutter. Also that
betting shops 'should not offer any facilities which might
induce people to enter them for any purpose other than to
bet' but should have lavatories and be allowed to sell light
refreshments. The commissioners could not come to any
agreement about 'paternalism' – protecting compulsive

gamblers from themselves – though 'some members of the Commission believe they have a duty positively to protect people from overindulging' and 'some members of the Commission feel that local authorities should have the opportunity of preventing housewives from being deflected into prize bingo establishments during their morning shopping in the high street'.

The Finer Report looks altogether less fun, and was a comprehensive study of every aspect of single parents and their often humiliating struggles to support their children and themselves. The Report takes a sympathetic line on parents ending up without a partner, quoting John Stuart Mill's famous comment that 'Marriage is really, what it has sometimes been called, a lottery: and whoever is in a state of mind to calculate chances calmly and value them correctly is not at all likely to purchase a ticket.' Some single parents had not purchased a ticket. Most were simply unlucky in the marriage stakes. After interpreting data from the census of 1971, the DHSS estimated that nearly one-tenth of all families with dependent children had only one parent – 'by reason of death, divorce, separation or births outside marriage'. Over 500,000 children were involved. And something had to be recommended to help families who hadn't enough income, either from work, runaway breadwinners or the state, to manage from week to week. This task was no picnic whatsoever.

Professor O. R. McGregor, now Lord McGregor, chairman of the Press Complaints Commission (Marje calls him 'Mac'), is the sociologist and historian with whom lawyer Morris Finer co-wrote the Report. Like La Proops, 'Mac' is not short of pithy observations about the work. In a talk on his experiences as a 'frustrated' member of numerous official committees, he quotes an exasperated Winston Churchill as saying that Britain was overrun by

committees as Australia was by rabbits, and suggests there
should be 'a Royal Commission into official inquiries'.

Those in particular which overlap between law and
social policy, like the Finer Committee's remit (because it
included legal action against absentee spouses who refuse
to pay maintenance), 'are among the most likely to be
left in the pigeon holes'. The Scottish Law Commission
refused point blank to co-operate, saying Scottish law was
none of the committee's business, and the English Law
Commission considered it none of their business either
to suggest that family law should be heard in special
family courts and not, like petty crime, in magistrates'
courts. The Home Office agreed with the lawyers. And
the DHSS, who made a great show of providing piles of
unhelpful data, thought the committee were a bunch of
spies who might snaffle some of their work.

Lord McGregor: 'Marje's role was as a very well-known,
highly respected member of her profession, applying to
what Morris and I wrote her own brand of common sense.'
Marje may not have contributed to their painstaking writing and fact-finding, but she was a boon in the ding-dong
debates. On the committee were two noted experts in the
field of social work. The late Morris Finer couldn't stand
them and had no patience with their unmoored ideas.
'Morris and myself and I'm sure Marje were sceptical
about their kind of theoretical, psychoanalytical social
work that refers to people in need as "clients". So
there was a fundamental split on the committee and
many acrimonious debates, with Morris Finer and the
social work theorists losing their tempers. And Marje was
exceedingly valuable as a mediator, despite having all her
sympathies with one side.' She wasn't much interested in
all the wrangling or the complex analysis, but she had a
passionate desire to help people by the shortest route.

Neither Sir Morris nor Lord McGregor was at all

optimistic about the Report's recommendations being implemented. 'What we thought was that the effect of the Report would be to raise discussion about one-parent families on to a new plain. The fact that they became the subject of a report and that their situation was massively analysed I think changed the way in which members of one-parent families are perceived, from being the casual victims of unhappy relationships into a major and serious social problem. The Report also made a significant contribution to the development of family law. Its very heavy emphasis on the need for family courts demonstrated that we will never get them in this country until we have a Ministry of Justice.'

Marje thinks all their work of the 1970s is gathering dust somewhere in Whitehall:

I came to the sad conclusion that the Government sets up these committees and commissions as a kind of public relations exercise. It's like a Band-Aid to soothe the population when people get worked up about one-parent families or whatever it is. The thing now is homelessness, and I dare say there'll be a Royal Commission on that any minute now, and that'll take another three years, and then people will think something is being done. And in the end very very little is done. Sometimes the Government enacts a little bit of legislation just to keep everybody quiet. I don't know if that's true in every case [apparently not] but it was true of the two that I was involved with.

I think there was a *little* bit more done about one-parent families than about gambling. Because at the end of that gambling investigation, we all threw up our hands in horror and said, What can we do? The answer is nothing. You can enact certain laws to do with casinos or racing, but in the end gambling is a neurosis, a bit like alcohol addiction. The interesting thing about those two commissions is that all the time I was on them, six and a half years all told, I continued to work at the *Daily Mirror*, and do my advice column and my articles – in fact everybody on the committees did their normal jobs. And when I think back, I don't know how the hell I did all that and ran a household and tried to be a gracious hostess for Proopsie.

Proopsie in fact retired from Bovis in 1973 at the age of sixty, though he was still a consultant and kept busy. The Monday morning after his official retirement was traumatic, because he had to see his wife off to work. Marje:

He had one moment when he came to the front door and said, 'Have a good day at the office, dear,' and went back into the house and closed the door. And I worried about that all day. But when I got home that night he put his arm round my shoulder and said, 'Come on in – you must be tired. Come and have a drink. What would you like? Come and relax and tell me what sort of day you had.' And from then on, he was just as supportive of me as he had always been – in fact more so, because he took on the entire job of running the house. He did all the shopping, cleaning, cooking, organizing – he was a terrific organizer and list-maker. He made lists of every bloody thing. His first day at home, he went through all the store cupboards, the fridge and the freezer, listing and analysing and doing a kind of work study. Then he organized shopping lists, separating out certain foods instead of writing haphazardly on the back of an envelope, which is my method. Just like a quartermaster – absolutely.

We had a couple of au pairs in those days – one,

called Maya, was Yugoslavian. The other was Belgian,
I think. The au pairs were his sergeants I suppose, and
had to assist him and go shopping with him and help
him with the cooking. They absolutely adored him, and
one still comes to see me. She used to call Proopsie her
English daddy and me her English mummy. She was
heartbroken when he died. I loved them both. I've never
had a daughter and I'd always wanted a daughter. So
these girls I suppose really supplied that need in
me. I absolutely idolized my son. Nevertheless there
is something very special about a woman-to-woman
relationship, which thankfully I now have with my
family because of Anya, my granddaughter. She's a
smashing girl and we have great times together – it's
like being with somebody my own age. It's true she's the
most mature twenty-one-year-old I've ever met – she's
twenty-one going on fifty. And Daniel, my grandson,
is twenty-two, and he's the most enchanting boy, and
an artist. I have his first effort on my noticeboard,
drawn when he was two. It's a bunny rabbit with
the inscription 'Happy Ester'. I think I'm a very lucky
woman to have two such grandchildren.

Far worse for Marje than Proopsie's retirement was Hugh
Cudlipp's some months before. 'I went into mourning,'
she says. Marje on the payroll business:

Before he gave up the editorial directorship to become
chairman of IPC and now Lord Cudlipp, he took me off
the regular *Mirror* payroll and put me on what they call
'the special list'. The people on this short list are not
in a pension scheme, and we are not insured unless
we ourselves pay for it. In effect we are freelance, yet
we're not, because I do have a contract. Hugh drew
up a contract which I signed, which in effect makes

me still a salaried member of staff, but I don't have the other things, and I am able to continue to work for as long as I like, until I'm 110 if I want, unless I drop dead before then.

What is Marje paid? Silence. What *was* Marje paid? She will not say. Neither will any of her colleagues, either because she bribes them to keep their mouths shut or because they actually are rather protective of her. We shall try to find out in a later chapter.

In June 1974 Labour had ousted the Heath Government in the election with a little help from their friend, though in truth Marje had expressed some disillusionment with the lot of them. She had once been invited by Labour to stand as a candidate because of her huge public appeal – 'because my name was well-known and I'd win them the seat: I'm absolutely certain that they never thought I'd be much use as a politician'. But in 1973, in one of her regular pieces for the *Sunday Mirror* under the headline 'Let Down – And By My Hero', she had told her readers how the recent Labour Party Conference had upset her over its lack of commitment to women's rights. Even cuddly Wilson was 'patronizing'. 'Hopefully I listened for a firm declaration from Harold Wilson that women, who add up to 54 per cent of the population, would get a better deal from the Labour Government. I waited and listened in vain.' Never a card-carrying member of the Labour Party, Marje had half a mind to defect over the business. Eventually, this was what she would do, though not before cuddly Wilson had delivered a more mortal blow, as we shall see.

1975 was International Women's Year, and the Sex Discrimination Act and Equal Pay Act became law. 1975 was also the year in which Margaret Thatcher became Leader of the Opposition. But in real terms, women knew that little had changed. Marje, whose stock as a journalist had risen since her gongs and whose prose was now increasingly purple, wrote a withering piece in *The Times* contrasting the take-home pay of female factory workers and the Woman in Blue.

She asked, 'What will Margaret Thatcher's victory really do for the countless women who tell me of their problems, the women who describe themselves as "mere" house-wives, whose lifelong vision of themselves and their daughters can, indeed, be described as "mere"? Will it change their lifestyle in a flash? Or in a year? Will it make their husbands kinder, their children less demanding, their chores easier, their sex-lives more fulfilling? Will they dream of glory on the front bench, musing, as they fantasize with their duster in their hands, that Margaret's achievement could be theirs?' Of course not. They would simply feel small and hopeless, or smaller and more hopeless than before.

'Marje versus Margaret' was a confrontation worthy of the Royal Albert Hall, surely. Were teeth dislodged?

I first met her in her Finchley constituency where a cousin of mine had been a Tory councillor, and there was a memorial service for him at the local synagogue. I was just going to pay my respects, despite the fact that he was a Tory, and she was standing there beside me. She tapped my arm and said 'Miss Proops?' I said yes. 'I'm Margaret Thatcher, MP for this constituency.' We shook hands, and she said to me, 'Do you mind if I come in with you? Because I'm not quite sure of the form at a synagogue and I don't want to do it all wrong. I don't know really when to stand, when to sit and when to kneel.' I laughed at that because if there's one thing you don't do in a synagogue it's kneel. So she said, 'Well, anyway – I'll do what you do!' I said, 'And I'll do what everybody else does because I don't know either!' So we stood and sat when the others did, and then we emerged together and stood outside talking for a while, saying we must meet again.

Now when I first met her, I rather liked her. I thought she was a nice, positive woman, the strong sort that I rather admired. Despite her politics. And after that we met quite frequently, mostly doing radio, though we did a few television slots together. We were both on the panel of *Petticoat Line* – and although I can normally hold my own in a barney, I could hardly get a word in. Afterwards we'd go and have cups of coffee that tasted like mud in the BBC canteen and eat our sandwiches and gossip and argue. And we agreed that we'd never convince one another, but despite our differences I think we liked each other: I because I admired this strength of hers and her determination and her purposefulness, and I don't know why she quite liked me but clearly we got on very well together. And then in 1975 she became leader of the Conservative Party, and the *Mirror* editor said to me, 'Why don't you go and interview her as you know her?' So I did, and she was very friendly. It was just like one of our nice, normal meetings. We had tea and we talked in a very relaxed way.

Marje had already warned *Mirror* readers and brainless critics of Thatcher's hair and hats not to be misled by the 'Tory garden fête image' – 'She is a woman to be taken very seriously indeed.' The interview itself took place on the fiftieth anniversary of female suffrage (in July 1978). Marje's centre-page spread was a paean of praise to Maggie, who certainly seemed warm and caring. The Iron Maiden noticed that Marje was limping and took pains to find her a very safe seat. Fun-loving Proops had brought along a photo of some suffragettes to make trouble, and pointed out that Mrs T. was enjoying the benefits of their violent struggle fifty years before. Mrs Thatcher ran her index finger thoughtfully over the picture and said she could never hurl herself under a horse. She talked sympathetically about female underdogs, though of course she herself had never been under any dogs either: 'It never occurred to me to think that because I am a woman, I'd be restricted. I didn't think of it. So I wasn't.' She smiled a lot, seemed awfully 'nice' and reminded the *Mirror* inquisitress of a sugared almond – smooth and sweet with a tough nut inside. Marje starts out viewing everybody through a rose-tint in her spectacles and only spots flaws later on (her great friend Felicity Green apparently does it the other way round, so they make a fine pair). She was to meet the inner Thatcher soon enough.

The limp that Mrs Thatcher noticed was arthritis. Marje had had twinges since she was young, but during the seventies the crippling disease became the bane of her life. 'It got so bad that I was unable to stand. I used to fall over and Proopsie used to have to pick me up off the floor because I couldn't get up.' She borrowed a zimmer walking-frame, a wheelchair and a chairmobile, though the latter was painfully slow and Marje was always in a tearing hurry. She managed to carry on working only because the *Mirror* provided her with a chauffeur, Fred, and a car to ferry herself and her metalwork to the office. Unfortunately Fred was claustrophobic, which meant that he couldn't go in the *Mirror* lifts. He had to ring Marje's secretary, who would descend from on high and wheel Marje in and out of the elevator. Being a wheelchair-person changed Marje's whole outlook:

I led quite a fascinating life in that wheelchair and learned a tremendous amount. The experience made me very much aware for the first time what it's like to be disabled. Poor Proopsie, who had arthritis himself, used to push me around the shops on Saturday mornings. The interesting thing is how people treat you – as if you're not there. They used to stop Proopsie and say, 'How is she today?' as though I were absent or deaf or had lost my marbles. And I used to sit there smiling foolishly. But they never looked at me. I came to the conclusion that this is how a lot of people treat the disabled. They're so embarrassed by somebody else's disablement and so unable to cope with it that they simply cannot look at the victim. The only ones that I got on friendly terms with during our shopping expeditions were dogs and small children. I had eye-level contact with those.

What you feel in a wheelchair is very very vulnerable. Because suddenly you're not in control. When you're in hospital having an operation, at least you know that there will come a point when you'll get out of bed and get better, and there are always people around to look after you. But in a wheelchair, you can't escape. For the first time in my life I felt physically helpless. Being the sort of person I am, I used the experience in my work. Every single experience of my life I mark down as something useful for my work – the same as those life classes at art school when I saw naked bodies. I used my time in that wheelchair to understand other people's disablement, and over the years since then I've had a lot to do with organizations for the disabled. I'm now a vice-president of Arthritis Care.

One very valuable learning experience for Marje was seeing how Proopsie loved and cared for her. He would bath her, wash her hair, dress her, do everything for her. No husband could have been kinder, and this physical and affectionate bond between them was to have a profound effect. Marje valued Proopsie as never before.

The men at the *Mirror* had their own rough brand of therapy, and would refer to Marje as 'Mrs Ironside'. Brian McConnell: 'The *Mirror* without Marje just isn't a possibility, and the newspaper humour was designed to encourage her to get better. Printers used to yell out, "How much for the zimmer frame, Marje?" and crack jokes about it to egg her on.' Photographer Doreen Spooner: 'It used to make me laugh because she always had the dishiest man in the office pushing her wheelchair. I often wondered if she went in her wheelchair purposely to get attention, because the young men used to race her through the building. It was quite a thing for them, this wheelchair racing.' *Wheelchair racing?*

Marje: 'My colleagues at the *Mirror*, unlike people I met on shopping trips, used to make great jokes about it. They used to put bets on who could get me from my office to the editor's office in the shortest time. The picture editor nearly always won because he was entitled to go through the dark room. The others had to go the long way round. So he was always in there with a chance, provided he got there before anybody else to start the push. They used to play wonderful wheelchair games. I was turfed out or fell out a couple of times. They used to haul me up saying, "Come on, Marje! Keep going! Don't fidget!"'

Later on Marje 'got very independent' and said she would manoeuvre on her own. This led to two moments of pure fear. She got trapped in one of the corridors when the chair wheel caught in the carpet. 'The feeling of panic-stricken helplessness was quite extraordinary, even though I knew someone would be along in a few minutes to give me a shove. And on another occasion I got stuck in the lavatory. And that was most terrifying because I simply could not get out. I'd got sort of jammed inside the door. I couldn't get out of the chair to release myself and open the door. That was a moment of absolute panic.

I yelled and shouted and eventually somebody came to let me out.' These glimpses of terror were foretastes of a blacker darkness that would threaten to engulf her in 1986. For now, her problem was mainly a physical one.

The doctors told Marje her affected hip wasn't yet sufficiently destroyed for a replacement operation, but not to worry as she would 'learn to live with the pain'. Marje didn't want to live with it. She didn't see why she should, and told the doctors they would just have to do something. Eventually she was seen at St Bartholomew's Hospital in London and began having hydrotherapy and epidural injections. She also had shots in her knees and right hand. These were agonizingly painful in themselves and Marje had to count to ten to avoid hitting the ceiling. But when the pain subsided and she was back in the car sucking a boiled sweet, it all seemed worthwhile. It meant that she could get about without using the wheelchair or the zimmer. She still has the odd injection in her hand.

Marje carried on working throughout her ordeal. She was answering more letters than ever through her 'Dear Marje' page, and the cries of her desperate readers were becoming increasingly close to her heart. She began a 'Stinker of the Week' feature, to highlight what inhuman beings had done to some of her letter-writers, and the item brought in fat postbags of woe. She was attacked by the Curate of St Mary Cray in Kent for saying to distressed wives who wrote to her that they should not be upset if they found hubby looking at porno magazines in the potting shed. According to Marje at that time, the stuff was therapeutic and fun, and instead of getting worked up, the missus should get in that potting shed and share her husband's leering delight.

She supported Harold Wilson's call for Britain to remain in the Common Market in 1975, saying she was inspired by concern for her grandchildren's future and didn't want them to be citizens of a 'tiny off-shore cabbage-patch of an island'. (She sees no reason to change her mind now, despite the spread of bureaucratic tentacles: 'I believe that unless we do join the prosperity of Europe, the poorer people in this country will once again be the victims of right-wing Conservatism.')

In 1976, Marje was granted an exclusive two-hour interview with Princess Anne and Captain Mark Phillips at their home in Sandhurst. The major feature was commissioned and published by *Woman* but was regurgitated in the *Mirror* in a centre spread. Rumours were rife that Anne was pregnant, but she told Marje that she was in no hurry to start a family until she had achieved her ambitions in Olympic showjumping. Bare-faced Marje asked all sorts of personal questions that would have made regular royal-watchers curl up their toes with embarrassment, and found out useful details of the marriage. Anne: 'He takes longer to get up than I do. We're very civilized in the morning: we hardly talk.' Anne turns to Mark: 'You are basically quite a chatty person and I'm basically a quiet person. You couldn't say I chat in the mornings, do I?' Mark: 'It's more like grunting than chatting.' Anne: 'Well, sometimes I can't get a word in edgeways.'

Anne revealed that she didn't think a married man should have to cook unless his wife was working, that she didn't like nightclubs one bit and that, contrary to myths put about by the press, she had to be 'dragged off by the scruff of my neck' to go to a party. There were hoots and howls of laughter quite uncharacteristic of the Princess, who has not only ridden the odd hack but ridden roughshod over the two-legged variety. Marje says that they couldn't have been formal if they'd tried, as Anne's slobbery dogs jumped about keenly, trying to lick their visitor. 'I got on very well indeed with Anne. Mark didn't say anything much – he wasn't called "Fog" for nothing. But I didn't ever feel intimidated in the presence of royalty or their dogs. Anne's leapt all over me and she kept shouting at them to get down. We had lots of jokes, mostly about the dogs who showed no respect for anybody, and it was all very relaxed.'

As if she wasn't quite busy enough writing for the *Mirror*, *Woman* and the *Sunday Mirror*, doing radio and television slots and sitting on endless Government committees in an effort to hatch them out, Marje had also blossomed into an author. In 1975 she produced a short, sharp study of the second sex called *Pride, Prejudice and Proops*, comparing women of Jane Austen's world with women of the 1970s. Females had come a long way from the downcast eyes and proper behaviour of Austen's heroines, who wanted romantic love and ended up in holy wedlock. Now they wanted romantic love *and* sexual fulfilment, and often ended up in an unholy armlock. Fewer girls were writing to Marje in the seventies asking how to get a man. The modern Elizabeth Bennets and Fanny Prices wanted to know how to get rid of one.

More important than *Pride, Prejudice and Proops* was *Dear Marje*, published the following year. This was a 200-page analysis of her agony mail, divided up into various key categories. Marriage problems accounted for over half the letters she received, and a third of these letters came from men. 'Many couples now, as in the past, stick it out for various reasons: children, money, possessions, jobs, relatives and religion. Even so, present figures indicate that one in four couples marrying now will break their ties in the divorce court.' Marje's sane replies were intended to help this insanity. Other desperate letters came from teenagers worried about their minds, their bodies and masturbation ('Will hair grow on the palms of my hands?' 'Will the habit damage my penis?'). Unmoralizing Marje reassures them, as perhaps

their parents should have done, 'There is nothing wrong
with you.'

Her book dispenses advice distilled from Marje's own
nous and network of experts and discusses with hard-won
common sense the anguish of loneliness, the pains of
parenthood, the grievances of sexual misfits, the worries
of ageing and the frustrations of women in a man's world.
And it provides a shot in the arm, a kindly cuddle, a kick
up the bum, a glimmer of hope for them all. As Marje
put it to me, 'I want to take all the ones that are suffering
into my arms and clasp them to my bosom, and look after
them, and say, "There, there, don't cry, you'll feel better
tomorrow," even though I know they won't.' But no one
can deny the survival value of someone to talk to, and
countless letters she has shown me say, 'I feel so much
better for being able to share it all with you.'

Bernard Levin, in his purring review of *Dear Marje*,
wrote in the *Observer*, 'Does Marjorie Proops do good?
I cannot see how anybody reading her book can be in
any doubt that she does an enormous amount, possibly
– of direct, practical good, at any rate – more than any
single individual in the country . . . To understand how
helpful Mrs Proops can be it is necessary to understand
that, whatever we are supposed to believe about the
permissiveness of our society, millions still cohabit with
misery and despair in a house of ignorance and fear.'
The *New Statesman* was equally impressed: 'There are,
naturally, those who scoff, and she has been attacked
by a lawyer, sneeringly referred to as the Queen of the
Agony Aunties and asked by what right she sets herself up
as an oracle. Let us answer for her. Anybody as reasonable,
helpful and open-minded has every right. For many years
she has been a positive cascade of wholesome good sense
and has done great service. Would to God she were in the
Government . . .'

Marje was not in the Government. The Labour Party was sinking fast, and its leader had perhaps seen the graffiti on the wall. Marje herself had her misgivings about Labour's commitment to women's rights, but she was still faithfully working for socialism. Loyalty shone like two lamps in her spectacles as she went to interview Prime Minister Harold Wilson at Chequers to honour his birthday in March 1976. 'Romeo, Romeo, wherefore art thou, Romeo?' trilled Marje from the stairs. Cuddly Wilson, sixty years young and looking slightly pickled in some of the press photos, appeared, beer in hand, to escort her to lunch, and sat knee to knee with his dear old pal Marje as they discussed the violence of the world, his disappearing paunch and his advice to shop for food after a good breakfast to avoid impulse buying. But the Premier's sozzled gaze concealed a strange and a terrible secret. Joe Haines, Wilson's press secretary at that time and in later years the *Daily Mirror*'s leader writer:

It had been Harold's intention to announce his decision to retire before his sixtieth birthday. He was going to do it on 28 February. But unfortunately, because of things happening within the Party, he had to put it off, and he decided to announce it on 16 March. I pointed out to him that we had Marje coming to interview him for his birthday on the 11th, and that this would be awkward and perhaps we should cancel it. He said that would be very difficult. Because if we were to cancel, it would alert the *Daily Mirror* to the possibility that something was up. I said the alternative was to take Marje into his confidence and tell her that he was going. And Harold said that would not be a proper thing to do to a journalist, to give her such an enormous piece of news and not expect her to tell her editor.

So with some reluctance on both our parts – I certainly

was against it – he decided to go ahead with the interview. Harold said that perhaps she was not going to ask the question about how much longer he was going to stay. And I said well maybe she wouldn't, but I thought the likelihood was that she would! And of course that was the very last question Marje asked. 'At sixty, which is a watershed age for most men, don't you think about putting your feet up?' And he said that depended on a man's faculties and good health, and he felt fine. But he was very concerned and felt guilty because he knew that he had misled Marje. On the other hand, had he told her, if she had then not put something in her article about how long he intended to stay, the editor would have said, 'Well, didn't you ask him how long he was going to be Prime Minister?' And she would have been put in the position of either letting Harold down or lying. Looking back on it, I still think he should have cancelled the interview.

It would have been a bitter pill for any journalist, but to one of Labour's staunchest supporters, one who liked and trusted and openly flirted with Wilson and had won the Party so much support for so long, it was similar to a knife in the ribs. Joe Haines: 'I once went to a Labour Party conference many years ago, even before Harold Wilson was Party leader, and I was sitting in a room off the conference having a cup of coffee when Hugh Gaitskell, the leader of the Party, came in. And nobody paid any attention to him. They were all gathered round Marje.'

How did the lady feel about what happened? Joe Haines: 'Marje doesn't bear any grudge.' Felicity Green: 'She never forgave Wilson for that. He misled her and even now when she talks about it she is filled with a sense of outrage. Because she is a heavyweight columnist, and underneath all the froth and bubble and fun, she is a very serious political writer.' Marje:

> Joe knew, and Harold knew, that the interview would appear in the *Daily Mirror* and that a few days later, when Harold resigned, both the *Daily Mirror* and I would look very foolish indeed. I don't know why Harold refused to cancel. It might have been out of vanity. It might have been that he didn't want to disappoint me and let me down, having promised. It might well have aroused suspicions at the *Mirror*. Anyway, the interview took place and I asked the question and he didn't answer. I was looking at his face but he's a politician, and absolutely any politician that I've ever met, and I've met a few, can look you straight in the eye and tell you the biggest whopper, and look so genuine and sincere that you'd be very cynical indeed not to believe him – what with Harold being very fond of Marje, and very nice and affectionate and warm and all that rubbish.
>
> Well, the piece appeared on 11 March, and then he resigned. I was angry and upset and every kind of emotion. I felt I'd let the paper down, that I should have known. I should have extracted the information from him. I felt very inadequate as an interviewer, that I hadn't got the truth out of him. Angry that he deceived me; even angrier with myself for being gullible. I don't know what I would have done had he told me. I've often thought about this. I think that I'd have told the editor, but I don't know.

Marje would go on supporting Labour in her articles; she would go walkabout with Labour MP Austin Mitchell in 1977, and do everything in her power to represent her millions of silent, skint, salt-of-the-earth readers. But she had suffered a bruising blow, both as a journalist and as a woman. Small consolation that her name should be bandied across the House. Small solace that Labour's Dennis Skinner, referring to Tory rebels in Thatcher's Opposition nest, should ask new Premier Jim Callaghan, 'Can you offer any advice on this matter, or would it be better for Mrs Thatcher to send a letter to Marje Proops?' Still, if you're, as it were, 'accustomed to agony', you can take a few knocks. When – as happened to Marje in 1976 – a man you don't know commits suicide leaving among his belongings several unposted letters addressed to you, all things are seen in their due proportion.

12

Magnum Ops

Girls butchered in kitchen-table abortions. 'Poofs' punched, kicked and arrested for their private relationships. Rancorous spouses condemned to live together for the rest of their lives. All of them had written to 'Dear Marje' at the *Daily Mirror*, hoping she could perform some miracle to help them. All of them were on her mind as she lay in bed in the witching hours, staring at the ceiling and wondering what the hell one woman journalist could do on their behalf. Clearly there was something wrong with the laws of the land, Marje reasoned, if they did such harm and caused such suffering. Clearly if this were so, these laws had to be changed.

Marje doesn't remember when she first started campaigning to right injustices. She remembers arguing as a little girl with her father about first and second-class bars in their pub. She remembers marching the postwar streets of Leeds beside the great Aneurin Bevan, celebrating tooth-and-nail victories for the poor, and she remembers the way grateful citizens hung out of their upstairs windows, screaming and cheering for the man who had given them the National Health Service – 'That was one of the proudest moments of my entire life.' She has always been on the side

of the desperate, from whatever cause. She has done her
best to champion the downtrodden and the unhappy, and
she has always fought for reviled minority groups, having
belonged to one herself, and having learned early on what
abuse felt like.

This was why, in the sixties and seventies particularly,
Marje spent much of her time campaigning to change
the law on homosexuality, abortion and divorce. It had
nothing to do with moral codes or Utopian theories.
It wasn't because Marje was a rebel or an iconoclast,
determined to sweep away old fuddy-duddies with her
reforming broom. She just wanted to place herself between
desperate people and their tormentors, and one of their
tormentors was the law. She had also, of course, fought for
women's rights, and supported MP Willie Hamilton's Sex
Discrimination Bill. But she very often fought for feminism
with one arm tied behind her back, because she loves men
too much really to Tyson them with blows.

A great ally of Marje in her compassionate endeavours
was poet and MP Leo Abse, who was instrumental in
changing the law on divorce, homosexuality and family
planning, and influential in altering the law on children's
rights. Marje: 'Leo was a very passionate man, and spoke
passionately in the House about all his campaigns for
new legislation. He was the public figure. He got up and
declaimed in Parliament, and I declaimed in print, though
I did go round talking and hectoring and lecturing anyone
who would listen.' Leo Abse: 'I think I met Marjorie
originally on some early television programme in the
south of England. And immediately I realized that this
wasn't the usual belligerent feminist of a journalist. She
wasn't working out her own problems in saying what
should and should not be. She impressed me then and
continued to do so all her life.' The issues raised by the
parliamentarian during the law reform debates were the

stuff of Marje's case histories. They were also, as Leo Abse points out, highly contentious: 'Always dynamite for the politician and I don't doubt, similarly dynamite for a journalist.'

Marje fervently supported Leo's homosexual law reform and helped to draft the new legislation, using her experience as a confidante to thousands of those persecuted (one homosexual letter-writer had christened her 'The Queen of the Gays' for her support). For this Marje was condemned by many of her regular readers ('You must be a lesbian yourself to want to make life easier for queers'). One of her remarks, suggesting homosexuality was 'in the genes' rather than a matter of personal perversion, incurred terrible displeasure. Marje was shaken, but would not shut up. She thought compassion a quite reasonable request to make in a newspaper.

Leo Abse admired the way Marje was able to handle such powder-keg issues. 'In all these arguments that were being presented and that I was involved with in Parliament, I always knew that I would pick up an article by her, and without taking an entrenched position she would allow facts and case histories to emerge in such a form that it would create a tolerant and generous public opinion. So that what I really respect her for is being a journalist without being an indiscriminate zealous missionary. Because of her talent and sensibility she was able to present things as they are, and consequently to tease out of public opinion a wish to have changes which would better our society but would not encourage heavy stupid campaigning and prejudice.'

Back in 1962 Marje wrote that divorce was 'an unrelieved disaster', and said she was wholly in favour of patching up broken marriages ('I know a lot about the stresses and tensions of divorced women. I know all about the devastating loneliness . . . I know of women, alone and elderly, living out their lives with nothing left in their hearts but bitterness and terror,' wrote Marje, remembering the Guinness Girls and the Lonely Old Ladies). Strange that such an avowed supporter of the institution should appear arm in arm with a man about to tinker with the divorce laws? Leo Abse:

> No. I think that's why I got on with her and why we became so friendly, because she realized that the manner in which I was seeking to alter the law was intended to buttress marriages rather than to take up any frivolous attitude towards them. She understood that a marriage can unhappily die, and if it dies, then it requires a dignified burial. She recognized that in order to maintain respect for the institution, I wanted to take away all the misery and downright lies that the legal process formerly involved. The Act, although there were many other things to be done, at least did take away the humbug and the hypocrisy and the cruelty that was embedded within the old legislation.

Mr Abse regards Marje's work as 'a civilizing influence'. 'The very manner in which she was presenting the "agony" has meant that she was illuminating a great deal of the issues and she was making the problems concrete.' This made Marje's column a useful sounding-board to test public opinion and discover possible pitfalls in the new laws. One problem she helped to highlight was the plight of deserted wives. The new humane divorce law accepted the irretrievable breakdown of marriage as sufficient and sole grounds for divorce, cleaving the chains on couples who, after three years, could not bear to live together any more. But it would, initially at least, cause a surge in abandoned marriages. And because women were frequently the unwilling divorcees and often lost their half

of the goods and chattels in the carve-up, Marje added her
journalistic weight to the Married Women's Property Act,
giving them respect and a fairer share.

But divorce was always a very thorny issue for Marje.
When the Reform Bill was getting its third reading, she
joined in the debate on whether one act of adultery should
be sufficient grounds for divorce. Her heart throbbing with
guilt and worry, she wrote, 'The realization that the one
you love has engaged in the deepest human intimacies
with someone else is devastating knowledge.'

Marje and Leo Abse worked in tandem on many liberal
law reforms, but on one she would go it alone. This
was David Steel's Bill to update the abortion law, and
Marje supported it with fervent conviction. It brought
her more abuse than any other single subject on which
she had campaigned, but Marje nailed her colours to the
mast and refused to take them down despite repeated
male-dominated attempts in Parliament to amend the new
Act and return to illegality – to backstreet abortions, to gin
bottle and knitting needle botch-ups for desperate women
who could not afford private terminations in posh clinics.
She wrote, 'It has been an issue I have felt more strongly
about than any other in my professional life' because her
mail told her of the degree of butchery and misery caused
to women by the old legislation. Of an estimated 100,000
abortions a year in the UK, 90,000 were of the kitchen-table
variety, putting the lives of all these women at risk in the
most squalid circumstances.

The Reform Bill asked for abortion to be legalized
where the mental or physical health of the pregnant
woman was in danger (vouchsafed by two doctors), or
in cases of sexual assault. When it became law in 1967
after a tumultuous debate in the Lords, Marje 'wanted to
stand up and cheer'. She thought that at last women were
being heard by male legislators in a matter that affected

them more deeply than any other – the right to determine what should happen to their own bodies. Unfortunately, she had not reckoned on the swift and shocking rise in abortions and promiscuity that followed the new Act, or greedy doctors doing as many abortions as possible. Nor had she reckoned on the strength of feeling of male MPs and lobbying groups, nurses, students, religious organizations and many gynaecologists who were concerned for the rights of the unborn baby, and who would now press for ever-stricter controls. Marje had every sympathy with their sincerity, but not with their calls for abortion to be prohibited again.

Of course she was not in favour of 'abortion on demand'. Women should behave responsibly, and avoid unwanted pregnancies by common sense if they could. She wrote that contraception should be taught in schools as well as newspapers. She also wrote that a child carried unwillingly and born illegitimate and unwanted stood every chance of being an unloved child and a battered child. Her *Daily Mirror* postbags told her which side her readers were on, and in a letter to *The Times* she summed up what she felt about abortion: 'When a young man becomes pregnant by a married woman who, on hearing of his pregnancy, leaves him to cope . . . I will be prepared to listen to men's arguments.' Until such time it must be a woman's decision whether she will carry and nourish a child inside her body.

And on this one issue, far more than on equal pay, sex discrimination or anything else, Marje identified herself as a feminist, whether it offended men or not.

Notorious Marje, famous Marje. Her likeness – or rather Hilda Ogden's likeness with wig and spectacles – was put in Madame Tussaud's in 1977 in a wicker chair. The sculptor had upset the model by showing her a large box of eyes 'like sinister marbles', and then making her legs

very fat. Her name had also been celebrated in a crimson
rose by Harkness and a couple of pop songs (one by
Max Bygraves). A Welsh sheep, an army truck, a boat, a
camel and assorted dogs, cats and budgies had also been
named after her, causing her sister Jo-jo to comment that
Marje had become a household name, 'like Vim, but not
so abrasive'. Having such a highly recognizable mug, La
Proops was mobbed by autograph-hunters wherever she
went. Des Lyons took her to Simpsons in the Strand,
where women were banned from downstairs. Des and
Marje were obliged to eat upstairs, followed by a throng
of well-wishers which nearly emptied the downstairs
restaurant. At Langan's, Marje was always invited to sit
at Michael Caine's special table when the Squire wasn't
using it, or the one next to it 'in pole position'. The *Daily
Mirror*'s Don Walker recalls how this led to an 'incident':

> Marje took me to lunch on one or two occasions at
> Langan's Brasserie, and guests like myself would be
> seated at Michael Caine's big round table, bathing in
> the glow of admiration from other diners. One day
> while she was there with Brian Bass, who should come
> up but Peter Langan himself, obviously the worse for
> drink with his shirt hanging out of his trousers, a bottle
> of champagne on his hip and his hair all awry. Seeing
> Marje sitting there he boomed, 'Hallo Marje! How about
> a fuck in Venice!' And Marje, completely unruffled,
> replied, 'Oh Peter, I'd love to, but it does play up
> my rheumatism.' Marje told us he was not averse to
> coming up and groping people, her included – 'and me
> a grannie!'

Marje:

That's right. Every time I lunched there, he used to

amble over drunkenly. On another occasion I was there with [the ex-*People* editor] Bill Hagerty, and halfway through lunch Langan came over as usual, drunk, and leaned across the table. 'What are you doing this afternoon, Marje? Fancy a fuck at the Ritz?' I said, 'I'm busy this afternoon,' and burst out laughing, but Bill was outraged. Immediately he stood up and said, 'Come on, we're going.' And out we walked.

Lucky Marje was invited to fly Concorde in June 1977 on a dream transatlantic daytrip with some *Mirror* contest winners. Editor Mike Molloy had managed to talk so persuasively about this once-in-a-lifetime opportunity to overcome her fear of flying, and had thrilled her so much with arguments about what tremendous publicity it would be, with Keith Waterhouse and other *Mirror* chums on board, and boxer John Conteh and a vanload of celebs, that Marje listened with her eyes practically on stalks before refusing to have anything to do with it. The editor had to take her to lunch and tell her how they were all depending on her, and how it would fall apart without her, and how they had the famous pilot Captain Walpole flying the aircraft, etc. etc., before at long last Marje agreed.

Mike Molloy: 'After I'd finally trapped her into flying, Captain Walpole was brought out to meet Marje in the airport lounge, with a drink in his hand. And Marje looked at him sternly and said, "I hope that's orange juice you're drinking, young man!" But during the flight they actually let her go on the flight deck, and I was saying, as she disappeared down the aisle, "For God's sake don't touch anything, Marje!" But she's utterly devoted to the paper, and would do anything for the *Mirror* – even this.' Fortunately, plane-petrified Proops found Concorde a bird she could trust. 'The captain invited me on to the flight

deck while we were driving,' glows Marje, absolutely
converted. 'When the stewardess told me of this offer I
was in a state of terror, but they strapped me in, and this
bloke was showing me all the knobs. They were very jovial,
with the flight lieutenant teaching me to fly the plane, and
I felt so much better that I actually ate an in-flight meal
afterwards.'

In 1978 Molloy promoted Marje to assistant editor of the
paper. She had been a longtime unofficial executive, and
Mirror Group News, the paper's internal news magazine,
said that she would join fellow assistant editor Joyce
Hopkirk in the planning of women's pages and features.
The concept of 'women's issues' in their own 'Mirror
Woman' corner of the paper is one that Marje has never
liked but Molloy insists that her brief was in any case
much wider than this. She would continue to cast her
beady eye over emotive topics and do her 'Dear Marje'
page every Thursday – 'putting on her poultices' as one
of her next-door neighbours termed the work.

Marje was certainly by 1978 'the highest-paid journalist
in Britain'. True or false? 'I bet I'm not now,' she says,
sidestepping niftily for a tin-hipped woman of undisclosed
age. 'I don't know that we ought to publish that. I honestly
don't know if I was the highest paid because I don't know
how much anybody else earned. I've no idea what Anne
Robinson earns but I would imagine it's more than I do.
On the other hand, she works for the BBC and she does
telly and radio so her earnings would be from several
sources, whereas mine are from one source. Basically my
salary is paid by the *Mirror* and anything else I earn, I'm
grateful for. And that can vary. It depends if you've got
an agent, which I haven't. Some get huge sums.' Marje's
son Robert is in charge of all her accounts. If she wants a
chair reupholstered she rings Robert and asks if this would
be an affordable move. Robert replies, sometimes using

the F-word, that it's her money and she should enjoy it while she's alive.

Undoubtedly Marje could have earned serious spondulicks from advertising and endorsements. But she was always very reluctant to use her name commercially because she sees her work as unexploitable. 'It would cheapen the job that I do. I can't say I'm not in it for the money because I get paid by the *Mirror*. But using my name for commercial gain I find somehow distasteful.' Readers occasionally send in gifts. One sent a locket and a gold sovereign on a chain, wrapped in grubby paper. 'The handwriting was very old.' Taking her chauffeur with her as bodyguard Marje raised £84 on one and £82 on the other, donating the money to an arthritis charity. Another reader sent a £20 note, thanking Marje for all her help over the years. She gave it to a little chap with a bucket collecting for a Guy's Hospital kidney machine.

'I do work for the BBC and all sorts of odds and ends for people, for twopence, if that. I often do it for nothing. The BBC will ring me up and ask for a short quote, or come to the office with a tape recorder and do a ten-minute interview, and I won't get anything.' Like the vicar. 'That's right. I think they do think that. The only appreciable sum of money I ever made was from an electricity board in the north who sent me a caption they wanted to publish. All I had to do was to agree to this use of my name for this particular purpose, and they offered me a £1,000 fee which I gave to a home for frail and infirm elderly people being built not far from where I live.'

1979 was an important year for the more commercially minded. Cutting great swathes through Marje's beloved socialism, Margaret Thatcher swept into Number Ten Downing Street with economic advisers in tow. La Proops had found it very hard to believe that the warm, sweet

Maggie she had interviewed during her reign as Opposition leader was the same ice-blue tormentor who had goaded Jim Callaghan across the House of Commons and reddened his rumpled cheeks. Now she was to learn new facts of life under Mammon Maggie:

> When she became Prime Minister in 1979 Mike Molloy said, 'You'd better go back and do her again now she's PM.' This time, though, I had to set up the interview formally through her press officer Henry James. And my goodness, the difference when I got to Number Ten! She was suddenly formal. She wasn't exactly unfriendly but she certainly wasn't cordial. She was very guarded. The interesting thing was the way she seated me. I was put on a low chair and she sat above me. This was the good old-fashioned psychological ploy to put me at a disadvantage. I was very amused indeed. And I was even more amused that this time Henry James was in the room with a tape-recorder. Never before had she taped any of our conversations. The atmosphere had changed. So far as I was concerned, that was the end of even the slightest bit of warmth between us. It was frost from then on. And it was then that I began to realize that underneath this rather attractive, rather pretty surface – and she was a pretty woman all those years ago, and very well-groomed and well-dressed if you like that kind of thing – there was somebody else. And the difference between Mrs Thatcher MP and Mrs Thatcher PM was tremendous and very interesting.

In fairness, one has to ask whether Marje was not partly to blame for this hellish freezing-over. Perhaps she unconsciously generated her disapproval of the wench from the front bench on the grounds of Thatcher's 'embourgeoisement'. Margaret had lived over a grocery shop; Marjorie's dad had been a greengrocer; both girls had had elocution lessons; both were now comfortably off with tidy incomes and living in posh London suburbs. Both flaunted a well-to-do image – Marje had not infrequently been seen in the *Mirror*, in life or in her own cartoons, wearing mink and diamonds and sporting her aristocratic fag-holder and going on exotic foreign holidays. But Mrs Thatcher had joined the seriously rich and chose to represent wealth and privilege, and Mrs Proops had retained her ties with ordinary *Mirror* 'citizens' and represented the moiling masses. Was Marje, deep down, an inverted snob? Did she secretly deplore the upper classes and vibrate her disdain?

Apparently not. Without exception, observers have told me she treats them all alike, the rich man in his castle and the poor man at his gate. Labourers love her. Lords leap to her side. The *Daily Mirror*'s leader writer, David Thompson:

During the Heath Government I was sitting in a bar in the House of Lords waiting for an important vote on a Bill which was being forced through the Commons. And I was talking to a Government whip called Lord Charles Edward Mowbray Segrave and Stourton, a premier baron of England who traces his ancestry back through the female line to the Norman Conquest and is one of the pukka aristocrats, with an eye-patch where he lost an eye in the war. And he told me that his greatest remaining ambition was to meet Marjorie Proops. I said, 'I will fix it for you' and I did. I bought them lunch in one of Marje's favourite restaurants and they had a splendid conversation. He was fascinated to meet her and asked her a lot of questions about her work, and she asked him about his background and whether he had any old family paintings. And he said no, the oldest had been

destroyed in the war. 'Oh, the blitz?' asked Marje. 'Oh,
no no no – the Civil War.' They got on really very well,
and he told me afterwards that it would be marvellous
if Marje went to the House of Lords, as she'd be very
valuable in their discussions.

At home in Barnes, life was humble by comparison.
Marje had acquired a disturbed cat called Benjie – 'ears
flattened back, eyes blazing' – and was awed by his unique
naughtiness and violence. He not only attacked Marje and
wrecked the home but relished television programmes
containing vicious fight scenes. Marje was woken at 7.10
sharp every morning by a nip on the nose, swiftly followed
by a clawful of hair wrenched from her slumbering bonce.
She was 'dotted with little bits of plaster and scarred like
a gangster's moll'. Benjie often appeared in her column
– at one point even doing an agony page of his own and
answering problems from troubled cats. Marje's white
dog Sophie was old and doddery (she died in 1980),
and toddling across the Common the Proopses and their
schnauzer made a picturesque group. None could walk
properly. Proopsie was crippled with arthritis, and spent
some time in hospital in 1977 having his hip attended
to (Marje visited him every day). Marje herself, despite
hydrotherapy and epidural injections, was grinding to a
halt. She desperately needed a hip replacement.

The operation was scheduled for March 1979 and Marje
went to see her doctor two months prior to surgery. 'My
GP was a very fussy lady and said, "I'd like you to have
a routine check-up first before you have the anaesthetic,
because it's going to be a long operation." She sent me to a
physician at Queen Mary's Hospital, Roehampton, in February, and he was going over me with his stethoscope and
kept coming back to my neck and frowning as he listened.'
Eventually Marje couldn't stand the tension any more.

'Is something wrong?'

'I suspect that you have a blocked carotid artery.'

'Oh – is that serious?'

'Very.'

'How do people get one of those?'

'How many cigarettes do you smoke a day?'

Fifty-a-day Marje, whose very trademark had been a fag-holder, was riveted to the spot. 'He frightened the life out of me because he personalized it. When a doctor suddenly asks you this, it's not like a telly ad, or warning stories in the newspapers saying smoking will damage your health. Smokers never think it's going to happen to them. They think such warnings apply to somebody else. But when you're suddenly threatened, it's like a knife pointing at your chest.' The doctor explained that Marje would have to undergo an emergency operation to by-pass the damaged artery. They would postpone the hip replacement and do this immediately.

Marje had answered letters from smokers trying to give it up ('They all want to be released from their addiction but not enough to do anything about it'). She had converted to small cigars to wean herself off the weed and made several attempts to escape from old Nick O'Teen, all to no avail. Running smack into the Grim Reaper, though, did the trick. Marje never smoked another cigarette. She would announce in the *Mirror* that she had finally packed up, and would be much photographed with a pen in between her teeth. She would tell her readers, 'I was a heavy smoker from the age of seventeen and stopping wasn't easy. Two previous efforts ended within a week or so. A couple of cigarette-holders in my drawer remind me I have kicked the habit. I have two unopened packets of the brand I always smoked. But the impulse to light up has vanished.'

When she woke up from the anaesthetic after the artery

by-pass, though, something had obviously gone terribly wrong. She was paralysed down one side of her face and her right hand was useless. Petrified Marje was told she had had a minor stroke. Bill Hagerty:

I went with Mike Molloy to see her, and it was very very bad. It was a lot worse than we'd anticipated. When we got outside, we looked at each other and I said, 'I know she's resilient, but just how tough is she?' In a joshing way, I'd told Marje something like, 'Come on, Marje – about time you got back to work!' I think people do that, don't they, when somebody's really sick. It's their way of saying, 'It's not that bad – you'll be all right.' But I'm sure most people thought that was it. Not necessarily that Marje was going to die, but that as a journalistic force, she was through.

Mike Molloy:

Bill and I came away from Westminster Hospital very depressed. We thought, 'That's it.' We thought we'd never see Marje back at work again. But the astonishing thing was her fighting spirit. She just bloody well fought back. She recovered from the stroke, and though her hand was gone she forced herself to write again. It was the sheer determination to get over it which was so impressive. Marje is a tough woman. When I met Mother Teresa, I was not surprised by her sanctity or her holiness – I was surprised by her toughness, and Marje is tough too. You can't take on a job like hers and not be tough as well as compassionate. To think that she's just a soft old jelly would be silly.

At first Marje had been very quiet and despairing in the hospital, and couldn't or wouldn't eat. She says that Bill Hagerty pulling her leg and telling her she was malingering actually helped her to get going again from a standing start. She was back at her desk by the end of May 1979, though she still couldn't walk and had problems talking, eating and writing. Her handwriting has never really recovered. Anyone ready to jeer at agony aunt Marje Proops and all she stands for ought really to see her today, carefully manoeuvring a large felt-tip marker in her painful fist as she goes through her papers. They might still scoff, but they would have to admit that here is a woman totally devoid of self-pity, who thinks she has important work to do.

Fiona Griffin, for twelve years Marje's secretary, arrived soon after the stroke: 'I was really shocked by her appearance. She was sitting behind a desk so I didn't immediately realize that she was in a wheelchair. She looked very ill. But she gradually got herself out of that wheelchair and off the walking sticks they gave her. She had two hip operations during the time that I was there as well, but no matter what happened to her, she came back. She had the most amazing powers of recovery.' Marje always wanted to get better. When she was most crippled, she was wheeled about by *Mirror* staff, sometimes at record speeds, sometimes getting her dresses caught in the wheels. Her first hip replacement was in 1980, after which she struggled to walk with one dodgy hip before Tin Hip Op Two in 1981.

Photographer Doreen Spooner recalls: 'We actually took a group of thirteen second-honeymoon couples back to Jersey in 1981 [the reassembled winners of a *Daily Mirror* Honeymoon in Jersey competition in 1958, now with thirty children and one grandchild between them]. It was just before Marje's second hip operation and afterwards we realized what a damn silly thing we'd done really, myself and another photographer. But we got her on roller skates, in this big indoor skating rink.' Marje was 'very nervous' but appeared in the *Mirror* next day surrounded by whooping second-honeymooners and laughing fit to bust with her legs swivelling under her.

Mirror readers (or 'citizens' as Marje invariably called them) seemed to love Proops more than ever when her long teenage existence was curtailed by all her ops. In 1978 she had begun sending out a Bouquet of the Week to some deserving nominee from among her citizens. It was intended to reward lovely deeds and cheer everybody up, as Marje had found the Stinker of the Week postbag rather demoralizing ('My faith in the innate goodness of the majority of people was badly shaken by the Stinkers'). *Mirror* reader Suzanne Edwards of Menith Wood, Worcester, responded by nominating La Proops herself for the Bouquet after her return to work from Tin Hip Op One. 'She deserves a very big bouquet from her readers,' Suzanne wrote to the paper. 'Can the *Daily Mirror* persuade her to accept it on behalf of us all? She deserves it for her courage and her concern for others . . . She is a great lady.' This meant a lot to Marje, who 'went red with embarrassment' at the presentation, and who has the metal plate of that particular 26 August 1980 *Mirror* page on her wall at home.

When Marje wasn't 'under the knife' or waxing mawkish over Charles and Diana's nuptials or helping to start up a *Daily Mirror* Bride of the Year competition in 1981 (the winner got a dress and £2,000), she was campaigning hard – for anonymity for rape victims as well as the accused, for an end to horrifying police interrogations of rape victims, for the abolition of the iniquitous VAT on sanitary towels, for housewives to stop calling themselves 'mere', and for greater recognition of women's achievements. In fact Marje's feminism got so uncharacteristically out of hand during this period that she was 'dodging irate men'. One young *Mirror* chap actually cornered Marje in a lift and kept his finger on the close-door button while he gave her a talking-to, and in a restaurant an older fellow leaned across from a neighbouring table and said (with a menacing glare), 'You're nothing but a troublemaker!' Proopsie was no help at all, and would usually go into huddles with other men, muttering darkly. Marje thinks they may have been planning to set up the first branch of the South-West London Male Liberation Group.

She had become much more of a home bod and had taken up Bargello tapestry (this replaced an earlier oil-painting craze with an easel in the sitting room). She thinks this might have been due to 'a subconscious urge, at a time when more and more of us women are questioning our feminine role' to prove she still had her feminine skills. In fact, with all the home-bodding and honeymooning and royal and *Daily Mirror* weddings going on, Marje got rather carried away. In August 1982 she suddenly attacked the 'trendy' Bishop of Winchester for saying adultery wasn't as hard to forgive as some marital sins. Marje's banner headline trumpeted 'ADULTERY IS FORGIVABLE? RUBBISH'.

Between ops, Marje was still being wheeled out – sometimes quite literally – at Labour Party conferences. One year, when she had evidently recovered some of her mobility, she and Proopsie gave former *Mirror* chairman Ernie Burrington a terrible fright in their hotel. Ernie Burrington:

We were all staying in a new hotel at Bournemouth: a number of us from Mirror Group and scribes from other organizations. And Marje and her husband Proopsie and ourselves had attended a dinner, and we saw them before they went upstairs to bed. Anyway, we hadn't been in bed long when there was an almighty ringing of klaxons and bells and stamping about in corridors. Apparently the place was about to catch fire, so we belted down the stairs in common with the others. A rag, tag and bobtail crowd had assembled on the pavement, including this fellow Cole, the BBC commentator with the wonderful voice, looking at extension ladders going up to his bedroom. People were asking, 'Is everybody down?' and I said, 'Has anybody seen Proops?' No sign of them. Oh God – they'd be roasted alive! But just at that moment, down came Marje, with some kind of dressing gown on, followed by what could have been the Ancient Mariner, followed by Proopsie, with some sort of snood on his head, and bedsocks up to his knees thick enough for climbing the Matterhorn. Refugees from the Towering Inferno, which never actually ignited.

The new 'raging feminist' Marje was feeling restless about some of Labour's policies and their lip-service to women's rights. One day in 1981, while Marje's feminist dander was up, who should ring her but Shirley Williams. Marje: 'Shirley told me about the Gang of Four and that they were going to form a party. She said, "Will you join us?" And I didn't have to think long about it because at that time there was a feeling in the country, and in the Labour Party actually, that there was a need for a more right-of-centre left, if you see what I mean. And I thought Shirley's was a very good idea.'

Shirley Williams (herself a former *Mirror* reporter):

Marje was very sympathetic towards the SDP when it started out. It was her kind of party. I got the impression she was very keen on the steps we took to try to make sure more women were put forward as candidates. (This was why we had a higher proportion than any of the parties by quite a big margin in 1983 and 1987.) Marje was very keen about that. She was also keen on the written constitution, and that we said there should be more emphasis on the devolution of power, human rights and freedom of information. When the party was founded I went and had a long interview with her. We had got on well in the past. I've always thought her extremely humane and sensible, warm-hearted and magnanimous. She wrote a long piece about me when I was engaged to Tom King and I couldn't marry him because I couldn't get permission from the [Roman Catholic] church to do so. Marje was very, very sympathetic and nice about that, and I'd always liked her a lot.

And Marje and I were part of the battle of women to be noticed and get some place. I'll tell you what she is: she's a feminist who likes men. It's a very important difference. She understands men as human beings, as much as she understands women. And so although she believes that women haven't been given a fair crack of the whip, the great thing about Marje is that she's a loving woman and that she loves people. She sees everybody, men and women, as human beings and it does show. I think there's a certain kind of hard-edged feminist who really doesn't like men, who resents them, blames them, sees herself in competition with them, and wants actually to have exactly the same position that men have had *vis-à-vis* women, except the other way round. Marje really isn't like that. She really does want a world of neighbours and friends and equals and it's a very different form of feminism. To me, it's one which is much more attractive.

And so it was that 'Labour's Own Girl' became a card-carrying member of the SDP in the 1980s. Marje would return to the Labour fold eventually, but it must have sent a chill down their hustings to think that one of their most devoted socialists was missing. Because she had probably taken some of the 'citizens' with her.

13

The Arterial Aunt

'Some people get into print and their next ambition is to be editor. I don't want it. I should be terrified. What I've always wanted was to be the best columnist, the best agony auntie. It's not quite the same.'

So said Marje Proops, talking last year about her position at the *Daily Mirror*. She seems to have got what she wanted. If there were a gong for Best Auntie, Marje would surely have won it a long time ago; certainly by 1981. That year, her 'Dear Marje' column had been running in the *Mirror* for a decade. Through this *Daily Mirror* page alone she had answered more than 300,000 letters – part of a running total, through all her advice columns since 1959, of over two million – from housewives, homosexuals, pregnant teenagers, rape victims, paedophiles, compulsive gamblers, alcoholics, baby-bashers and lost souls. She had ministered to the depressed, the desperate, the depraved, the degraded and the docile victims of wife-battery. She had tackled anorexia and abortion, impotence, masturbation, premature ejaculation, jealousy, paranoia, incest and drug abuse. She had boosted the shy, hugged the unwanted, snapped at the snobbish, mended marriages, found homes for unwed mums, rescued abused children, allayed young terrors, assuaged elderly loneliness and arranged belly-dancing lessons.

She had saved several people from taking their own lives and made other lives worth living by a few of her forthright suggestions. She had had thirty-two page letters, even seventy-two page letters, from people with nobody else they could talk to, or trust. She could have shown you problems sent in on coroneted notepaper and problems on tear-stained scraps, problems so shocking they'd have made your hair stand on end, and so deeply demoralizing they'd have made you feel like going out and getting drunk. The only problem Marje hadn't had by 1981 was one from a man with two penises. Everything else she'd seen. And sundry press folk around that time took stock of her work and arrived, by different routes, at the same conclusion. Dear Marje was now the doyenne of them all. So in this chapter we shall be looking at La Proops's role as Britain's shoulder to cry on. Sometimes she would have needed to have been God Almighty, or at least to have had a magic wand, to find a solution. She is not divine, as we have seen. She does have a magic wand – it's a stick given to her by a group of university students – but she has wafted it about several times to no avail.

In the late seventies and early eighties Marje was getting an estimated 40,000–45,000 letters a year, with seasonal fluctuations (more loneliness at Christmas, more romance in spring). That peak figure has now levelled out with the drop in *Daily Mirror* circulation to a steady 25,000 a year in the 1990s, with the staggering ongoing total unknown ('I've never kept records'). Her published letters were, then as now, mere snowflakes from an avalanche of mail, all of it carefully sorted and considered, all of it privately replied to. One printed cry might snowball into several thousand similar inquiries, all deserving the same care and attention. Marje and her staff constantly consulted experts and authorities to find further sources of information and help. Suicidal cries were given top priority. One was from a girl in a Notting Hill telephone box who had swallowed a bottle of pills. Marje kept her talking while her team alerted the emergency services in a pre-planned drill. The girl was found unconscious, revived and saved.

Agony aunts had traditionally been prissy. Nothing prissy in Marje's column. Even thirty or forty years ago, when a lot of women still thought sex was part of the housework, prigs and prudes had got on her nerves. To the woman asking, 'What are the limits to which a wife ought to go to please her husband . . . I mean sexually?' Marje replied, 'You sound as if you are a pretty inhibited girl. Countless marriages fall apart because nice mothers bring their nice daughters up to regard sex as a rather nasty duty. Countless husbands learn to loathe wives who "allow" them sex as a kind of privilege, even a favour . . . You know, sex is like cooking. No woman can be a cordon bleu cook all the time – but every so often she achieves a perfect dish. The rest of the time she can, if she tries, produce something satisfying.'

Over one-third of Marje's mail was still coming from men. La Proops had been writing about masturbation since the year dot telling them not to worry, but some were still ashamed of themselves (the insult 'wanker' possibly didn't help). Marje said simply, 'Go ahead and enjoy it.' However, sexual indulgence that caused pain to someone else was quite another matter. Though she often advised letter-writers to 'forgive one foolish act of infidelity', a woman who wrote in saying her husband wanted permission to sleep with other girls as he was bored in bed is told, 'I never heard such cheek!' A mother who suspects her husband is abusing one of their children is urged to seek help from the NSPCC – 'Waste no more time.' And as a dog-lover Marje was not even printing letters about bestiality, though she certainly received them, and even had a phone call from a tearful woman who had found her husband raping their unfortunate pet.

In 1981 Marje made an assessment of her letters so far, to see what they were all about. Readers of this book who immediately put their hands up and shout, 'Sex!' are to go to the bottom of the class. 'If you asked me if there was any one thing common to them all, I'd have to say *love*. It's the need for it, the lack of it, the quality of it, the depth of it, the pain and joy of it, the giving and taking of it which is the motivation behind almost every letter that falls on my desk.' This love was hard to define, blind, and different from lust.

Her mail had undergone certain changes. Whereas women used to ask her timidly about 'submitting' to their husbands' sexual demands, now most of them were Pill-liberated, had rights, expected orgasms, and found their hubbies were suffering attacks of impotence with the worry of it all. A woman who wrote saying she'd never had a climax in five years of happy marriage asked, 'Is it really so strong a need for women, or is it something we're being conditioned to demand?' Male-adoring Marje replied, 'The strongest need for most women in love is to do what you do – help their men to achieve ecstasy. This statement will no doubt heap upon me the wrath of all good Women's Libbers, but it is true.' She does go on to explain, though, that there are ways and means for both partners to achieve fulfilment, and disputes that women have been 'conditioned' to demand anything. Indeed, the same week she was praising Germaine Greer, in a centre-spread article, for 'demonstrating her own liberation' and giving 'the rest of us the courage to demand it'.

But if Marje's letter-writers had changed, so had Marje. In 1976 she had written, 'Ten years ago, I would have stated flatly that group sex could only spell disaster.' Now she was agreeing 'with reservations' with a psychologist giving evidence in the Linda Lovelace court case who said group sex 'does no harm and brings some pleasure to those concerned with it'. Provided, added Marje, that any marriage involved was a very secure one indeed.

There was also a shift in shock-value. 'A few years ago, the shock element was very strong indeed throughout the letters people wrote. Phrases like "we are living in sin" kept cropping up; divorce was still a condition which brought shame and guilt; and homosexuality was something people wrote about anonymously. Many of the letters began, "This will probably shock you . . ." Girls who slept around told me how used and cheap they felt. All they wanted was to find Mr Right, get married – in white – have a good husband and children. Their promiscuity was no more than a search for love. There was a feeling, in the letters, that people felt victims of an intolerant society which failed to take into account their weaknesses and didn't understand their special plight.'

Marje's sympathetic articles on unmarried mums and homosexuals had reaped a whirlwind of indignant wrath from many of her readers. 'Imperceptibly, it's all changed. I cannot put a date on it, or note that any particular event was a watershed in our tolerance towards other people. But here we are, in the run-up to the eighties, and we no longer point the finger and cry "shame".' Marje rejoiced, in 1981, that her own 'live-and-let-love' philosophy had caught on, and that people could now tell their stories without shame and 'follow their chosen lifestyles without guilt'. Living in the shadow of AIDS and the remorselessly guiltless nineties, she might now phrase that rather differently.

Some of the letters were (and are) hoaxes, from simple fellows who get excited seeing their mental masturbation in print and hopefully shocking a lady. Marje has an eagle eye for such stuff, and a sharp beak. She inherited her

grandmother's ribald sense of humour and her shock
absorbers have never failed the MOT. 'A lot of the letters
are intentionally salacious. I get more of that sort now
than I used to. A lot of people live out their fantasies
in letters to people like me, and they get their kicks
that way. But I take the view that these people have a
problem.' And Marje's advice on sexual problems, unlike
that of her predecessors, has always been unflinching,
non-moralizing and down-to-earth. As one critic wrote,
'She isn't a writer for the squeamish.'

Most of the two-million-odd letters Marje had received
by 1981 were not hoaxes. They were serious. Those
who look down on agony aunting tend to assume such
letter-writers must be wobbly women, neurotic ponces,
whingers, publicity-seekers, pathetic people with no self-
respect who discover a molehill in their affairs and immediately write complaining of Mount Etna in the back garden.
Why don't they sort themselves out? Why don't they see
a doctor, ask Auntie Maud, have a drink, take a pill? The
answer is, unfortunately, that most of them seem to have
tried such remedies for months before they got to the
humiliating pass of appealing to a total stranger from a
newspaper. Many are deeply ashamed of having nobody
else to turn to, and nothing left to try. Many say something
like, 'If I read this back, I know I won't post it.' Marje:

A lot of readers start their letters by saying, 'I finally
plucked up the courage to write.' I had one from a
homosexual yesterday who said he'd been plucking up
the courage for four years. I once had a letter written to
me by a housewife on the back of a laundry book, all
tear-stained, and you could see the ink had run. And
she started by saying, 'It's three in the morning, and
I'm sitting writing to you in the kitchen.' It's difficult to
imagine the anguish that a person goes through before

she gets to the point where she sits in the kitchen at that
hour, dropping tears on the back of the laundry book
writing to me.

Some of the most desperate pleas were anonymous, oblig-
ing Marje to print the gist of the letter in the newspaper
and advise the frantic inquirer to write in again, this
time giving an address where Marje could send a proper
answer. She was willing to reply to a friend's address, or a
post-office box, rather than compromise the writer in any
way. Frequent cryptic messages appeared in the column
asking those about to commit suicide, or about to do
something equally drastic, to send a forwarding address. A
sixteen-year-old girl even posted Marje a specimen, hoping
Mrs Proops could tell her if she was pregnant.

There were occasional inquiries from paedophiles. Marje
confessed to a reporter that she found these particularly
worrying. 'I advise them to get help because a paedophile
is at great legal risk and the very best thing that he can do
is to belt round to his doctor and ask him to get him a
psychiatrist or psychotherapist to help him control these
impulses.' Equally perplexing were letters on incest, one
of which came from a frightened fourteen-year-old girl.
Marje knew that if the allegations were true, the father was
committing a felony. She also knew that if she withheld
information she would be an accessory, even though she
might simply want to avoid breaking up a home. In such
cases, Marje has a fall-back position. Relying on her
excellent relationship with the police, she rings them
up and asks them to handle the situation sensitively by
sending round some nice plain-clothed young lady rather
than a flat-footed Plod.

Not every letter required sensitive handling, of course.
The chap who wrote in to tell her he was falling in love with
an otherwise nice girl from Birmingham got a surprise. The

stricken fellow had explained in some detail how his family
were 'wincing', and wondered 'if there is some tactful way I
could get her to take some lessons to get rid of that accent'.
Marje, who had had elocution drummed into her as a lass,
replied, 'The best lesson she could learn is how to get rid of
you.' A woman nursing a secret passion for a homosexual
wrote asking what she could do for the best. Marje tells her,
'There is absolutely nothing you can do for the best.' Often
Auntie Marje would use her column to air a particularly
testy problem. One was, 'How do you get your own back
on a loved one?' One lady had the solution. Having found
out her husband had a date, she hid his false teeth.

Equally imaginative responses followed a recent article
on what a desperate battered wife ought to do. Not all of
the ideas could be printed. One woman reader suggested
the victim should 'put a tight rubber band on his willie'
while he slept. Another said she 'should put on a sexy
nightie, put a sleeping pill in her husband's drink, give
him a good bonk, and then when he was fast asleep,
as he soon would be, find a heavy object and bash his
face'. The reader herself had tried this method with some
success, having used a frying pan. 'The husband was taken
to hospital with a broken nose and some bits missing, such
as teeth.' Afterwards he was afraid to go to sleep, much less
batter his wife.

On the whole, Marje's published letters tend to be less
silly, less inarticulate and, although frequently about sex,
less titillating than those in some other publications. Why
is this?

> You have to remember that those letters you see on my
> page are selected. I've got some here now in my tray
> that I wouldn't use in the paper. There was one I was
> considering yesterday for quite a long time, wondering
> whether to use it, and I decided against it. It was a fairly

inarticulate letter from a young man who is worried
because every time he has sex with his girlfriend, she
cries out in pain. Well, clearly she's suffering from
vaginismus, poor girl, and she should go and see a
doctor because it's a condition that can be remedied
fairly simply and then it won't hurt her. But I felt that
this was not an appropriate letter to print for various
reasons. First of all, I think of my page in relation to
the other sections of the paper and this verges on the
medical, which I try to avoid. Also the subject was
somehow slightly distasteful.

A column like mine has to reflect, as far as is practi-
cable, the paper's readership as well as those who write
in. So you have to select on the basis that it has to
be readable and encourage other letter-writers, and it
also has to give practical, sound advice and information
where necessary. But you are trying to entertain the
readers and ensure that they buy the paper. If you don't
do that, you serve no valid purpose at all. On the other
hand, I don't make mine up! There are one or two advice
columnists who do, I have reason to suspect, make up
sexy letters in their publications. Well, I've claimed all
these years and years to be in charge of this page and
what goes in it, and I know the editor is the editor, and
if he said, 'Your letters are a bit boring, Marje – can you
zip them up a bit?' I might have another look at them.
But if any editor at the *Mirror* said to me, 'Make up some
sexy letters, Marje,' I'd say 'Ta-ta!'

A depressing job? 'Doing the advice column can be
very depressing indeed. It's such a heavy responsibility.
Because you're very much aware that you're giving people
advice and the chances are they are going to take it. In
fact I know they take it because sometimes they write
back and say, "Thank you – I did what you suggested,"

and so on. And you think, "My God! I hope I've given the right advice! Have I destroyed this man's life? Have I added to this woman's depression and hopelessness?" You can't know, but I lie in bed at night worrying about them. You can't shake it off. No way. In fact, I think if you did – if you were the sort of person who could say, "Well, that's it," and slam the office door and go home, then you shouldn't be doing the column.'

There was a lot of praise for Marje's decade-old page in the *Mirror*, but also the usual derision. Marje thinks even the term 'agony aunt' is derisory and has always preferred 'advice columnist'. What about the *Sunday Telegraph*'s Paul Jennings writing, 'The advice business must be the greatest (and to my mind the most useless) growth industry in postwar Britain'? Marje: 'It's funny, because they don't look on any of us as journalists. And I argue, if I can be bothered – and I can't always be bothered because I think poor things, maybe one day they may have a problem – that I've been a hack. I started off doorstepping for the *Daily Herald* and I've done as much journalistic training and a damn sight more writing than many of them. And yet they still don't regard me as a professional journalist. We're all a joke.'

Marje's opposite number on the *Sun* is Deidre Sanders, supposed by millions to be a great rival. In fact most of the advice columnists have regular get-togethers, and chat on the phone. Deidre: 'I have great admiration for Marje and we meet up for lunch. I think most of the agony aunts appreciate one another as colleagues and we have a support network of our own. Even the agony uncle on the *News of the World* maintains a friendly relationship with the rest of us.' Deidre has had her share of sob-sister abuse, but some contrite critics too: 'I often get letters from people saying, "I thought it was a joke, but now I'm writing to you because . . ." Some of them even say they normally read

The Times or the *Telegraph*, but now they have this problem.
I think it's very easy to jeer, not only at the columns but
at the people with problems – until you've actually been
there yourself. The smugness that some of us have in our
early twenties can wear away.'

Some of the derision undoubtedly has to do with snob-
bery about women's magazines, and about the readerships
of papers like the *Mirror* and the *Sun*, where agony columns tend to flourish. According to legend, the longest
word in the vocabulary of such readers is 'hamburger',
and they don't know nuffink. They certainly don't feel
nuffink, or have complex emotional problems. Deidre
Sanders, like Marje, looks down on the snobs, and fiercely
defends her non-academic readership: 'I find such people's
appreciation of the ingredients of an emotional problem
have grown dramatically more sophisticated. They may
sometimes struggle to find the vocabulary and I might
have to straighten up a word for them that they've got
slightly wrong, but they know what they're saying, and
they're expressing very sophisticated emotions. I really get
very angry when people think that subtle emotions are the
prerogative of *Guardian* readers.'

What do other problem page editors think of Marje?
Former teacher and 'Relate' counsellor Suzie Hayman is
one agony auntie with an English degree. She does the
network's newsletter: 'I think Marje is wonderful. I think
she is the person who started it all. I tend to refer to her as
the doyenne. She's the agony aunt who made us respectable. Everybody knows Marje. You say "agony aunt" to
people, and that's the name that springs to mind.' When
one points out that Dorothy Dix, Abby van Buren, the cosy
'Evelyn Home' (Mary Carn and Peggy Makins in *Woman*),
and the moralizing Mrs Marryat (in *Woman's Weekly*) all
pre-dated Marje by many years, her fellow aunts reply that
Marje altered the concept of problem pages, turning them

into mass-media newspaper fare. Quite apart from her
no-holier-than-thou approach, she has been humorous,
snappy and abrasive in her replies. In other words, she
took some of the sentimentality out of the job. Suzie
Hayman: 'I've often referred to it as slapping knuckles,
and we do have to do that occasionally! Marje has been
the leader of that sort of style.'

Oh dear, not one claw extended among the sisterhood.
Not wishing this book to be a hagiography, I approached
Claire Rayner (who has 'aunted' for the *Sun*, the *Sunday
Mirror*, *Woman's Own* and *Petticoat*). She at least must see
Marje as an arch-rival. Claire:

Codswallop! We're not trying to cut each other's throats.
We're all on very good terms, so much so that if one of us
gets a bit of information we think the others would find
useful, we pass it on. And I'll tell you something else,
lovie – every so often when I'm out in the streets, at the
theatre or in the shops, someone thinking they're very
witty will shout across, 'Watcha Claire – I got a problem!'
And I've learned to answer: 'Oh, I'll tell you what. You
write to Marje! She's a wonderful woman.' And I told
Marje this and she says, 'Oh I do the same thing. I tell
them to write to you!'

I've got enormous affection and respect for Marje.
We go off to lunch and natter, and there is a more
formal lunch circuit now, organized by Suzie Hayman,
which I often don't get to. We have all got our own
personal networks obviously, but we all talk to each
other. We are always a fair old target for a joke, but
what the hell. We know that we are good at what we
are doing. And I will tell you something about those
same male journalists who laugh at us. They are very
good at buttonholing you in the lift or round the coffee
machine. I've talked to more of those male journalists

than I've had hot dinners, kid, and I'm sure Marje has
as well!

The fact that Marje was for so many years a campaigning
journalist sets her apart from other advice columnists, no
matter how intelligent or humane. For thirty of her years
on the *Mirror*, Marje Proops wasn't just in the comforting
'there there' business. She was in the middle of a reforming
newspaper, constantly able to quiz millions of readers
about their feelings and opinions (there were sex and love
surveys by the dozen), and constantly updating readers on
her involvement with pressure groups and enlightened law
reform on divorce, abortion, child abuse, homosexuality,
racial prejudice, women's rights.

If you kept up with Marje's stuff in the *Mirror*, you had
a fair idea of current thinking in Britain. And this put
her in an excellent position to give advice, because she
wasn't just sympathetic and sensible. She was in touch
with the heart and the nerve centres of her society in
a way that well-meaning aunts drafted in from other
professions could not possibly be. What's more, Marje
was using the whole volume and impact of her mail
to urge experts and politicians to tackle the underlying
causes of discontent – the prejudice, the bigotry, the smug
cruelty and intolerance. In this her importance as an artery
for reform can scarely be exaggerated.

Former features editor of the *Mirror* and erstwhile editor
of the *People*, Bill Hagerty:

She's known as an agony aunt but she's a great journalist, without any doubt. She's done everything from
fashion drawing to major interviews, the lot. One of the
things that impresses me about her is how wise she is.
I will never forget, when we were in hot-metal print
and the place was full of printers, how there would be

guys from the print area outside her office knocking politely on her door and waiting to talk to her about their problems. She is so good at that. She's had some problems in her own life, but she'll always listen and do her best. I've had problems, like we all do, and I pick up a phone or go and see her because she is extremely wise – common sense mixed with compassion.

I cannot imagine why, even bearing in mind that we've had a Tory Government for many years, she's never been made a dame, when you think what her contribution has been. Because she's been such a tower of strength, both to the public and in her private life, and I don't think she's got a nasty bone in her body. I'm amazed Margaret Thatcher didn't see fit to honour her, because apart from the fact that it would have been very well-deserved, it would have been bloody good PR for the Tory Government – and I'm a Labour supporter from a Labour newspaper.

Former *Mirror* editor Mike Molloy:

The point about Marje is that she's immensely wise. We always used to refer to her as the Heart of the *Mirror*, because she had a direct link with the readers, more so than anybody else. Apart from knowing them so well, she kept in touch. A lot of journalists get very out of touch with readers, but Marje never did. She has known how they've changed over the years, reflecting the fantastic changes in the country, since the permissive society, in manners and behaviour patterns and beliefs. And Marje has always been attuned to that, and she's understood how people live, what it's like to be a housewife, what's affected people, what their real worries are – because people generally don't sit at home worrying about the bomb:

they worry about paying the gas bill. Marje understands that.

And because of this empathy she has a great hot line to the readers. She's been able to change readers' opinions and expectations and to reassure them, certainly as far as sex is concerned. In quite a brief period people have gone from not knowing about sex or not talking about it to the most incredible explicitness, but that's comparatively recent. People used to have terrible fears about masturbation – would they go blind? Would it drive them insane? Marje was reassuring. She was the mum or the aunt that people could talk to. 'Agony aunt' is in many ways a very honourable thing to be. It's used as a pejorative term and a laughing term often by the smart and the sophisticated and the cynical, but for many many years, for millions of people too frightened to ask questions, there was nobody to turn to but Marje, or someone like Marje.

What about her status as a journalist? 'Marje is a newspaper woman. Her advice is particularly valuable about what effect a story will have or how one should report a story. She was always there for guidance. I would call Marje and ask her advice about such things, and very sagacious advice it was as well. She had wisdom – it wasn't simply about "Should you allow your boyfriend to kiss you on the lips on dates?" or anything like that. Her influence on the *Mirror* over the years has been profound.'

Felicity Green: 'Marje has saved more souls than the Salvation Army.'

Former chief sub-editor, *Mirror* features, Des Lyons:

I used to think cynically that she would be as I visualized all agony aunts – a hard nut who really didn't give a damn about her readers' problems. Going through her copy with her in her office every week, I was amazed to find out she really *did* care – and worried about them, even. She would quietly get herself in a right old state, especially with the 'Help!' letters which were agonized appeals, sometimes from people threatening suicide. Yet she always kept calm. She would pour me a glass of wine and we would read over the copy. At one time, she said she wanted livelier come-on headlines on her page, and could I help her with that? I think the first one we came up with was 'THE DAY THE MILKMAN CALLED THREE TIMES'. She was a thorough professional, with an amazing knowledge of the mechanical side of newspapers.

Former *Sunday Mirror* editor, Robert Edwards: 'Her column is extremely highly read. All those columns are. But there's no question about it – much though I personally admire Claire Rayner who was her successor on the *Sunday Mirror* and tremendously famous, hardworking and diligent too – *the* doyenne of them all is Marje.' Lord Cudlipp: 'Her deep understanding of the human problems that baffle and distress ordinary men and women and families, and her sincerity in dealing with those problems, are her principal virtues. She is unshockable. She is also the best-known journalist in the country.'

— 14 —

Bonzo

*A*loft in her crows-nest office with her two secretaries and five assistants, Marje remained virtually undisturbed by a series of upheavals that was to change her future and turn the *Daily Mirror* from a campaigning newspaper into a personal publicity stunt. In 1984 Reed International floated off the Mirror Group – cast it adrift according to many – and left it prey to any enormous ego with sufficient capital to gobble it up before the flotation went ahead. In the dark depths of Fleet Street lurked a kraken, larger and more terrifying than any that had ever swallowed a floating bark before. So gargantuan was his appetite that he had already gorged a fleet of international companies and made one or two previous attempts upon passing national newspapers, opening his vast jaws only to see them snaffled away by other bidders. When the Mirror Group hove into view, however, the kraken was ready.

Robert Maxwell, or 'Bonzo' as Marje was pleased to call him, bought the paper for £113 million. From a journalistic standpoint it never looked forward, and by 1986, 2,100 of the 7,000 workforce had been paid off with a so-called 'surplus' Bonzo had discovered in the pension fund, opening the way for the new technology without hindrance from the greedy, strike-happy print unions. But Marje, who would do her utmost to sort out the problems of the devil if he wrote to her in confidence, took a liking to the man who made pensions a thing of the past. She was actually in hospital having one of her numerous bits of surgery done when the paper was sold, and watched the event on television. Unlike many of her colleagues, she wasn't horrified by the kraken. She had met him in the seventies, when he was a Labour MP. Marje:

It was at a Labour Party conference, at one of the *Mirror*'s big annual receptions for Party members, MPs and trade union leaders. Maxwell was there at this party having a drink, and we simply started talking to each other, as you do at a party. In those days he didn't have that great huge bulk. In fact he was a very, very good-looking man when I first saw him. His hair was very black and he was very tall. I've always been attracted to tall men. Mmm. He was glamorous and very impressive. And he was also very affectionate. Always affectionate to me. Whenever I met him, his arms would go round me and he would kiss me.

The pair would be seen smooching shamelessly at *Mirror* get-togethers. Bonzo would kiss La Proops on both cheeks and La Proops would say, 'And one in the middle.' The editor noticed something going on. Mike Molloy: 'I think Bob realized that she was one of the essential parts of the *Mirror*. I think he was genuinely fond of her because he liked her, but it was also part of this enormous respect that he had for icons. And he couldn't control Marje. He had no power over her in that sense. He could have fired her, but Marje would immediately have been hired by another newspaper. I think he always respected anyone that he couldn't bully, and he couldn't bully Marje.'

He didn't have to. This is Marje describing one of their typical romantic interludes:

Amusing, but he had no sense of humour. When the *Daily Mirror* went public, we had a big meeting of all the directors and executives, and I sat near the back with Stotty [Richard Stott, former *Mirror* editor]. We were huddling, hoping nobody would see us there, and in lumbered Maxwell with all these bankers and people that were going to launch the share flotation, making for the platform. Suddenly he spotted me. He halted his progress and came lumbering over to me. Pushing Stotty to one side, nearly crushing him, he leaned over and kissed me. 'How is my beautiful darling girl today?' he said. And I replied, 'Why don't you go and ask her?' At this he leaned back and stared at me as if he'd never seen me before. 'Marje?' And I said, 'Yes, Bob?' And I patted him on the cheek and he gave me another little kiss, and then he moved away to the platform, and sat down right smack in the middle. But all the time the meeting and the speeches were going on, he was craning his neck trying to see me, to make sure that I was in fact me. Because with that little joke, he wasn't quite sure whether he'd kissed the right woman!

Maxwell's *Sunday Mirror* editor Robert Edwards: 'I hope this doesn't damage Marje, as this is the last thing I would want to do, but I did have the feeling that Maxwell actually succeeded in genuinely admiring her! Most of the people he cultivated, he cultivated because he thought he could get something from them. He was extremely self-centred. But I think he enormously admired her success and her empathy with the readers, and of course he recognized most of all that she was useful to him, because she somehow typified the spirit of the *Mirror* so much.'

The *Mirror*, meanwhile, was earning its daily bread, rendering first aid to the institution of marriage. New divorce figures had shown that one in three marriages was scheduled to collapse and that the seven-year-itch was now the three-year-itch. Marriage – 'a public commitment, an acknowledgement of mutual and proud possession' – was now in peril. 'I am passionate in my belief that marriage can survive, *must* survive,' proclaimed La Proops. Prince Charles kissing Diana was a cause for dewy-eyed rejoicing over royal wedlock, and Marje was producing centre spreads, impressively illustrated by Michael Frith, suggesting how to solve particular marital problems. The Bride of the Year competition, still going strong, was bringing 'colour, glamour and excitement into the lives of people for whom life was grey and grim'. Banishing grimness, Marje was pictured at a Brides of the Year reunion with a lapful of their squawking babies, celebrating the joys of family life.

The divorce statistics gave Marje the willies. With Proopsie now so kind and caring, and Phillip having retired to live in Hove near his beloved Brighton, she was now more married than ever before. Indeed, Proopsie was so devoted that Marje revealed in an interview with *Woman's World*, 'I am consumed with guilt about what my disability has done to my husband. It has trapped him.' It had also, of course, trapped Marje, and prevented her from pursuing her physically passionate love affair with Phillip. This could not be said. What could be said was that Proopsie was not only proving a splendid househusband but a very fine district nurse as well, bathing and shampooing Marje and putting her tights on her. And if she tried to explain to Proopsie how guilty she felt, his only comment was, 'You talk the most utter rubbish and you know it. Why should you feel guilty? I regard it as a privilege to look after you.'

Of course, Marje may have been trying to tell him something else as well. That she was herself very privileged to know such tenderness from a man who had always been secretly rated second-best. And that this sexy writer and accomplished flirt was grateful beyond expression to a man who had perhaps turned a blind eye to her own conduct, and his own needs, for so many years. In November 1985 the Proopses would celebrate their golden wedding anniversary. And a golden wedding, after all, it had proved to be. Proopsie seemed content. He'd found that one of their next-door neighbours in Barnes was a recently retired brigadier, with whom he could have long conversations in Hindustani because 'the Brig' had also served in India. Both were passionately fond of the army. Marje: 'So they were chums. Mates. And they used to chatter away in Hindustani, teasing me because I couldn't understand what they were talking about. Proopsie used to say, "We're talking about *you*."'

The missus was now billed by the Maxwell *Mirror* as 'Britain's Best-Loved Columnist' and 'The World's Greatest Advice Columnist' – a heady responsibility. The 'Dear Marje' page (now shortened to 'Marje') was busy trying to help those living miserably ever after. Interviewed about her work by the *Guardian* in September 1984, she confessed that the letters were now disturbing her sleep. 'Last night I woke up at four in the morning worrying over one woman's particularly dreadful problem, and I stayed awake till six, but there just didn't seem to be any answer.' She told the journalist Polly Toynbee, 'No, don't write that down,' but Toynbee wrote it down anyway. Marje said, 'Proopsie keeps having to remind me that I deal only with the miserable ones. Most people aren't unhappy, but at times it's easy to forget amongst all this.' Margaret Disher, who in the old fashion days had been regaled by Marje with hilarious one-liners, recalls meeting her again around this period, when they were both guests of Ted Blackmore in a *Sporting Life* box at the races. 'I was struck by how much more seriously she viewed things. It was as if the cares of the world had descended on her shoulders.'

Nearly half the anonymous letters Marje now received were from children sexually assaulted by their fathers or other men they knew. The NSPCC confirmed the rising swill of perversion and cruelty. Rape, like divorce, was on the increase. Marje sat before the tide like Queen Canute, writing: 'The final and ultimate privacy of her body is a woman's inalienable right.' But it was all becoming too distressing for one well-meaning journalist to bear, and when, in 1984, mother-of-umpteen Victoria Gillick sat opposite Marje in a BBC studio and said that doctors should not prescribe contraceptives to young girls without telling the parents, Marje finally exploded. She told her *Mirror* readers:

Usually I'm a fairly easy-going, peace-loving citizen, rarely roused to anger. But lately, I've been getting roused to fury more and more often. It began a couple of weeks ago, when I blew my top in a studio at the BBC. The rage, broadcast live, was heard by a lot of people who later said, shocked, 'Not like you to shout, Marje.' The woman who drove me into a rage which made me white-faced and breathless was Mrs Victoria Gillick, a mother of ten, who is mounting an eccentric campaign against doctors. She is a pretty woman whose face turns ugly with hatred just as my unpretty one turned livid with anger. Mrs Gillick, you may recall, is campaigning to get the law changed so that doctors would be prevented from prescribing the Pill to girls under sixteen without their parents' knowledge.

It is a totally potty idea. Anyone who thinks that

by denying young girls safe contraception they'll be
good little darlings and say no to their sexually excited
boyfriends doesn't live in the real world. Maybe her
children are obedient. They have a stable home and
loving parents. Which is more than can be said for the
countless distressed kids who write to me – kids with
indifferent, neglectful or hostile parents, kids who face
physical brutality in an unstable home, kids abandoned
and alone. They often take sex as a substitute for the love
and tenderness they've never had from their parents. Do
we send those children away, do we tell them the doctor
mustn't help them because Mrs Gillick says so?

Unfortunately the General Medical Council was to say
so (in February 1986). But it wasn't just Mrs Population
Problem that was the problem. It was Margaret Thatcher
and her obstinate, heartless, persistent kicking away at
the soft underbelly of Britain, damaging those who could
not defend themselves but who cried out by writing to
Marje. 'I'm talking about the young people, demoralized
and despairing, with no future to hope for. I am choked
with anger about the wasted lives, the lost talents, the
endless misery, the dead marriages, the marriages that
will never take place because you can hardly set up home
and start a nice little family without the means to buy even
a second-hand bed . . . I share the anger of the wives who
write to me about the humiliation and ignominy their men
feel when the wives have to get a job (low-paid, of course)
. . . I share the misery when those wives describe the
once-happy marriages, dying now under the burden of
poverty and despair.'

Anyone wondering what can be meant by 'socialism'
in the context of Marje's comfortable lifestyle and public-
school-educated offspring – indeed, anyone wondering
what socialism can mean at all, in view of its abandonment

by the Labour Party – need look no further than this for
Marje Proops's manifesto. Socialism may well be dying all
over the world. It is certainly unfashionable and unsexy
in our cash-crazed, grab-all, up-the-Wall-Street ethos, and
welfare states and 'governments by the people' are dropping
like dead flies from its poor old carcass. But to those of us
who regret its passing, like Marjorie Proops, socialism was
an ideal meant to succour the shirtless and ennoble the
nobody, remembered with sobs, and deeply mourned.

The letters weren't all gloom and doom. A woman wrote
in concerned about her best friend, a forty-two-year-old
widow, 'making a fool of herself' over a divorcee boyfriend. 'What would you advise me to do?' asked the
woman. 'Mind your own damn business, that's what,'
replied Marje. Another touching letter came from a bald
gentleman, aged sixty-two: 'I have this flipping hairpiece
that I've worn for more than ten years. I am utterly fed
up with it and want to get rid of it and look like my own
normal self again. But how can I shed the thing without
making myself a laughing stock? I am quite well known
in our local community. I have colleagues at work and
I also have grandchildren. Can you imagine the general
reaction if I suddenly appeared with a bald pate? I'd be
grateful for any advice you can give me.' Marje replied:

After much nail-biting and deep thought, I reckon you
should give a jolly good burn-the-hairpiece party. Yes,
honest, I mean it. Do not delude yourself that your
friends, family and colleagues have been fooled by your
hair these past ten years. However well made, male wigs
and pieces are easily detected. And I believe that if you
can make a jokey end to it all, you will gain everyone's
respect as well as your own. Your wife knows about
the hairpiece. I'm sure she'll co-operate. Make the party
simple – some wine and cheese or beer and sausages

– and send out notes saying: 'Please come round for a little celebration to drink to the end of an old friend' – or words to that effect. Then, at a prearranged moment, whip the beast off and set fire to it. I bet your friends will cheer and slap you on the back and cry, 'Thank heaven you've got rid of the ruddy thing at last!'

Her Bouquet of the Week had proved a huge hit, but now she decided to start a new readers' nomination prize called 'My Special Man' as well. Marje explains: 'I thought it would be rather nice to send a bottle of champagne to a deserving male, because I sent flowers every week to a deserving lady. So it was a nice balance between the sexes.'

Backpedalling her feminist bicycle, Marje was telling Britain's twenty-three million females over sixteen that she disagreed with a TUC study showing women were harassed by soft porn pin-up pictures and media pressure to look gorgeous. Only sexually hung-up and self-conscious women were bothered, according to Marje. Strange sayings, considering most women and even a few men had been bitten by the gorgeousness bug. One twenty-two-year-old called O'Dowd, for example, was anything but dowdy. When Marje met him in 1984 she was struck by the unusual combination of huge clomping feet and heavy make-up. But then Boy George was not 'your ordinary transvestite, camp or limp-wristed'. He wore Y-fronts on his botty as well as ribbons in his hair, and seemed to Marje to be 'asexual', loving both men and women in a cuddly way.

Surprisingly for a socialist newspaper with an allegedly socialist owner, the *Mirror* increasingly toadied to that most bingeing and undertaxed of privileged families, the House of Windsor – a thing that would never have been tolerated in Hugh Cudlipp's day. Marje's nose was unfortunately browner than most. When the Canadians criticized the Queen's attire as she toddled on tour in 1984 in her fifties outfits, Marje let fly with the screamer 'MAJESTY' and told them to 'mind their own bloody business'. Somewhat debasing the headline Cudlipp had used to castigate Khrushchev at the Paris summit in 1960, La Proops boomed from the front page, 'DON'T BE SO BLOODY RUDE!' She had been just as fierce in her defence of Elizabeth Two's togs when the Americans had compared her unfavourably with Jackie Kennedy. Indeed, Marje celebrated royal weddings, birthdays, babies and beanfeasts as though she were a member of the Firm. She saw the royals as a symbol of family stability and marital steadfastness – a reputation now rustier than my old banger.

None of which troubled Marje's new 'socialist' boss. The Bonzo Years at the *Mirror* have become the stuff of legend, because despite his pledge to the editorial staff that their integrity was assured, he seemed unable to let a day go by without poking either his nose or his entire anatomy into one of his papers. Vast sections of the *Mirror* were given over to Bonzo's personal attempts to resolve the miners' dispute and act as sugar daddy and spiritual lighthouse to common folk. A bizarre *Mirror* railway train carried Marje and other perplexed journalists round the country in 1985 to meet sprinklings of people in vast hired halls, and space allotted to such Bonzoisms far outstripped the print given to genuine news and campaigning features which had earned the *Mirror* its circulation. Readers sensed that they were being talked down to, and decided that they would rather be talked down to by the *Sun*, which at least had big boobs. Sales began to plunge.

In an attempt to attract the labouring droves back to his sheets, Bonzo gave them bingo like the *Sun*, and other games he thought might appeal. Touchingly, his favourite was the £1 million 'Who Dares Wins', partly of his own devising, which could transform a poor, working-class *Mirror* reader overnight into a millionaire like his good self. When at long last a winner materialized, in the shape of elderly, poor, hardworking Maudie, Bonzo's joy was boundless. Maudie and her daughter's dog Thumper were ferried about in a Daimler and taken to Marje's house for tea. Marje: 'I was her minder, and spent quite a lot of time with her. She found it very difficult to understand that she could now spend money on herself, because she'd never had a lot and felt she didn't deserve it. Part of my job was helping her to adjust to her new wealth, so that she felt happy rather than guilty about it.'

Mirror columnist John Knight viewed all these goings-on with a poisonous gaze. 'It all climaxed, I seem to remember, when we found Maudie. The whole thing was a sort of ghastly charade. Maudie was taken up to the Labour Party conference, and the zenith of her life was being photographed with Maxwell on some sort of roller coaster at Blackpool – that was the height of the Maxwell Madness. It was during that period when everyone was flattering his ego. And alas, Marje, not to her discredit but certainly not to her credit, was part of all that. To no one's credit, incidentally.'

Bonzo's back was bad. Sometimes he would lean down to his *Mirror* Woman and bellow softly, 'Rub my back!' Marje: 'So I had to stand there massaging his aching back, and he had his arm round my shoulder. It was almost a kind of lover-like situation. But it wasn't just with me – he was like that with women. He liked women very much indeed. He was much more comfortable with women than he was with men. I feel sure that he slept with endless women – not with me, I can tell you.' His secretary Jean Baddeley has reportedly denied it all, saying any woman would have to have been Houdini to have got past her security system without her knowledge. Marje: 'I'm quite sure that if he wanted to have a sexual relationship with a woman, he'd have got past Miss Jean Baddeley very easily indeed!'

La Proops, no stranger to a spot of amorous subterfuge herself, talks about her Bonzo period with the utmost warmth, cloaking her admiration beneath a veil of humour. Tough though she is, and worldly-wise though she may be from all her agony mail, there are times when Dear Marje sounds strangely like a total *ingénue*, liable to be kicked to death by butterflies. This was one of the times. You can tell a lot about her character from listening to her talking about Maxwell. And one should let her have her say. After all, seeing the best in everybody is a gift not to be derided, and she must be one of the few people left in Britain who can still speak of him without spitting on the floor.

I had a very close relationship with him. And possibly one of the reasons was that he was Jewish, and a very special case at that. He mesmerized people, including me. You couldn't fail, actually, to be mesmerized by him. I remember one occasion when Mike Molloy had written a book and his publishers held a big launch at Groucho's: it was a very crowded party, and you couldn't get a playing card between the people all drinking and talking at once. And suddenly Maxwell walked in, and everybody stopped talking. The buzz stopped – just momentarily – and then it started again. And one of the reasons of course was his towering height and bulk and this very impressive appearance. But there was a hint of menace in this intimidating presence. People parted to let him through, and they felt honoured when he stopped to talk. They would probably never admit it now, but you could see their heads turning to look at him, hoping for the beneficence of his presence.

Then he left, and I decided to leave shortly after. My new chauffeur Eddie was waiting somewhere outside, but being a bit disabled with my tin hips it was difficult for me to fight my way through the crowds. So Glo, one of the secretaries, said, 'Come on Marje – I'll fight a way through for you and help you down the stairs.' It was a very dangerous, long, narrow staircase down to this front hall, and when we arrived at the top, Maxwell was still there on the landing talking to a couple of blokes. And when he saw me come out with Glo, he stretched out an arm and said, 'Wait there' in this imperious way of his. So I waited. And he went on talking to these two blokes, and I wanted to go, and my hips were aching, so I said to him, 'Bob, I'm off now – I'll see you soon. Bye-bye for now.'

'Wait!'

So I muttered to Glo, 'What shall we do?' and she said, 'We'd better wait a second.' So I said to him, 'Well, what do you want me for?' He replied, 'I shall take you down these stairs!' So Glo said, 'Don't worry, Mr Maxwell – I'm looking after her. I'll take her down.' But he repeated, 'I shall take her down! Just wait a minute! I shall take her down!' And Glo answered back, and the two of them started arguing about which one of them would take me down the bloody stairs. Meantime I start off down on my own, and I manage to negotiate these stairs and get to the bottom, and they're following me, the pair of them, still arguing. And I go through the swing doors, followed by Maxwell and Glo. And Maxwell said to me, 'Go back inside! Immediately! It's cold!' 'I just want to look for Eddie,' I told him. But he replied, 'I will find Eddie and your car! You go back in there and sit down!' I said, 'Well there's nowhere to sit.' He repeated, 'Go back!' So back I went. And Glo put in, 'I'll get the

car, Mr Maxwell.' Very few people would talk back
to him the way she did – Glo would argue with anybody. And he and Glo continued this slanging match.

Meanwhile I went back through the swing doors and
stood behind them, and I could see Eddie coming along.
And I waved to Eddie. Eddie pulled up. I got in the car.
Maxwell and Glo were still arguing about who was to
look after me and I was already in the car when a copper
came along. The copper started shouting at Eddie to
move out of the way, because this street was very narrow
and the traffic was everywhere. And Eddie was trying
to get out from behind Maxwell's huge Rolls Royce,
and Glo was shouting at the copper, saying, 'Can't
you see we've got a disabled lady here?' And Maxwell
said to the copper, 'Clear off!!!' And I said to Ed, 'For
Chrissake, Eddie, put your foot down!' And so Eddie
swung round and we disappeared smartly without trace.

But that was a demonstration of Maxwell's behaviour
and his very very protective attitude towards me. He
always used to bellow at poor frightened Eddie, 'Are
you taking care of her? Are you looking after her?' and
he'd turn to me and say, 'Who's looking after you?' He
would say that whenever I spoke to him on the phone,
and I would reply, 'And who's looking after *you*?'

Slightly less protective was Maxwell's number two son,
Ian. Seeing Marje hobbling down the corridor, Ian would
call out, 'Here she comes – the geriatric teenager,' to which
Marje would reply, 'I'll tell your father!' She didn't mind
Ian teasing her and preferred him to number one son,
Kevin. 'Maxwell was very close to Kevin, more so I think
than to Ian. He once fired Ian for keeping him waiting at
the airport. I've always felt that Kevin was rather a hard
nut, a tough boy.'

Of course, not everyone at the *Mirror* viewed the Marje

– Bonzo liaison without cynicism. Her close friend and colleague Geoffrey Goodman:

Maxwell used Marje. I told her so many times. I warned her. I tried to persuade her that Maxwell was bad. The fact that he was Jewish, like myself and Marje, somehow made it worse. But she was immensely fond of him and he exploited that in the most appalling way. I said, 'Of course we all like Bob, Marje, but don't be misled, because he's a shit.' She knew what I thought about him and about the people who cringed around him. But she was genuinely seduced by his charm, which oozed from every pore of his body. He would be dismissive of Marje as of anyone else out of earshot, though to their faces he would croon. Marje really couldn't distinguish between those who were genuinely fond of her and those who were trying to use her. She was far too kind. She would try, because of her nature, to find the best in people and discard the worst. She was a sucker for feeling sorry for people. She's not realistic about the people she likes. She wants to shut out the possibility that they might not be quite what they seem. But then, if she'd been harder, she'd be like the rest of us cynical buggers.

In fairness to Marje's judgement, Maxwell had an awful lot of people fooled. Even beady-eyed journalists thought they were witnessing a surge of finer feeling in Bonzo, quite apart from his customary 'greed to use'. Some even thought Marje was toying with Bonzo, rather than the other way around. John Knight: I've known Marje for many years, and she has always liked to see herself as the power behind the editor's throne. And it was the old mafia, to be honest with you. When Maxwell arrived, he rather took to her almost as if she were his

Jewish momma that he never had. And he immediately
made her a director, without calling a board meeting.
He never called any board meetings. The Robber Baron
tried to conduct his court with grace and favour. He saw
Marje as the good public figure, but there was also his
own emotional attitude towards her. And Marje played
that all up for as much as she was able to do.'

Mirror Group directors were supposed to retire at sixty
or sixty-five. Marje wasn't *made* a director until she was
well past retirement age. It happened in 1985, not long
after the acquisition. Marje:

> I was entering the building one morning and Maxwell
> came in behind me. He took me up to his office for
> a drink, and we sat on the sofa for half an hour or
> so, talking about the paper. Suddenly he said, rather
> reflectively, 'Are you a director of this company?' And
> I said, 'No.' 'Well, why not?' 'Nobody ever asked me
> to be,' I answered. So he said, 'From now on, you're a
> director of MGN.' So I said, 'You can't do that, Bob. It's
> illegal. You have to have a board meeting, with people
> putting their hands up and saying Aye, and all that. You
> can't do it.' So he said, 'If I say you're a fucking director,
> you're a fucking director.' I continued to protest, but
> he threw me out and said that the company secretary
> would come and see me that afternoon and tell me
> what my duties and responsibilities were. I thought
> I'd never hear another word. However the company
> secretary did turn up, and we discussed the illegality
> of it all, but the company secretary said to me, 'You
> know Maxwell – you can't argue with him. If he says
> you're a director, you're a director.' And the rest of the
> board was ignored. Some announcement went out.

Editors have always come and gone through the revolving

doors of Fleet Street with refreshing speed. Bonzo gave
the doors a good hearty shove, rotating his editors with
new velocity. Out went Robert Edwards on the *Sunday
Mirror*. Out went Mike Molloy on the *Mirror*, to become
'editor-in-chief'. In came Richard Stott who then went
to the *People*. In came Roy Greenslade. Out went Mike
Molloy. Out went Roy Greenslade. In came Richard Stott,
again. Marje watched it all philosophically, though she
swore allegiance to each one as he came flying through
the air. Marje:

> When the *Mirror* had changed hands before, it made
> no difference to my life at all. I didn't know who
> owned us, and I really didn't care. It wasn't until the
> Maxwell reign that we had a proprietor who played
> such a positive role in the newspapers. But even then
> I always considered the editor. I was brought up, as
> journalists of my generation were, to see the editor as
> the pinnacle. His word was and is law. And although
> I've seen lots of them come and go, it's not so much
> the man as the office. Whoever's in the office I hold in
> high esteem, and I'm consummately respectful. I might
> think that a particular editor is an idiot or a shit, if you'll
> excuse the bad language, and some of them have been.
> Nevertheless they're still the editor, and I'll do what
> they say and what I'm told.

However, Marje was completely loyal to Bonzo, and saw
nothing wrong or sinister in his interference in editorial
policy:

> Most proprietors, on account of the paper being their
> train set, will involve themselves in editorial policy. If
> we were about to publish a leader with which Maxwell

disagreed, or one in which he wanted the emphasis changed, then he would talk to the editor, and the editor would talk to the leader writer. I don't think 'interference' is the right word. Roy Greenslade came close to blows on many occasions with Maxwell because Roy Greenslade was very determined that he was going to have his own way. He always referred to the paper as 'my newspaper', and this was the thing that clearly enraged Maxwell, because it's not – the editor of a newspaper is a caretaker.

I can't remember how many editors I've sat through in thirty-eight years here. I don't remember half of them. They're here for a while, and they do what they have to do, and then for some reason or another they come unstuck, or they get fed up or they get a better offer, and they move around the Street. But in the end, it was Maxwell's money that paid for the train set. And anybody who failed to recognize that was being a bit daft, because Maxwell could take the train off the rails and stop playing. Or get rid of the driver.

I sit here now, after all these years' experience of seeing them coming and going, and I realize that in this trade it's no use your getting your knickers or your Y-fronts in a twist. You have to be as objective as you possibly can be, to maintain your standards and integrity as much as you can, or as much as you're prepared to. Some people aren't prepared to. They'll sell their integrity to the highest bidder. And the ones that do that don't live to a ripe old age in Fleet Street. Because they sell it to somebody else, and it doesn't work. I can understand a man like Maxwell: if I owned this great newspaper, and I sat in my penthouse office looking at some of the stuff that goes in it, I would blow my top, and I would say, 'This is not the sort of newspaper I want. And as it does come out of my back pocket, either you do it the way I want, or we shake hands and say goodbye.'

Roy Greenslade Ph.D., who often went fifteen rounds with his proprietor, nevertheless got on very well with Marje. She remembers his arrival with amusement:

Shortly after he joined, he read one of my columns on his screen, and in the reply – it was a very explicit reply to a very specific letter from a man anxious about his small penis – I was writing to reassure this bloke, saying that if you've got small feet you can still walk along, and if a man has a small penis he can still perform with it. And in the reply I mentioned 'penis' possibly three times. And I got a very hesitant request from the new editor, via the sub-editor, saying would it be possible to remove one of the penises? So then I had to tell the sub-editor to tell the editor that I had performed the operation successfully. And when I saw Roy, he stuck his foot out and said, 'Look at the size of my feet! I've got good big feet!' And I was greatly reassured by that.

Roy Greenslade: What I think is so interesting is that Marje was astonished, first that I had read the letter – because she said not many editors had ever read her letters before – and second that I should be so prim that I wanted fewer penises in it. But I just felt that it was a bit too explicit.' Did he think it odd that Marje had been appointed as an MGN director without consulting the board? Roy: 'No, that sounds absolutely bang-on right. Maxwell once announced that he was pleased that we had just bought two Canadian paper mills. Virtually the whole board were there having lunch, and he just told us that we had committed £300 million. That was what he would regard as "backing of the board".'

We still don't know what Marje, the new Mirror Group director, was earning – except that it wasn't as much as Anne Robinson. John Knight:

Well, Anne was earning £40,000, the same as her husband, who was a colleague. And when he fell out with Maxwell and was fired, Annie went to see Maxwell and said, 'Look Bob – you've fired my husband and halved the income in the family, so I'll have to get other work.' And Maxwell said, 'Oh, I'm very sorry about all that. How much were the pair of you earning?' '£80,000.' 'Oh well – let's pay you £80,000 then.' That's absolutely true. Salaries between about £50,000 and £80,000 for newspaper columnists and executives are not uncommon these days. They're not common, but they're not uncommon. I'd be very surprised if Marje was getting less than about £60,000, because she is a great star and she's still rattling it all out.

Roy Greenslade:

She was paid very little, really, for her contribution and her name, and for what she brings to the paper. When I went there she was paid, I thought, very badly indeed, and I got her a major rise – and despite any arrangement you say she may have made with Hugh Cudlipp, her wages were definitely on the regular payroll that I administered. I won't mention the sums if she doesn't want to mention them, but she was paid less than any other columnist on the paper and less than a number of senior feature writers. She was paid a great deal less than Anne Robinson, less than Joe Haines, less even I think than Michael Parkinson, who I believe was then just a one-day-a-week contributor, and less than my wife, who was a senior feature writer. But she did have, in fairness, a chauffeur-driven car.

This wasn't so much a perk, though, as a face-saver for the *Mirror*. The sight of Marjorie Proops driving a mechanized wheelchair in heavy traffic round Holborn Circus might have caused a murmur among the prols.

— 15 —

Double Widow

*I*n 1986 Marje Proops, the worldly-wise, the institution, the embrocation of Britain, became mentally ill. The circumstances can readily be explained. What she went through during her illness, though, is not easily disseminated in a biography. We could of course skip the episode by saying, 'Marje had a breakdown for this and that reason', and leave it at that, as many biographies do. But this would scarcely be appropriate in a book on the life of an agony aunt, of all people. Our innermost fears are her stock in trade, and she has been reassuring her flock about mental illness for decades, telling them it is not a thing of shame. Besides, her black period was not just some strange quirk. It came about because of the life and work described in previous chapters. So if we are to follow Marje through her story here, we shall just have to try to use our imaginations.

If you say the words 'advice columnist' dozens of times, they begin to sound like unfamiliar gibberish. And if you were foolish enough to apply this alienation technique to lots of other words, and then to habitual ideas and customs you take for granted, and then to the regular routines and tasks of your daily life, the same unnerving meaningless-ness might begin to pervade your perception of reality. A

wave of futility might numb your senses. And then a void
might well open up beneath your feet, and give you an idea
how scared it is possible to be. Of course, nobody really
does this deliberately. Most of us are pleasantly preserved
from thinking about such matters. Most of us can think
about death and madness without losing our poise. But
this is because we are merely scanning the surface of
these subjects, and not really understanding, or wanting
to understand, what they mean. If we understood them
– that is to say, if we brought our full intelligence and
imagination to bear on such concepts – the emotions they
would engender in poor little mortal beings like ourselves
would shake us to our very foundations, as they shake
those whom we call 'mentally ill'.

In 1986 the ground gave under Marje's feet. She tried to
carry on as normal, but the more she clung to normality,
the more normality came away in her hands. The meaning
both of death and of madness became stark and clear. By
dint of plain courage and forty years in journalism, her
advice column and occasional articles were still appearing
fairly regularly in the paper. But their writer was gripping
the desk in terror, picking her way from one moment to
the next hoping not to forfeit her sanity.

Her readers had no idea what was going on. Neither had
colleagues at the *Daily Mirror*. Proprietor Robert Maxwell
and editor Roy Greenslade, although they knew something
was wrong, could not be allowed to know the seriousness
of Marje's condition, and even at home there seemed to
be nobody whom she could lean on. Proopsie had grave
health problems of his own, and for reasons which will
soon become apparent, they had begun to fight. Marje's
lover Phillip was away in Hove, in the last year of his
life, obsessed with the vain hope of having his book on
the Press Council revised. Robert had his own family to
take care of, and so did sister Jo. So Marje turned for help

first to her doctor, who prescribed drugs, and then, when
these seemed to make matters much worse, to psychiatrist
Tom Kraft, whom she had consulted before in connection
with her work.

Marje's secretary Fiona, who has been a Samaritan and
is now a trained counsellor herself, covered for her boss
during her anxiety attacks in the office and fended off
inquiries. Fiona Griffin:

She was just so ill. I don't believe she knew what was
going on half the time. I protected her from anyone
knowing. I remember exactly when she became ill,
because I came back from a holiday and she was totally
different. Prior to that she was coming in every morning
and confessing about this guy Mr Levy, and telling me
everything about her marriage, and it was quite a lot
to carry around with me because people used to think,
'Oh isn't Marje wonderful – she's been married all those
years and she's an example to us all,' and she was writing
about how to keep your marriage together.

But later on she became upset because Phillip had
gone to live near Brighton, and she never saw as much
of him as before. He used to come up every now and
again but he was a doddery old man by this time. And
also I suppose when people get really old, you don't
get any feedback from them. When they used to speak
on the phone, he wasn't as concerned as before, simply
because he was so old. He was a very independent man,
but just wasn't capable any more of the things he used
to do. And that upset her too, I think. He used to take
us both to lunch sometimes, and he was a lovely man.
He was sweet. He'd send chocolates to Marje, and some
chocolates to me, though he hardly knew me. I thought
he was gorgeous actually: he had a real twinkle. He was
quite funny, a fantastic-looking sort of guy, very tall and

well-dressed, rather exacting. He liked his soup piping
hot, and he would send it back if it wasn't steaming.

Marje may have been worried about Phillip, but I think
the main cause of her illness was one of the drugs she
was taking that was making her really bad. She lost
an awful lot of weight – she was so anxious all the
time. She wasn't phobic when I first knew her, so maybe
that was brought on by anxiety. But when she began
to have these problems getting around the building,
her driver Eddie used to have to bring her up to the
office. Before, she used to talk to me about all sorts of
problems, but when she became ill she didn't say very
much at all. She was very nervy and shaky. As soon
as they took her off this particular drug, she started to
put weight back on. I think they gave her the drug for
anxiety and depression, but it had a really bad effect
on her. It gave her nightmares. So she was very tired
and she'd sometimes sleep in the office, or in the car.
When she wasn't asleep, she'd be in an anxious state
– terribly agitated. You couldn't talk rationally to her
saying, 'Come on, calm down,' because she was so very
frightened. When you're a bit down, you think, 'Oh
well, I'll talk it over.' But when you're that depressed
and frightened, you can't. And Marje had the terrors.

When the time came for Marje to discuss her period in the
tunnel with me, she called for tea through what she calls
her 'fish and chip hatch' in the wall between her office and
her secretaries'. She joked grimly, 'I'd better have a biscuit
to give me strength if I'm going to talk about this,' and sat
back in her executive chair:

Well, I had this terrifying fear of death. And anything
to do with death. I couldn't pass a hearse in the street
without terror and cold sweats. I used to turn to my

driver and talk to him to distract myself from the funeral.
And I couldn't bear to pass funeral parlours. I had a real
terror in the pit of my stomach. And I told Tom Kraft
about all this because I was frightened of the fear, and
the terror was so strong, and so powerful, that another
fear I had was of losing control of myself, because of
this fear.

I also had an obsession with numbers. I would add
up car numbers. I still occasionally do it: not very often
because I laugh at it now. Tom Kraft managed somehow
to make me laugh about it.

Marje had actually had this compulsion before; indeed, she
had mentioned it in an article in the *Mirror* in 1970 headlined, 'WELL, JUST WHAT IS NORMAL?'. In the piece,
which reassured readers about so-called abnormalities,
she wrote that she hadn't dared mention her car-numbers
obsession before, for fear of being thought 'deranged', but
that she had recently read a book on compulsions and
discovered it was quite common. During her black period,
however, the compulsion became much worse.

I've no idea why I did it. Tom thinks that it may well have
been something to do with my childhood lack of any
kind of skill at maths at school, and being ridiculed by
everybody including my own mother over it. My sister
could add up and I couldn't. And I think that when you
get neurotic – because any fear like this is neurotic – the
only way to get rid of it, or to cope with it, is to track
it down, hopefully with somebody's help, or to track
it down yourself, and that's very hard to do, because
self-analysis is extremely difficult.

So I used to prattle on to Tom, sometimes for an
hour uninterrupted almost. And sometimes he'd say
something to me like, 'How did your father react, then,

to your lack of mathematical-skills?' And I'd say, 'Well, they would have made my father laugh, because to my father I was perfect anyway. No matter what skills I lacked.' And then Tom would laugh. Because he was quite well aware then of the importance I put on my mother's approval. I had my father's anyway. I didn't have to work for that. But I didn't have the capacity to earn my mother's approval when it came to things like doing maths. I simply couldn't do it. And I couldn't look different either. So that I knew I was a constant source of disappointment to my mother. And I think that one of the reasons why I did try very very hard indeed in those early days to be good at what I was doing – my drawing and so on – was to prove to my mother that I was as good as my sister. But it was only by talking through the subject with Tom that I began to think about it with reason and clarity.

And then the fear of death and funerals was again to do with my father. And the memory, which will never leave me, of my mother at the time of my father's funeral. And the anguish at losing my father, which was greater than the anguish at losing anybody. Losing my father was like having been wounded – a pain that you could almost feel as a physical injury. Whereas losing Proopsie and Phillip, as I was soon to do, was an ongoing grief, which is different. Losing Proops and Phillip is not related in my mind, and never has been, with the fear of death, or funerals or funeral parlours. I went to a funeral quite recently, and I went with equanimity. I sat beside the widow comforting her. The fear of funerals and wreaths and hearses and all that had disappeared, or I'd come to terms with it.

Marje had no religious beliefs to support her through her ordeal. 'We all I think have a conviction that we're immortal, and a lot of people become religious or more deeply religious as they get older. I get the feeling that it's a bit like taking out an insurance policy!'

It is rather unusual for a biographer to be told by his or her subject to 'talk to my psychiatrist'. For a start the analyst in question has to be given written clearance by the patient to disclose such highly sensitive confidentialities to a third party. Then, contrary to all your instincts and experience as an author, you have to pay – I was charged the same fifty-minute session fee as if I'd gone to Dr Kraft with my personal lunacies. And to top it all, you are then liable to end up being labelled Kitty Kelley the Second for worming the facts out of people. But I put no pressure on Marje to make this information available to me. Having come clean about her double life, she wanted to tell the truth about everything else as well. Perhaps the shattering details of her breakdown and her recovery may serve to heal and comfort some of the millions who write to her for help. Perhaps they may feel a little less alone, seeing their problems laid bare in their famous counsellor's life story. In any case Marje is now at an age, never mind what it is, when she sees no reason to lie. Dr Tom Kraft:

Marje was quite severely phobic when I took her on. She could not walk round the corridors of the *Daily Mirror*, she was so frightened. And as for anything to do with death, funerals, funeral parlours or hearses, she was absolutely terrified. She was going very rapidly downhill, and her own GP at the time asked me whether I would see her [as a patient]. She felt dreadful. She was depressed, she was miserable, she couldn't cope, she couldn't do anything really.

I was asked should she retire or not – that was really the point. Even her son said to me, 'Don't you think she should retire? After all, she isn't coping. Don't you think she ought to give it up?' And I said no. I said I would see her for a few weeks, and see how we got on. In the state she was in, nobody could make decisions, because she was far too ill and depressed and unhappy. Once she started to recover from all this, then we would see whether she needed to retire. But not at this point. One shouldn't make decisions when one is at such a low ebb.

And Marje asked me quite frequently in those days, 'Don't you really think I ought to retire?' And I said no. And that was my attitude throughout. And she's ever so pleased now that she took my advice and that she did go on working. I felt that really her work was the most important thing in her life. I felt that if she stopped working, she might well die. I thought, 'Well, either she will continue working and her graph will go upwards, or she'll retire – and I don't think she'll live very long after that.'

Robert insists that he never at any time suggested to Dr Kraft that his mother should retire. In fact, he thinks it would have been disastrous for her. But Dr Kraft continues:

Now, why was she at this low ebb? Well, she had become quite severely phobic. Why was she severely phobic? Her relationship with Phillip was no longer in its heyday. She was leading what in general terms would be called a double life. We would call it a 'combined relationship'. That means that you've got two relationships going on at the same time. Of course it is very common, though you usually hear of it the other way round: in fact it's called 'the wife-mistress syndrome'. What happens in this process is a splitting between the two relationships, which are completely different. The two components of marriage are split down the middle.

In Marje's case, these were the living component and the sexual component. And the only way the sufferer can function is to have one partner to live with, and one to have sex with. There is a division, which Marje showed quite dramatically actually, in that she'd got a lover, Phillip, with whom she had had an ongoing extramarital relationship for twenty years [nearer thirty if we count Phillip's retirement], and at the same time she was having an ongoing relationship with her husband. And if you look at these two relationships, they are quite different. The one with Phillip was a loving, sexual, enjoyable, warm relationship, and the one with her husband was a very different, thorny, aggressive and non-sexual relationship.

Clearly, Marje was very frank with Tom Kraft:

She's been terribly open about everything actually with me. She saw very soon that unless she told me what was going on, there was really no point to the whole business. And we mustn't forget that in 1986 she was very ill. Not physically, but mentally. Her illness was nothing to do with her physical disability at all. Her disturbance hinged on the fact that she had one partner to live with and one to have sex with. And that's all right, as long as that situation continues. But presumably the sexual aspects of her relationship with Phillip had reduced very considerably at that point. So she had lost out on that component of the Phillip relationship – and that's really when the thing starts to go wrong.

In therapy altogether, one encourages the person to bring the feelings into the session, so that instead of feeling them outside, they can be worked through here. And it worked to a certain extent, but we still got a lot of angry scenes [at home]. When I took her on, she was too timid, too frail and too depressed to do anything, but as we continued, she became more and more angry with her husband. She had a very thorny relationship with him at this time. She was really quite unpleasant. They were constantly at each other's throats. She was very aggressive towards Proopsie. Mind you, he was irritating her to distraction too – it wasn't one-sided. But they had a very stormy relationship.

Marje had answered letters from readers afraid of death. One reply said, 'When someone we know dies, the fear leaps into our hearts and minds and brings it all so much closer than when we only read about loss and tragedy . . . It's perfectly normal, everyone does it. But most people soon realize that they simply have to go on living and indeed enjoying life to the full.' Does Dr Kraft consider Marje's illness had anything to do with her agony mail?

In a way I think you've hit on something which is quite important there. She has said very often that although she writes all these letters, she feels that she cannot offer much in the way of help. She can give a certain amount of consolation. But she cannot actually take these people for treatment herself. She cannot be of tremendous help to them, and this is very worrying for her.

After all, she signs hundreds of letters a week. But she knows that the amount of practical help that she can give to each individual is relatively small. I'm not minimizing the value of her work. But if you look at some of the letters she receives, they are quite alarming. She's not that hard-boiled. Marje is in fact quite a soft egg under all that surface veneer. It affects her quite deeply. And I think the reason is that she knows she cannot really do a tremendous amount for each of these people in distress.

Marje saw Tom Kraft twice a week, from 1986 until 1990,
then once a week. What form did the treatment take?

> I decided from the very word go that I would only use
> a psychodynamic approach with her: I would not give
> her any 'homework' at all, or anything of a behavioural
> nature. I felt that it was not appropriate for her; that she
> wouldn't like it, and would only resent me. A sixth sense
> told me what approach I'd use. Obviously the aim was
> that she should be able to walk along the corridors,
> that she should be able to cope with the dark – she
> was terrified of the dark, and not until recently did
> she recover from that. But I didn't give her any sort
> of exercises to do. Now transference has developed in
> some large measure here. I got a very strong, positive
> transference from Marje. She thinks terribly highly of
> me. Mind you, I did help her go from virtually rock
> bottom, right up to stardom again. And she knows it.
> I said, 'It was your work as well.' But she knows. And
> she feels better now than she has done for years.

Although Kraft gives himself a lot of credit for having
pulled her through, neither Fiona nor Marje's son Robert
was enthusiastic about his contribution to Marje's recovery. Indeed, Fiona felt that the demarcation between
patient and therapist was not sufficiently clearly main-
tained, and that Marje mistook the relationship for a
friendship. 'You never make friends with your clients,
because if you're involved, you can't treat them. I feel
he must have helped in some way, but she pulled herself
through. She pulled herself through everything else. But
she became so dependent on him, particularly when she
lost both men in her life. She used to come back from
there as though she'd been on a date sometimes. That
used to really annoy me because she was so vulnerable.

She used to mention that she saw flowers in his office and he said, 'Oh I only buy them when I know that you're coming, Marje.' You have to know where to draw the line to help someone, otherwise you're not helping them. Particularly when someone's paying you. You don't pay for friendship.'

Marje's son Robert was convinced that most of his mother's health problems during this period were caused by some of the drugs she was prescribed and to which she was quite obviously allergic: 'Most of the apparent breakdown that she had was, I am absolutely certain now, not psychological in the obvious sense. It was almost all drug fallout.' He was dubious about the prolonged psychoanalysis his mother was receiving, and when she became very much worse after the death of Proopsie, he confronted Kraft about her treatment, as we shall see. There are also one or two other imponderables. Both Marje's mother and her sister Jo-jo suffered from 'phobic disturbances'. In neither of these cases was there any connection with what Dr Kraft calls a 'combined relationship'. Marje did discuss Jo's agoraphobia with her sister; she was worried that Jo might become as seriously agoraphobic as their mother had been.

It is also rather difficult to give credence to the idea that Marje was adding up car numbers because of some childhood difficulty with maths. One might more simply suggest that numbers hold special power because they are connected with age and the passage of time, and as Robert says, 'That's a big issue for her, ageing.' Marje not only conceals her age, but avoids consideration of dates and years altogether. By ignoring age and advancing years, she had perhaps hoped to avoid worrying about them. And when this escape mechanism could no longer be sustained – because Marje was visibly ageing – she began to address her fears by adding up numbers for good luck, as a protection against their power to scare her. Marje has always been extremely superstitious. She admitted in a letter to me, 'Have I ever told you how superstitious I am, despite the fact that when I write to readers I tell them it is all a load of rubbish? Nevertheless, I touch wood, cross my fingers, avoid walking under ladders and throw spilled salt over my left shoulder three times – all this is a legacy from my very superstitious mum.'

There is also the question of Marje's 'double marriage' as a symptom or cause of mental instability. Such double relationships are surely so common that we might almost refer to the phenomenon as 'biogamy' (as distinct from monogamy or bigamy), and suggest that while it may not be socially acceptable, it is nevertheless ordinary, human and normal. The search for an idealized or romantic partner, whether actual or imagined, goes hand in hand with domesticity because a domestic partner, seen in unglamorous circumstances with hair standing on end and worrying about the mortgage, is no longer the stuff of premarital dreams. Even where no romantic or illicit partner exists, one is often found through fiction or fantasy, simply because it is very hard to discover one single human being who answers all our needs, and only a small minority hit the jackpot. The rest of us have to manage as best we can. We are creatures of dreams as well as reality, and this dichotomy pre-dates Freud by many centuries.

Despite having championed marriage and monogamy for decades, Marje is quite open and honest about this subject. After all, she had once written (in the *Sunday Mirror* in 1974), 'A good many wives are very ripe indeed for an affair. But that is one thing; having the nerve to conduct one is something again.' She had also (in the *Mirror* in 1981), told her readers, 'The human capacity for love is immeasurable. "Is it possible," I'm so often asked, "to love two people at once?" It's certainly possible. It happens more often than you think. A man loves his wife and secretly loves his girlfriend. He also loves his parents, children, best friend, dog, cat and possibly his budgie. Different kinds of love have different kinds of depth. It's not so much who you love and how much, as what you do about that love.' This is what she had to say to me about her own 'biogamy':

When I compare Proopsie with Phillip, and what I got from them both, and therefore was able to give to them both, they are two very distinct areas of my life. With Proops I had a relationship based on friendship and to some extent on fear, because I was always frightened of him. I was never frightened that he would hit me, and he would never have done so, but I was just frightened of his authority and his bullying. So I spent my life with Proops doing what I was told. But with Phillip I was able to express all the emotion and the love that I had in me to give, that I couldn't give to Proops. And although we had a very physical relationship, Phillip and I, which I didn't have with Proops, it was based on real and very deep love. And if Phillip had become impotent after a fortnight, I'd still have gone on seeing him. So although sex was part of it and clearly enjoyable and terrific, it was only the icing on the cake.

The large majority of people have to settle for one. I was lucky, because the job I had and the life I lived meant that instead of being trapped in domesticity and being a housewife at home, I was able to split my life into two areas and keep them separate. So I was very fortunate. But the majority of women – and indeed men, although men have a better chance because they traditionally go out to work – have to settle for only one deep relationship. But because I was in a well-paid job and able to pay somebody else to look after Robert while I wasn't around, I was able to have the best of both my worlds.

Isn't it unrealistic to expect to find all one's needs fulfilled in one partner anyway?

Could be. I wouldn't otherwise have all these letters, would I, about all these people's relationships. Looking at this batch waiting for me to sign, they're all about partnerships, or looking for somebody if they haven't got anybody.

I'd hate my relationship with Phillip to be seen as a kind of trivial pulp-fiction, hands-across-a-candlelit-table office affair. It was so very much deeper, more significant and more intense than that. There was, of course, an element of romance in it, at least for me, although he wasn't a romantic man. He was austere and outwardly undemonstrative. It was difficult for him to express his feelings but they were immensely deep and genuine.

He added a great dimension to my life and personality. The rather foolish and frivolous woman I was when we met changed and matured under his influence. He stimulated and encouraged my interest in the law and in politics. He took me seriously as a person, not merely as a mistress. He gave me, I realized later, the education I'd missed and for which I'd always yearned, the music and the reading. He helped me to learn to think and to analyse as well as to love, to channel my unruly emotions. He guided me intellectually and underpinned my wobbly self-esteem. He was my friend as well as my lover.

Proopsie bullied and cowed me; Phillip gently led and supported me and gave me the reassurance and strength that helped me to do my job and lead my difficult life. I only hope that he was happy and fulfilled by what he got from me. We were both very seriously and deeply committed to each other. Whatever I did, whatever I am now, I owe mainly to him and to the other central figure in my life, my son, Robert.

My relationship with Rob has always been and is very, very special. There couldn't be a more loving son or a more supportive one. He's seen me through all the tough times. I depend on him. We depend on each other. He's had tough times, too, and we are always there for each other. We see each other often, he comes round with his dogs – my three wild granddogs – at least once a week and he rings me every night, not, he says, out of duty, but because he wants to and I believe him. He is a scrupulously truthful and honest man. He is also fun. He makes me laugh. There's a lot of banter between us. He has the sort of ribald sense of humour I respond to. When he rings and asks me how're things and I say I'm busy he says, 'Good, it'll keep you off the streets.'

His childhood and adolescent years were very difficult for him, not only because of the stresses caused by his parents' disastrous marriage, but because of his father's antipathy and jealousy of him. I was very protective towards my son when he was young. I tried to compensate him for the harm the marriage was doing.

Gradually, over the years, we've swapped roles. Now he is fiercely protective towards me and an immensely loving as well as practical son. I've been a very lucky woman to have known such love and friendship from these two men. It's a lot more, I guess, than I deserve.

By a cruel irony Marje was in hospital having some surgery when her hidden half, Phillip Levy, died of a heart attack at the beginning of 1987. She was unable even to go to his funeral, supposing she could have coped with the prospect, though Levy's colleague Hugh Corrie attended.

Hugh Corrie: 'I was the only one there from the *Mirror*. He went to his grave thinking that nobody in the office knew about the affair. For about two years before he died, his great thing was that he wanted to revise his book on the Press Council, and he kept a lot of cuttings about it. He wanted to get the *Mirror* to pay for the new edition, which they wouldn't do. In the end he wrote to me and said, "Come down – I want your help over this: I've got all these cuttings" and so on. I went down and had lunch with him, but it was quite clear to me that he couldn't concentrate on anything. He kept on producing documents which were years old, and it was apparent that he'd really gone to pieces.'

Marje: 'I didn't even know he'd died: someone in Hove got in touch with me. Towards the end of his life he was beginning to get a bit frail. He was not the sort of man who would admit to illness because he would have regarded that as a weakness of character. So he would never admit that he felt ill. He tried until he went to live in Brighton to sustain our relationship physically. And in fact he managed very well. He was sexually a very virile man, but the signs of ageing were beginning to show. He also got much more tetchy towards the end of his life. There was a tendency anyway for him to be tetchy. But when he died, there were no arms to rush into any more.'

After Phillip's death, Marje began to explode at Proopsie, not at first realizing why. 'The quarrels got very severe. And I would scream and beat my fists against him with anger.' Among other things, she blamed him for the fact that she was never married to the love of her life. Her resentment towards Proopsie grew, and Marje was too ill to manage her emotions. Her whole system was poisoned with guilt. She says now, 'I must be the most guilt-ridden person going. I've always been guilty.'

The spectacle of Proopsie's moral uprightness, the fact

that he never strayed or acted dishonourably, and always tended to Marje's disabilities; the fact that he was always in the right, that he was arrogant and domineering; the fact that he wasn't in mental terror and turmoil and she was, all combined with her sense of outrage at herself that she could not now come clean to her husband about the past. He was in his late seventies and physically ill already, and Marje was worried about his health. Whatever would she do if he died, and left her alone? He had severe arthritis, and he'd had one hip replaced but was in a lot of pain. He also had serious circulation problems, had been diabetic since the war, and was always disciplined about his diet, putting on a brave face. He wasn't a man to elicit pity. And because Marje's sessions with Kraft were drawing out emotions she had long kept hidden, in her distress she took it out on Proopsie. 'I showed compassion to strangers,' said a breaking voice into my tape-recorder, 'but none to him.'

Despite Dr Kraft's advice not to retire, Marje's situation as a Mirror Group director was becoming untenable. Proopsie had never liked the way she had been appointed, and sensed something odd was happening at the *Mirror*. His son Robert believes he always had 'second sight'. 'My father knew things he couldn't possibly know. He was a totally logical man who was a humanist; he did not believe in ESP at any level. Yet he would tend to know who was on the phone when it rang, and once absolutely shattered me with his accurate knowledge of some people in Mitcham whom he'd never met. He was perfectly capable of having no information and saying, "I think this should happen now," and for some unknown reason turning out to be right. Now, my father wouldn't let my mother have a Mirror Group pension, and before he died, he told her she should resign as a director of Mirror Group Newspapers.' Marje's former colleague, John Knight, adds mysteriously, 'Proopsie probably had good antennae.' Marje:

Proopsie was always a bit worried and uneasy about my
directorship, and in the summer of 1987 we went to
Majorca for a holiday, and while we were there I had a
call to say that I'd got to meet some official at the airport,
to sign something, because all the directors had to sign
this particular document. So I went to the airport and this
bloke said, 'Quick – sign here – I've got to get the next
plane back to London.' I signed. I didn't read it – there
was no time. To this day I don't know what the blasted
document was. And he snatched it away from me and
tore off to get his plane. And when I told Proopsie, he
was absolutely outraged. And he said, 'Don't you *ever* do
that again. Signing without reading! You must be mad.'
And he said, 'I want you to resign. I think there's too
much pressure. You've got enough pressure as it is with
the advice page and all the other work that you do, and I
don't want you to have the additional pressure that this
position on the board is imposing on you.' So on account
of I was always one for a quiet life and no arguments
with Proopsie, I went back to the office and I wrote up
my letter of resignation.

The letter, on MGN Intermemo notepaper, is addressed
to the company secretary, Mr A. Stephens, and says: 'I
hereby tender my resignation as a director of Mirror Group
Newspapers (1986) Ltd., to take effect from 1 June 1987.'
Another version of the letter tendered Marje's resignation
from Mirror Group Newspapers as a whole, though she
doesn't remember why, and after asking two of her
secretaries thinks it may have been on legal advice. Marje
says that Bonzo seemed distressed by the news. 'Maxwell
was very upset when I resigned. He didn't want me to and
he argued with me but I told him, "I can't keep upsetting
Proopsie and having troubles." So he said, "OK, all right,
but you will continue to have director's status and you will

have all the benefits that you had as a director without any of the legal or other responsibilities." So that was another demonstration of his kindness to me.'

Maxwell is not known to have suffered from schizophrenia. But a man who could give his employees fat salaries and golden handshakes whilst purloining their pensions is a contradictory cove. Anyone who could sack his own son for keeping him waiting at an airport, and protectively promise his boys that he would leave them precisely nothing, as that was what he started out with himself, is hard to plumb in affairs of the heart. Even his death was both fish and fowl. He has been condemned as a crook and a robber baron, but this is to oversimplify him. In fact he seems to have had a duel nature, combining both good and evil in the same entity, rather like Herman Melville's white whale, Moby Dick.

One of Marje's secretaries told me how he could make a diligent young assistant cry over the phone with his rudeness and contempt, and yet come breezing into the office like a kindly uncle and forgive them for idling about and sitting cross-legged on the desk. They never knew what to expect. Various colleagues of Marje have explained that he was extremely generous, cold, charming, mean, warm and cruel. All of these qualities, it seems, were genuine. The strange oxymoronic nature of the man made him hard to fathom and even harder to defeat in business or boardroom, because he wasn't just a shark. He was a mystery, a white whale. Tony Boram: 'Maxwell never told anybody anything. He operated very much on a need-to-know basis.' Even Marje herself, who seems to have trusted him implicitly – 'I never had a moment's disquiet' – also says, 'Nobody knew him, not really. You just knew what he presented to you. He was always manoeuvring people.'

An example of this manoeuvring was that he apparently

had the bright idea of asking Marje if he could buy her
name, so that he could carry on using it after she was dead
– rather like 'Disney'. This was either immensely heartless,
or a deeply felt compliment to her greatness. As this story
reached me from three different sources, I asked Marje to
explain. 'Well, he never said it to me. Nobody actually said
it to me. It was rumoured that this was what he wanted to
do, and the rumour went round the office. I just laughed.
The answer to that would have been "not bloody likely".
When I'm dead and I'm no longer writing, then the name
Marje Proops will die with me as a writer. I've never ever
allowed anything that anybody else has written to go under
my by-line because I think it's highly dishonest. Absolutely
awful. And the whole idea to me was bizarre.' I put it to
Marje that he might have meant to give her everlasting life.
'Oh yes, indeed. Perpetuate this great quote name!'

Roy Greenslade: 'I think it says a lot that when Maxwell
first went to the *Mirror* he decided that one of the icons was
Marje Proops, and he would always be seen hugging her in
public and making a great fuss of her. Now, I have got a
real difficulty here, because Marje doesn't know about this.
But it is an absolutely true story, one of those disgusting
episodes, and I'm glad it's over.' This is the story. 'Maxwell
asked me to get rid of Marje. He tried, just before I arrived
at the *Mirror*. Mike Molloy, who was then editor-in-chief,
had come up with a plan to get Marje to write a book called
The A to Z Manual of Sex or something, and when I arrived
Molloy said, "You must convince Marje to write this book,"
and I said, "Yes, right, fine, I think it's good for the *Mirror*
if she does this."'

Maxwell, however, saw this book as a means of putting
Marje out to grass, a means to 'shift her out', as he phrased
it to his new editor. Greenslade: 'There were two things.
One, if she didn't go quietly, it would probably have
caused a public outcry, so he wanted to make it look as

if, by getting her to do the book, she had so much work that she couldn't possibly carry on with her column. That was what was going on. I asked Marje about doing the book, but when I realized what he was luring me into, I decided to foil the plan. I started saying that I thought the book was too much for her to deal with and so on. I asked why he would ever want to get rid of Marje Proops? It seemed to me that that was the last thing the *Mirror* could do. It was all very well and I was very happy to kick the Old Codgers into touch and to get rid of the "Jane" strip cartoon, but I baulked at the very thought of getting rid of Marje Proops.'

What was Bonzo's reasoning? 'I think Maxwell was convinced that she wasn't wholly his person. He didn't like that. [Compare his reaction when spurned by Marje at the flotation launch.] And the second thing he considered was that her page, or her contribution, cost a lot because she had a big back-up staff, so it was a cost-cutting measure. Anyway, a month or so later Molloy was sacked, and the plan was put on the back burner and never dealt with again. I certainly wouldn't have done it, and I made sure that Marje never knew.'

It would be easy to see this as just another axe-stroke from Butcher Bonzo, but perhaps this is not entirely fair, even to him. Maxwell's strange cost-cutting notion may have been part of an undisclosed but far-reaching self-rescue package. He knew what Mike Molloy and Roy Greenslade did not: that his ship was taking on water, and that if he didn't start getting some of his belongings over the side pretty damn quick, the City would begin to notice he was riding low in the waves. Cost-cutting was a top priority. However genuine his feelings for Marje, he couldn't muck about being sentimental: he had to look after his business. Ironically, as often happens with people who divide heart from head, he made a misjudgement, quite seriously underestimating just what a hard asset his 'beautiful darling girl' was to the paper – as we shall see.

My own guess, for what it's worth, is that Bonzo was fond of Marje; that in his two-faced, white-whale way, he even cared for her quite deeply. But he was desperate, and digging for victory, and in the past, ruthlessness had always paid off. Of course, he may have got wind of her illness, and seen the possibility that she might have to resign, or retire, in less than flattering circumstances. In 1987 this had certainly been on the cards, and may explain the mysterious second resignation letter. Perhaps the book idea, like the name idea, were his gross ways of covering for her, and protecting her from unpleasant publicity. In any case he was not a man to discuss such things with his 'creeps', as he called them, and once told Marje, 'You're not like all the other creeps that work for me.' So who knows? The answers are all at the bottom of Davy Jones's locker.

On Friday 30 September 1988 Proopsie died, as Phillip had done, of a heart attack. He was eighty. Marje's young secretary Emma Field, who had joined her staff in 1986 as Fiona's junior: 'Mrs Proops was going from the house to the hospital, ringing us from home. She wouldn't stop worrying about the office, and although she was upset she always managed to call in to make sure everything was OK. On the Friday we didn't hear from her and wondered why, so lunchtime we rang, and he'd died. It was terrible. I think he'd had a stroke, then a heart attack. He was really ill. Robert had been away on holiday in Greece, but he flew back two or three times to visit Proopsie in hospital.' Robert:

> He probably didn't have a real friend in the world when he died, though he had quite a few acquaintances. To most people he appeared charming, lovely, a little sweetie. But to people very close to him, he was quite

the reverse. To those who didn't know him, he put himself out as an old English gentleman, particularly in his latter years. He seemed very gentle and friendly. It was only people who knew him really really well, and who knew his capacity to cause emotional damage, which was massive, who would say anything against him. But he fell out with everybody in the family. He ended up the most friendless person in the world.

We got very close the last time I saw him before he died. I flew back from Greece when I thought he was dying. He seemed to get better, and we spent a lovely day together, and were very happy, and actually in a strange way – it was a most strange experience for me – we buried our differences that day. I then went back to Greece and I'd been back at the hotel for twenty minutes when my mother rang and said that he was very ill again. I turned round and came straight back to London, but he was not *compos mentis* when I got there, and I was with him when he died. So it was only the last day that I ever saw him *compos mentis* that we actually buried our differences. And it was lovely for me that we did.

Marje, already frail, was knocked sideways. Even now, she says she misses her bossy husband more than Phillip. 'Proopsie was admirable. The most honest man I've ever known in my life.' She paid tribute to him in the *Daily Mirror* after her return to work a month later: 'Sorry I've not been around for a few weeks to help with your problems. But I've had my own. I still have. Many of my readers know that my beloved husband Proopsie died at the end of September . . . We had had a very long marriage. It had its ups and downs, like most marriages, but it worked a treat, and I can't begin to describe my feelings now.'

She kept his books and 78 records as mementoes, but she cleared out all his other things, and sent his clothes to Oxfam. She needed the space for a live-in housekeeper, because she was very disabled, very afraid of being in the house on her own, and very scared of the dark. She read in bed: whodunits, sloppy novels, biographies, anything. Her nightmare scenario had come true: she was alone, like the Guinness Girls and the Lonely Old Ladies. In the space of just eighteen months she had gone from being a woman with two adoring men, to a woman with nothing, a double widow. Robert: 'Losing them both in a relatively short period of time was very difficult for her.'

Fiona: 'She was frightened to be in the house on her own once Proopsie had died. She was much worse after his death – that was the really bad time, and I think there must have been a lot of guilt there, as well as the fact that she couldn't cope alone – she was frightened. She had to think of the practicalities of her life, and I think that threw her. Any widow would be in the same boat if she had let her husband take over to such an extent, but on top of all that, she had the guilt.'

Robert considered the terrors that she endured now were the culmination of long-term misprescription and drug side-effects.

Over a period of years she had been given the wrong drugs, and drugs that interfered with her psychologically. Eventually I got so angry about it that I rang up Tom Kraft and lost my temper one afternoon. Because I thought she was going to die. She was painfully ill and in such a state that she was too frightened to go upstairs or downstairs on her own. I happen to have some knowledge of prescription-drug side-effects and what they can do to people, and three years earlier I had tried to see my mother's doctor. My father stopped me. I told my father on the phone that I was going to see the GP and that my mother wasn't to know because

I thought she might be unnerved by it. And my father put the phone down and went and told my mother, who then got on the phone herself and got hysterical and said I mustn't go to see him.

Eventually, when she got very seriously ill after my father died, I rang Tom Kraft and let rip. It was a Monday, and I'd been round to my mother's on the Sunday and she was so ill I didn't think she was going to live a month. I really didn't. My mother was screaming through the night. She would go to sleep and wake up screaming at the top of her voice, so much so that the neighbours both sides were kept awake by it. And it was all drug fallout. I'd listened to all the advice about being sensible, and I thought, ignore it, bugger it. And I got hold of Tom Kraft and I went absolutely barmy.

A week later my mother went to see a neurologist at the Hospital for Nervous Diseases in Maida Vale. He ordered a brain scan and discovered that she was mildly epileptic. She had been given beta-blockers. The specialist took her off the beta-blockers and put her on another set of drugs. A month later she was well. All the symptoms lifted. I think most of the apparent psychological effects were the result of taking the controversial sleeping drug Ativan, and then because this caused problems, being prescribed other drugs.

Robert will never forgive himself for not having acted sooner, and wishes he had ignored his parents' advice to keep out of it. 'I blame myself terribly. I knew what the problem was, and if I had been prepared to interfere sooner, my mother would have been well two or three years earlier. It makes me angry because those drug side-effects took four or five years out of her life. I feel very bad that I didn't tell my father to stuff himself and go and see the doctor anyway.'

Whatever the real cause of Marje's inner torment after Proopsie's death, she had to fight both her mental illness and her physical helplessness. She'd never been a handywoman and always relied on Proopsie for everything. Marje: 'One of the reactions that I felt when I got over the shock and grief of his death was anger. Fury with him. When I have to change a light bulb, or when something goes wrong in the house, I feel fury at Proopsie for leaving me to cope with all these jobs that he used to do and that I took for granted.' All the residents of their little close in Barnes were thrown into confusion because Proopsie was no longer there to take charge of things. According to Marje, the directors of the residents' association would sit gloomily trying to sort out their accounts saying, 'If only Proopsie were still here!' Their gloom, and Marje's anger, were strange tributes to a sorely needed man.

— 16 —

A Mortal Remains

*I*n 1989, Maxwell and Mike Molloy held a mammoth dinner party to celebrate Marje's thirty-five years as a *Mirror* columnist. Bonzo himself stood up in front of all his minions and made a rather moving speech. He also gladly made a fool of himself in a *Daily Mirror* special edition, being depicted by brilliant cartoonist Charles Griffin as a roly-poly Sir Walter Raleigh paying court to his 'Good Queen Bess', Marje. The originals of the cartoons were never returned to the artist, who was, incidentally, married to Marje's secretary Fiona. Mrs Griffin tells me that Maxwell particularly wanted the portraits himself, to put on his wall. The celebration issue contained pictures of La Proops at various high points, with sundry editors, Cary Grant and Harold Wilson. 'They put on a lovely dinner for me,' says Marje, who was surprised by all the fuss. Bonzo didn't mind being represented as one of her courtiers. 'He loved it. He absolutely loved it. And he made a wonderful, wonderful speech.' No doubt he meant every word as well. Moby Dick was at it again.

The following year he was worried that one of his other star columnists, John Diamond, might not be earning his keep. He talked to Roy Greenslade about the matter. Greenslade: 'To stop him banging on about it I said,

"I'll tell you what I will do, Bob: I will commission some market research on this with your own dear firm AGB, and then we will see whether your columnists are recognized or not." John Diamond came out about equal with Joe Haines. But Marje Proops was way out in front, at every level of reader interest. It's just a wonderful document, and it hurt Maxwell in every way.'

The survey summary says of the top-rated writer, 'Marje Proop's [*sic*] column is well known and always read by well over half of *Daily Mirror* readers and read at least sometimes by most of them. Almost half rate it as very interesting and over half indicated it is a very important part of the *Daily Mirror* for them. She appeals to all demographic sub-groups.' Her nearest rival, with a two-fifths regular readership, was neither Joe Haines nor John Diamond, but Anne Robinson. Maxwell's gob was smacked by the research. It showed that with all his business acumen he had got his sums wrong on his 'beautiful darling girl' and her appeal to the *Mirror* public. Roy Greenslade: 'It confirmed what a triumph it was having Marje on the staff, and it angered him that his own beloved hackiographer, Joe Haines, was not as well liked as he thought.' (Joe Haines attracted a regular third of readers compared to Marje's half.)

There was, though, something else. Maxwell had done his utmost to curry favour with *Mirror* readers, and plastered himself all over the paper as their working-class hero, their rags-to-riches sugar daddy, who had plied them with soft socialism, gorgeous girls and hard cash. They still didn't like him. And here was this Marje Proops – who wasn't what you call pin-up pretty, who had never offered the sods the chance to win a million pounds, and who in any case was loved by her own circle, and probably didn't need all this public warmth coming in – winning their hearts and minds with a bloody felt-tip pen. This may have rankled. Indeed, it may have troubled poor Bonzo during the 'shift her out' phase, however kind and kissy-kissy he may have seemed to Marje's face.

Marje was working hard following her illness. She had never neglected her journalism and clung to work when everything else was disintegrating. The Bouquets of the Week were still going out to deserving women, as well as bottles of bubbly to 'My Hero' and 'My Extra Special Man'. From the bottom of the abyss she had been writing about child abuse, and warning the public not to panic and suspect innocent fathers and grandpas of perversion when they showed affection to little kids. 'It is a wicked slander on millions of decent men.' She had reassured readers about mixed marriages, saying that one she knew (Made's) had been going strong for years, and she questioned the wonder of fertility drugs following recent tragic cases of multiple births and deaths, and stirred up a hornet's nest of criticism from readers who believed in babies at all costs.

Well or ill, Marje had never shirked controversy, though lately she was receiving a few more jolts than usual. She crossed swords with her beloved Labour Party, and with Jo Richardson, over a proposal to appoint a Minister for Women if they won the election, because Marje furiously opposes sectioning off women's interests and 'putting women in the ghetto'. More personal sparks flew when, in 1989, a baby named 'Claire' was left outside a hospital X-ray department in a Marks and Spencers carrier bag. Marje wrote a two-page 'open letter' to the mother, urging her to be brave and come forward, because as the baby's real mum, she was the best person to care for her. Marje's phone never stopped ringing. Irate adoptive parents and adopted children told her she was a fool, and that 'substitute' parents could be more loving than natural ones. She apologized. 'I'm truly sorry to have caused such distress,' wrote Marje, omitting to mention her own during this period. But she stuck to her opinion about Baby Claire, and again called for the natural mother to claim her.

Marje had occasionally resorted in the past to the notorious 'open letter' format, even though the unsolicited advice, addressed in a national newspaper to various public figures, did not always reflect on her very creditably. She had written an open letter to Bernadette Devlin in 1971: 'You are pregnant, you say – and you are unmarried . . .' and followed up with various tart moral observations. Though Marje had a point – that the new MP was evading her public duties – the letter upset readers across the political spectrum because of its moralizing tone. But worse was to come.

In 1974 she had written an open letter to David Frost, 'an old friend', about his being jilted. 'David, honey, listen to your well-meaning old mate; next time you fall in love, try to settle for a girl-next-door type . . . Don't tell a soul (including your mum) . . .' and so on. There had also been open letters to Queen Elizabeth II (in 1972, in answer to a fictional plea for advice), and to Princess Margaret, purportedly in reply to a note saying, 'My life is a mess . . .' and discussing her affair with Roddy Llewellyn. Marje's reply on this occasion was: 'At the risk of sounding unsympathetic, you have only yourself to blame for your troubles . . . You showed early signs of being emotionally insecure, that's why you fell for an older – and unattainable – man' – referring to Peter Townsend. Even to a republican like myself, this was, as they say, 'a bit orf'.

Under Maxwell, the unsought advice lark became a feature. An open letter to Andy Capp's wife Flo was all well and good, but Marje also wrote to Ivana Trump on her wayward husband, to Princess Di's brother, Charles Althorp, and his wife about their marriage problems, and to Sarah Johnson, mistress of Jilly Cooper's husband Leo, saying (astonishingly), 'You, Sarah, were simply his bit on the side.' She had both England manager Bobby Robson and soccer star Paul Gascoigne on the couch, discussing their so-called emotional problems. The centre-page piece on Robson, headlined, 'YOU NEED HELP, BOBBY!', actually took the form of an interview with agony aunt Marje by Ian Gibb about the football boss, and carried a cartoon of Robson on a psychiatrist's couch. It suggested, 'He could get relief from psychotherapy,' and that 'He's probably having a lot of sleepless nights.' All very amusing, until you remember where Marje had been reclining twice a week.

The article on Gazza, also a centrefold, featured an imaginary desperate plea from 'tormented' Gascoigne: 'Dear Marje, I am sitting here, still in my strip, with the tears streaming down my face, wondering what I've done to deserve that red card I got on Tuesday . . . Now I feel really choked. I'd be obliged if you could give me a bit of advice, please.' Marje replied, 'Dear Paul, If you were my son, I would take you by the scruff of the neck and give you a real ear-wigging . . . You are only a daft, spoilt kid, I reminded myself – and I found my heart melting with pity for you.' Marje talked about fame ruining him, tantrums, effing and blinding, and his mum and dad – all across seven columns, suitably illustrated by cartoonist Griffin. The spread was followed up by another piece, in May 1991, in which Marje has 'Gazza on the couch' and writes, 'Paul Gascoigne needs help – the Spurs star has got to sort himself out . . . He will need psychiatric treatment as well as physiotherapy.' Hilarious stuff, so long as you weren't Gazza or his family.

In August 1980 Marje had been asked by *Woman's World* magazine what advice she would give to Princess Margaret on her many problems. Marje had replied, 'I never proffer advice to anyone unless they ask for it. If they write to me and say, "Please help me," then fine. But until, or unless, Princess Margaret writes me such a letter, I would think it highly impertinent of me to suggest how she might survive her problems – or solve them.' Unfortunately Marje has not always obeyed her own code of practice, and when she slips, one suspects an editorial forefinger has been inserted in her copy.

Another strange Bonzo period lapse occurred in a retrospective article on Marje's famous 1976 Anne and Mark Phillips interview, following news of the Princess Royal's marital crisis. At the time of the original exclusive, you will recall, they had lots of fun with Anne's dogs, Moriarty and Pleasure, and loads of laughs and hoots from 'warm, funny, easy-going' Anne, leading Marje to conclude that this was a 'normal and nice' couple. In fact she wrote that, barring accidents, they would present us with 'no surprises, no sensational headlines, no scandals'. Suddenly, though, under Bonzo's captaincy in April 1989, we read of 'ANNE'S ANGUISH'.

Marje writes, 'I know that anyone can be wise after the event, but even all those years ago, I promise you, I had several little doubts about the marriage and whether it would last. As a couple, they seemed somehow too good to be true. The fixed smiles, the atmosphere they created . . . Even then, the notion of unbridled passion seemed out of place between this well-bred, well-dressed, well-mannered pair.' In a piece headed 'Marriage, Mark and Me' [*sic*], Marje went on to reveal some of the hitherto unprinted 'Sad Secrets the Princess Told Her', and to comment, 'Her husband certainly didn't appear to be knocked out by her looks' and 'I remember thinking even then that he was probably more interested in horses than in his attractive wife.' As Marje's friend Lord McGregor would say of press speculation on the Charles–Diana marriage, this was 'dabbling fingers in the stuff of other people's souls', and not like the royalist Mrs Proops at all.

But Dear Marje was still very much herself in her own advice column, where her deep empathy with other people's distress coloured everything she wrote. As she told one woman whose husband had confessed he'd always hated her, 'I can feel your pain and turmoil as if you were sitting here beside me.' This was Marje's real work now, and she poured her talent into it, despite all the riveting pain of her life, with something like heroism. Her replies are never sloppy or sentimental, but always disciplined, bringing order to discord, and offering detailed practical advice wherever she can, as well as compassion. Of her motives she says simply, 'I want people to need me and depend on me.'

A disabled lady of sixty-eight, who has divorced her husband of fifty years, is encouraged to look after herself, enjoy her new home, get involved in speech therapy. Life goes on. She tells Marje, 'You have restored my faith by being concerned.' A young man tells Marje he's afraid to have a relationship because he's a virgin and fears his lack of experience will put a girl off. Marje tells him, 'A girl who is attracted to you and likes you a great deal has nothing to gain by humiliating you.' A couple who have lost their business and their home are asked to try to put it behind them, however hard. There was no alternative, and 'It would certainly upset me to think of you and your husband being unhappy and allowing yourselves to be made miserable over a length of time.' A woman who fears Marje will dismiss her as barking mad has been left utterly desolate and lonely by the death of her closest pal, a dog. She is told, 'Not for a moment do I think you're a nutter. Your loss is as poignant and as sad as if your dog was indeed a person.' The letter set off a chain reaction. Hundreds more came out of the woodwork and wrote to tell Marje about their grief at the loss of their pets.

Often she says, 'My heart goes out to you,' and it does. But she is always frank. A man writes that he's been a rotten husband and that his wife is now fed up with him. What can he do to win her back? Marje tells him, 'I receive so many similar letters from other husbands who have done little to make their wives happy and it is not until the poor women decide they have had enough that panic sets in. I have to say that you are not going to be able to make up for the years of neglect in a few short weeks or months, if ever.' She shares her private thoughts with her letter-writers, listens to what they say, is never trite, and doesn't pretend life is fair; only that we're all in the same boat. A wife who has been faithful and kind tells Marje that her husband has 'dumped me and my little boy', and left them with debts and the threat of repossession. 'No one,' says this lady, 'is entitled to cause so much pain to another human being.' Marje replies, 'You say that sometimes it seems as if the good, loving, and decent partners always end up married to the ones who couldn't care less. That is, of course, a gross generalization, but sometimes I begin to feel it is true as well. Sometimes I can be heard muttering to myself after going through a whole pile of correspondence that it is the wrong person who wrote to me . . .'

What Marje in fact does, rather than romanticize the pain or provide an instant solution, is to glue the lost soul back into the human race. She explains: 'Everybody with a problem thinks that he or she is the only one that's got it. The wife who's deserted by her husband is convinced that she's the only wife in the world with this terrible heartbreaking trouble. People in distress are in a kind of tunnel. They can't think about anything outside of their particular problem. And they need somebody to say to them, "Well OK, darling – you're not alone in all this. There have been other broken marriages that have been mended. Women deserted like you have started life again. Have found somebody else. There is always life after divorce, if you look for it." So I think that somebody like me supplies the essential little slap on the back, saying, "Come on now, be sensible: look at it this way." I think that's the value of this sort of column. All agony aunts agree that this is our function in life.'

In 1991 Marje highlighted the plight of battered wives. She had done so before, in 1975, when Erin Pizzey's Chiswick refuge was threatened with closure by council bureaucrats. Now statistics came in that 'violence in the home accounts for 45 per cent of all serious crime, including murder and manslaughter'. Marje looked up from her desk. 'Here we go,' she said calmly. 'You see what I mean?'

She had just run a full-page feature, sparked off by the plight of a pseudonymous 'Mrs Hurst', that had 'opened a can of worms'. This unfortunate lady had written to Marje to say that her husband was beating her up, and had done for years. She couldn't stand it any more. The doctor had told her to go to a shelter. Last time she did so, her daughter went missing, and she'd lost her job. She was afraid to go to a solicitor, as her husband would beat her senseless. Marje stared at this letter for some time, wondering how to help. Then she decided. And in the classic, ruthless, tear-their-hearts-to-bits style of tabloid journalism at its best, she wrote up the story and asked her readers what they thought this woman should do. There was an avalanche of mail. *Daily Mirror* readers offered support, free legal advice, money, marriage proposals, even housing. One offered a bungalow. Marje passed all the goodwill, cash and letters on to Mrs Hurst, who rang her and sobbed down the phone with gratitude at people's kindness. One down, several thousand bruised and bleeding wives to go.

Some of the most distressing letters are from people who hate the world and everybody in it, like the young man who bombarded Marje with reams of self-loathing, who threatened suicide and seemed to despise all women on the grounds that they might look at him and find him unattractive. 'His first letter was horrendous,' says Marje, 'all to do with his hatred of his looks and hatred of himself. His second letter is not quite so full of hate for everybody, including me, so that's a hopeful sign.' Sometimes, even the very fact that the letter-writer has not committed suicide and writes again is a minor miracle, something for Marje to build on with her powerful common sense. God knows how many she has eased away from the car exhaust or the pill bottle, just by being there. She seems acutely fond of everybody in a jam, and sexual problems, of whatever tone or type, hold no fears for her whatsoever. There is still, after all these years, no embarrassment, no reproach, because Marje reserves all her comtempt and cunning wit for the sin of cruelty. Anything else is salvageable.

She has her own theory of human sexuality, and the differing attitudes of males and females towards sex:

I dare say Tom Kraft and co. would laugh their heads off at it, but I think it has got something to do with the biology of men and women, and with the fact that men's semen, once there's an emission, is waste matter; in biblical terms it falls on stony soil. But women are at the receiving end of this stuff, whether it goes in them or not. They are the stimulus and they also bear the children, so it puts women sexually in an entirely different category. For a man sexuality is often stirred and stimulated by touching either a woman or another man, and then up comes this penis and they can't do anything about it. And I've written several times, to the horror of various editors, that one thing you can't argue with is a stiff penis. Some editors have refused to allow me to use this expression. Some have laughed and said go ahead. But it's a fact, isn't it? If a woman is stimulated sexually, nobody but herself knows that there's a little damp patch going on down there, and she can still go and buy the potatoes.

One of the problems I have to cope with a lot in my job is men's anxiety about their penises. They send me drawings, measurements, descriptions, with spots and knobs on. Emma, my secretary, comes in and says to me, 'There's another bent willie for you.' But these boys and adult men have nobody they can talk to, to express these anxieties. They don't have the words. They're much too embarrassed to go to the doctor, although I'm forever telling them that doctors have seen it all and heard it all, and it's absolutely *everyday*. I say, 'Your willie means nothing more to a doctor than a cucumber means to a greengrocer.'

Transvestites are equally run-of-the-mill. 'I have a lot of letters from women who write and say, "I've discovered . . ." – they nearly always "discover", it's very sad – "that my husband wears women's clothes. I walked into the bedroom unexpectedly and I found him wearing my underwear!" And these women are distraught when they make this discovery. And I have to write back and try to explain to them that it doesn't mean there's anything wrong with their husbands, and that it doesn't mean they won't be able to perform like a man. All that it means is that for some reason, which we don't clearly understand, there are certain men who need to wear women's clothing before they can get sexually excited. They are not usually homosexual – because this is the immediate first thought. It's possible, but very unlikely,

because very few homosexuals actually do dress up like
women. Homosexuals are perfectly happy to wear trousers
and shirts.'

To listen for any length of time to Marje talking about
her agony work is rather unnerving, like taking some
psychedelic drug that enables one to see through doors
and walls. You alter your perception of what is 'normal',
and take weird wonders in your stride. Given this perspective, it is hard to look down on anybody. We are all rather
a mess. Some are on the floor. Some are up the wall. Some
are on the ceiling. And there, behind a desk in the centre
of the room, sits Marje, glasses glinting, huge felt-tip pen
in hand, calm as a pond and smiling philosophically.

Baroness Alma Birk, who started *Nova* magazine and
worked on the socialist *Daily Herald*:

> I think Marjorie is a very able writer and a very confident
> writer, and she can turn her hand to most things. She
> can be funny or she can be scathing. But I think that it
> is as an agony aunt that she will chiefly be remembered.
> She lays the trail there. She sets herself such amazingly
> high standards in that area, and I would say that she
> has turned the form into serious journalism, as serious
> as somebody writing about the economic situation. But
> what is so important is that she is actually helping
> people. Not just giving them the opportunity to read
> something amusing or something that catches their
> interest, but literally doing something to help. She
> has a very sympathetic and empathic way of doing it.
> She has that measure of empathy and sympathy with
> people. I've always felt that she rather puts herself into
> their skin.
>
> There are thousands of people who haven't written
> to Marjorie, and who will never write in to anybody,
> but they are able to say, 'My God, that's me! That's my

problem!' And though you may not necessarily give them a solution, you have to get people to understand – which is what Marjorie does and what I was trying to do at *Nova* though in a different way – that everything doesn't always necessarily work out one hundred per cent in life, whether it's marriage or anything else. It doesn't all end happily ever after. I think it can be very downbeat for a lot of people who have tried their best and can't really see the light at the end of the tunnel, to realize that there are many others in the same situation. It really does give some solace.

At home, the doyenne of aunts had very little solace herself. Even her precious punk cat Benjie died in 1990, leaving her all alone. 'But now I've got my Fred,' she says. Fred is an enormous, short-haired British blue tom with fat cheeks, yellow headlamps and a pompous mien. His ambition is to eat more than any other cat has so far thought possible. 'He's very aristocratic,' says his owner and servant. 'His antecedents are much more impressive than mine.' Every so often during tape-recordings at her home, Marje would interject admiringly, 'Look at Fred. His silver feet. The most beautiful pussy-cat boy in the world, aren't you, Fred? He knows I'm talking about him. His tail's wiggling.' Fred is never off his food, not even when doting Marje is in hospital. 'Oh no. Food comes first in his life. He knows all his mealtimes and races into the kitchen. And sometimes he lies on that sofa staring at me, and doesn't take his eyes off me. A slightly baleful stare. Are you a good boy, Freddie?' No response.

Fred has never forgiven his owner for the Arranged Marriage. Marje:

My old mate Christine Garbutt is a feature writer on the *Mirror*, and she and I were talking about our cats, and she asked me if Fred had been 'done'. I said, 'Not yet, but he's going to be,' the next week I think it was. Christine said, 'Oh Marje, before he's done, wouldn't it be wonderful if Fred and my Pebbles could get together and get married?' Of course neither of us thought anything about Pebbles having to be on heat. That didn't occur to us. So we got very excited and arranged this wedding in a flash. My job was to order the flowers and Christine was going to order the cake and the bridal bed. We both wore a corsage of flowers on our fronts, and there was a beautifully made coronet of pink flowers for the bride. I even bought flowers for the room to make it look festive and weddingy.

Christine arrived with the wedding cake – shaped like a heart and made of minced chicken and cream – and brought along Pebbles in this bridal bed thing, which was actually a carrycot bearing a large pink bow and the words 'Just Married'. We put it down on the carpet and I grabbed Fred, and Christine held Pebbles, and we put the cake on the coffee table, and put the little coronet on Pebbles – which she wasn't too keen on. Christine did think I ought to put a white satin ribbon on Fred, but I said no, as he's a very macho cat, is Fred, and I didn't want to make him look a poofy pussy, so she could forget all those fancy notions about him. I sat on one end of the sofa and Christine sat on the other, and Arthur Sidey, our great animal photographer, who had come out of retirement especially to do the wedding pictures, stood ready and loaded.

First of all, Fred struggled and knocked the flowers off my lapel and trod on them. Then Pebbles, in her anxiety to get off Christine's lap, knocked her bridal coronet askew. We introduced them to each other. Fred took one look at Pebbles and cowered back in my arms, turning out to be a wimp in macho clothing. Pebbles took one look at Fred, and it was clearly hate at first sight. They spat at each other. Out came Pebbles's long claws. She bared her teeth at him, looking as savage as a lioness, with her coronet over one eye. Arthur Sidey, going mad, got some good snaps of Pebbles's claws, and I got so fed up with all the scratches I was getting from Fred, who was struggling to get out of captivity, that I let him down on the floor. Whereupon he spotted their 'Just Married' cot and went in to have a sniff round. So Arthur Sidey did finally manage to get a picture of Fred, emerging on his own from the marital bed looking rather disgusted with the whole thing.

Another – far more dreadful – disaster in the home occurred on Marje's birthday in August 1991. Its consequences were so serious that for a time it looked as though this book might have to be published posthumously. Marje's son Robert again blames what happened on a drug, this time Tegretol, which Marje had been prescribed at the Maida Vale hospital. 'Tegretol is a drug that I've seen used many, many times, and it affects your balance, and this I think was why my mother was suffering from dizzy spells and giddiness. And I am certain this was what gave her the fall.' Marje:

I was spending the evening with my next-door neighbour, the Brigadier. He'd asked me what I was doing for my birthday, and I'd said, 'Nothing. It's not a birthday I particularly want to celebrate.' And he said, 'Come and have a meal with me – I'll cook you a nice supper.' So we'd had this very nice meal, and when he went into the kitchen, I was sitting in a deep armchair in his living room. And I thought I'd better get up and give him a hand. So I got out of the chair and I stumbled, and fell against a heavy table. I screamed. He came rushing out of the kitchen and I was in a terrible state. The poor Brig kept saying, 'I shouldn't have left you on your own! I shouldn't have left you!' I said to him, 'I want to lie down. Let me lie down.'

He took me upstairs to his bedroom and I lay on his bed, but I was in agony, and it hurt to breathe. So I said, 'Take me home. Please take me home.' I've had a few operations and two tin hips and one thing and another, but I'd never known pain like this. Which I'm still having, four months later. I mean, now at this minute as I'm talking to you, I'm getting stabs. Anyway, I ended up in hospital, and I had cracked two ribs and punctured a lung. And that was on 10 August, which is my birthday.

Marje was given opiates, antibiotics and blood transfusions. She was sent home, developed a lung infection and had to be readmitted. She was then in hospital until the end of November. I was shocked when I saw her, having grown accustomed to the sight of Jaegar-smart Marje Proops sitting in her office with her make-up on and her hair done, looking indomitable and making people laugh. Now here she was, barely able to totter along with a nurse's support and two sticks, pale and frighteningly thin. Her cheeks were hollow, because she couldn't or wouldn't eat. Her brown eyes, normally twinkling with vitality, were empty, as though all her spirit had been siphoned away. There was no question of her talking about the book, or doing tape-recordings or anything else. She was just about with us.

At home, shortly after she had been discharged, she wanted to work, though she flinched and caught her breath a lot. Her sentences were shorter than usual. She said, 'I had every kind of painkiller and all sorts of treatment for the pain. But they can't do anything about broken ribs. They can't plaster them. In due course they knit back together. I lost a tremendous amount of weight. I had to have blood transfusions and be on a drip for goodness knows how long. I'm still taking the painkillers. I take one, and after half an hour or so the pain diminishes. And sometimes it goes away for a few hours. Then it starts again. One of the big difficulties is that I don't sleep for more than three or four hours at a time. And then the pain wakes me up. I can't remember the last time I had a night's unbroken sleep. But anyway, I'm operating again. I'm working. I did some "Dear Marje" letters this morning. I think it's good for me.'

Marje told the consultants she was fed up with sitting round doing nothing. One doctor got annoyed, and said, 'Now you listen to me. You have had a very very severe illness indeed. It would have knocked many much younger people out completely and finished them off. You may be a fighter and a survivor but you've got to take it easy.' The upshot of this advice was that as soon as Marje was able to travel she was back at her desk at the *Mirror*. She's still there as I write, working away. She has her arthritis, and a bad back ('I'm going to this osteopath who beats me up once a week'), but thinks that on the whole she's been lucky with her health.

She was undeniably lucky in one respect. She was in hospital throughout the Maxwell crisis, with Cap'n Bob overboard and the *Mirror* running on to the rocks. One doubts that she would have relished seeing the TV cameramen swarming the Mirror Building like cockroaches, looking for the carcass, if not the body, of her Bonzo. Had he ever told her his troubles? 'Never. No. I had no idea. I would think very few people knew. The boys probably knew – Kevin particularly. Maxwell kept his promise, didn't he, to those boys? He left them with no

more advantages than he'd had, except their education.'
What was Marje's interpretation of events?

I don't know what to think. I would have thought he'd
be the last man to commit suicide. On the other hand
I didn't know that he'd robbed the till to the extent
that he did, or that he'd been such a crook, or that
he was on the brink of discovery, or that all the banks
were about to call in their debts. I can't somehow see
him walking to the edge of that yacht and deliberately
throwing himself overboard to knock himself off. On
the other hand, I could never have imagined him being
crooked. The day he was found drowned I burst into
tears. I was distraught.

I take the view that he got himself embroiled to such
an extent that he became absolutely desperate, and his
robberies were the acts of a desperate man. And I think
he probably thought that he could manipulate all these
four hundred companies and these various accounts
everywhere, and that he could move money from here
to there to Japan to America to Russia and various other
countries, and manipulate the money and businesses
like he manipulated people. And I think that the whole
thing simply got too much for him, too big, totally out
of control.

I'm sure that he had with him some very crooked
associates, who helped him with the robberies. And
I can forgive anything, except the robberies of the
pensions. Eddie, my driver, who is due to retire soon,
worked for many years on the *Evening News*, and he
left to join the *Mirror*, and a few years ago he brought
his other pension with him to the *Mirror* pension fund.
He's got twenty years in the fund, and now he doesn't
know what the hell he's going to live on when he retires.

The whole saga is incredible. I was horrified about John Pole, the security man who bugged the phones, because I knew him quite well. I was always either losing my keys to the office or having to deal with a theft from somebody's handbag or something, and I would ring up John Pole, and he'd arrive at the office and unlock the door or investigate the theft. And I just thought he was a rather thick ex-Plod. I had no idea he knew how to bug anything, let alone bugging everybody's phones.

Unlike Marje, I was going in and out of the Mirror Building during the crisis, studying Marje's cuttings of forty-five years. News of Maxwell's demise was greeted by cheers and shouts of joy from some of his put-upon staff. One journalist apparently stood on a chair and yelled, 'I'm glad he's dead!' But Marje never condemns anybody, not even the man who lied and cheated and tried to 'shift her out'. She still remembers the decent Bonzo, the charming Bonzo, the kind Bonzo who was always so anxious to look after her. 'I felt then and all through his time here that he regarded me as being valuable to him and to the paper, and that he regarded me personally with great affection. He showed great affection for me, and warmth. In fact he used to tell me – he didn't say, "I love you" like a lover tells a woman he loves her, but the sort of things he would say to me made me feel that he had this great feeling for me. When he saw me, the arm would go round my shoulders, or round my waist. He hugged me; he kissed me. But it is a weakness of mine that I do see the best in people, and it's not until they demonstrate the worst that I see it. I'm the last to see it. And then I feel the disappointment.'

Robert: 'He was so kind to my mother, and so thought-ful. I remember her telling me of when he went to a party that she was at, and he arrived in his helicopter which

landed on the lawn, but he wouldn't leave until he'd
made sure that somebody was driving my mother home.
I'm not saying that Maxwell's motives in relation to my
mother were beyond reproach. He was an operator and
he wouldn't have kicked around a bankable asset. But all
I can say is that he was lovely to her, and very nice to me,
and so was Betty. And until what we now know came to
light, when he was being vilified in the press I used to
get very angry.'

Perhaps the Proops family are unbelievably naive. Or
perhaps all the rest of us are unbelievably cynical. Only
the angels know, and the creatures of the deep. All
that can be said with certainty is that Marje Proops has
never hated anyone, and she's not about to start now,
at the age of whatever-she-is. It is difficult to assess the
impact of her work, or her non-moralizing, all-embracing,
all-humanizing philosophy. But it is a philosophy; of that
there can be no doubt. A journalist who can influence
human affairs in the realm of intimacy and relationships,
marriage and divorce, domestic violence, sex, abortion
and contraception, prejudice, politics, childcare, feminism
and masculinism, is a philosopher, whether she is given
gongs and honorary degrees or not, and whether she
aspires to the title or not. A philosopher is someone
who pursues wisdom, and whose thoughts and writings
change people's lives. Marje Proops has done these things,
for forty-five years.

Whether she should have told the unvarnished truth
about her life I leave to critics to figure out. They will
always know everything about everything, and judge us
with unblinking ruthlessness. Marje won't worry. She'll
shrug and say, 'Perhaps one day they may have a problem.' The ones who thought Marje was an institution
rather than a human being will no doubt be upset. Noel
Whitcombe, when asked for an interview, told me he

wouldn't even want to appear in the index of such a book. Not to worry. The two people Marje consulted about allowing a no-holds-barred biography, her son Robert and her then editor Roy Greenslade, told her to tell the truth and shame the devil, and that if anybody thought badly of her as a result, well sod them.

We shall simply leave Marje in office, in her office. After all these undisclosed years, and all this agony aunting and agony, she has the work down to a fine art. Her chief secretary and personal assistant since Charles Griffin 'got Fiona pregnant', as Marje put it, is Emma Field. Emma told me: 'She makes me laugh. "If you have a baby," she says, "you'll just have to have it in the office. You can't have maternity leave." I said, "Don't worry – I'll hang some stirrups up." But I love this job. We've had loads of fun. We're always laughing, trying to make the best of a bad thing, with all the problems.

'She's tough with herself, though not with me. Of course, if she thinks you're wrong, she'll tell you. She doesn't beat about the bush, and she certainly wouldn't weep in a corner if anybody upset her. I never forget she's my boss, but we're friends, too.' They work as a team. When Marje ran an item on premature ejaculation and impotence, they received, quite literally, thousands of letters in a fortnight asking for a leaflet on the subject. There was a train strike on, which made things more difficult, so Emma and her mum had to help by sticking leaflets in envelopes, and the ones without stamped addressed envelopes all had to be carried back to the office to be franked. 'My arms grew a few inches during those weeks', says Emma.

After Marje had recovered from her accident, she was interviewed on television by Miriam Stoppard for BBC Television's *People Today* lunchtime chat show. One of the more astonishing questions she was asked was about death, and what she felt about the subject. Knowing about her medical history I felt my toes curl in my shoes, but Marje didn't miss a beat. She replied that when Proopsie died, she realized she had been telling thousands of women it would take at least a couple of years to adjust to widowhood, and that now she was taking her own advice. 'The *Mirror* is my second husband,' said La Proops expansively. 'I hope it's not going to be unfaithful to me.' Marje's very faithful secretaries, watching the programme in her office, were charmed by this news. Unfortunately, Marje sailed on: 'I've got to die somewhere, and I hope it's at the *Mirror*. Then in the morning the cleaners will find me and come in and sweep me up.' At this remark, about their employer intending to pop her clogs in the office, their young brows furrowed. 'And if she does,' said long-suffering Emma, 'I'll kill her!'

AFTERWORD

by Marjorie Proops

One of the by-products of this biography you have just skipped through was an invitation by psychiatrist Dr Anthony Clare to be quizzed for his on-the-couch radio show. I accepted with some trepidation. I'd heard he was a tough nut, that some of his guests ended up feeling like battered victims ready for collection by men in white coats, and I sat uneasily on the edge of the chair in a tiny BBC studio (not a couch to be seen) facing this small amiable Irishman exuding large quantities of Irish charm.

I wasn't fooled by the charm. The attack was swift. Smiling affably, the doctor put the knife in by asking me why I'd allowed myself to be subjected to such a frank exposure of my private life. Had I anticipated the grief I might cause, did I realize that the secret, illicit twenty-year love-affair of a generally-perceived-to-be-respectable and respected married journalist would cause the sensation it did when the book was published?

I got really mad with the man. Was he implying, I wondered, that, as a tabloid journalist, I'd have been aware of the commercial value of sex and was in it for the notoriety and the money? Dr Clare wasn't the first to question my motives for agreeing to tell all to Angela Patmore, the talented, sensitive and perceptive author of this book. The reason behind the steamy revelations was a lot less interesting than most people believe.

It began with Maxwell, the monster for whom I toiled when he owned (and robbed) the *Daily Mirror*. He knew nothing about my private life and didn't even want to know. He wanted to make a few quid whenever he had a chance and he figured he had a chance with me. He was very into rags-to-riches stories. After all, that was his story, too. He reminded me that I had started with nothing, knowing nothing, had the sketchiest of educations and training – a plain kid growing up in insalubrious London pubs . . . 'and here you are,' he boomed, 'right at the top of your profession.'

He wanted me to write my autobiography but I resisted that one. I wasn't, I explained, into all that ego burnishing, the 'I this' and 'I that' which is the inevitable result of a book you write about yourself. We compromised after several weeks of argument when I finally agreed to be 'done' by a biographer. Which is how Angela came to be spending hours, weeks and months sitting facing me, with her tape-recorder ticking over. Handing me the Kleenex when remembrance of the past became too much to bear, trying to console me and comfort me when I wept for lost love. It is a bizarre and immensely disturbing experience, re-living your life. It's a bit like reading your own obituary or like opening a novel and meeting in Chapter One the skinny, plain kid named Rebecca Israel ('Becky the Jew-girl' for short) who, as it turns out, is yourself. And objectively observing the development of this Becky as she grows from the plain toddler into the plain teenager and the plain woman she became.

I got the feeling that Dr Clare was particularly interested in my obsession with the lack of beauty which, if it hasn't actually blighted my life, at least coloured and influenced it. My younger sister Jo was the beauty of the family; damn her gorgeous large brown eyes, never to be disfigured, as mine were, by glasses. I don't remember whether I reminded Dr Clare that plain women are often achievers because they've got to find compensation somehow. Jo only had to gaze with those large brown eyes into the eyes of any callow youth and he was enslaved. I argued with them passionately about politics, which doesn't get a girl of fifteen or sixteen very far with the lads. I was lucky that the man I married was into politics, too. That was one of the reasons why I married him. The other was that he asked me, and I was amazed and immensely grateful to him for asking and for failing even to notice Jo's existence until she became his sister-in-law.

Poor Proopsie. If only he'd had a crystal ball that cold winter day when he proposed, less than a week after we met. When my journalistic career began to take off and by-lines appeared on my pieces, he'd say, with humour (but also some bitterness, I now suspect) that the reason I married him was because Marje Proops fitted neatly into a single column. He had a lot to be bitter about, one way and another. To outsiders, we were a well-matched couple – both from decent middle-class Jewish families, reared to cherish and respect family values, both diligent and with the drive Jewish parents at that time stimulated and encouraged. He'd had a better education than I'd had, or at any rate he'd made more use of it. He was bright and intelligent – brilliant at maths. And boring. A decent, boring husband who spent the early years of our marriage swotting after work to gain his engineering and building degrees while his bored wife sulked in the silence he demanded for his studies. Looking back, I'm amazed I remained faithful to him for more than twenty years before embarking on the life of sin that has shocked so many worthy, upright and presumably sinless citizens.

The moral outrage this book provoked amazed me. Of

the 334 pages in the original hardback edition, only 13 were devoted to a blow-by-blow account of the relationship I shared with the love of my life. It was a deeply committed relationship between two mature people with common interests. Sex was an important part of it, of course. That goes without saying, but judging by the outpourings of scorn and reprobation from journalists on rival newspapers, it seemed that Phillip Levy and I had far outshone Lady Chatterley and her lover in the gasp/pant stakes. Mainly, I think, their outrage was because, as several pronounced, I had lived a lie for so many years. Agony aunts, they implied, should be a bunch of Mother Teresas, pure and saintly. I could have quite easily invented a pure and saintly character – after all, journalists are inventive creatures. I could have censored my story for Angela and presented myself to her as a faithful wife, upholding all those standards and virtues my parents taught me. I could have put on a halo for Angela and no one would have been any the wiser.

But I had decided that if my story was to be told, it must be truthful. Before I sat down with Angela and the Kleenex, I told my son Robert the truth about my marriage to his father, about Phillip, about the years and years of carefully planned infidelity. I pointed out that revelations such as these in a book could cause him and my grandchildren pain and embarrassment, that people might criticize his mother's unconventional life-style. I said that if he'd prefer the story not to be told, or if he thought I should present readers a heavily whitewashed version of Marje, he must tell me and I'd apply the brakes and forget the whole thing. Rob patted my hand and said, 'Tell it the way it was and if anyone says anything critical about you to me, I'll tell them to f*** off. And your grandchildren know that word, too.' I also decided to tell the then-Editor of the *Daily Mirror*. He should be given a similar opportunity to halt the project if he felt it would have an adverse effect on the paper and if he thought mobs of angry readers would be stoning Jezebel Proops. He wasn't one for four-letter words, but he agreed absolutely with Rob's attitude.

In the event, the very large number of *Mirror* readers who wrote to me were marvellously supportive and kind. Over and over again, people said it was plain that my own experiences of pain, sorrow, guilt and regret had helped me to counsel those who sought my help. A tiny minority of readers, mostly men, denounced me as a liar and a cheat. Interesting that, I thought. Maybe men are outraged when a woman behaves the way men have always behaved, regarding such lying and cheating as their sole and exclusive right.

Many of the people who wrote to me regretted that my story didn't have a happy ending. But in a curious way, it did. For although I loved Phillip Levy with an uncontrollable intensity for twenty years, the last few years with Proopsie were tranquil enough. It was like living with an old friend. I'd hated him at times with as much intensity as I'd loved Phillip, but in the end, it was the old friend rustling his *Times* in the other armchair in the parlour who made me feel secure. In between the bouts of rage, I was comfortable with Proopsie and I believe he was comfortable with me, and it's odd that of the two of them, Proopsie is the one I most miss.

In this same parlour where I'm writing this epilogue, there are photos of both of them. And lonely as I am now without them, both of them enriched my life beyond telling. And while I appreciate my readers' concern that this life didn't have the kind of ending Barbara Cartland would surely have invented, I am not complaining. I've had a lot to be grateful for. I am truly grateful. Before I began these ruminations, I re-read Angela's book. Again I experienced that same kind of disorientation I'd had the first time I scanned her manuscript to re-check facts and dates. In a curious way, it seemed to be about someone else, someone vaguely familiar, someone, indeed, I didn't even like very much.

It is immensely difficult to be objective and to judge a book when the subject – or the victim – is yourself. If I could detach myself entirely and imagine it was the story of someone else's life, I would read it avidly and be unable to put it down. But I cannot relate to the Marje between these covers. I can't get to the bottom of this curious woman. I do not know who she is. I suppose I'm too close to the character I'd like her to have been to stand aside and make a cool judgement about her. I do not know if she's a decent woman or a foolish one, or maybe – God knows and readers will judge – an evil one. I still don't know whether or not I was right to submit so wimpishly to Robert Maxwell's bullying. Perhaps I should have remained forever an anonymous blurred face above a newspaper column. Or perhaps I should have invented a fictitious whitewashed character, veiled and saintly for those with delicate sensibilities.

Dr Anthony Clare, my inquisitor, concluded at the end of our long session that the truthful and honest telling of my story was therapeutic, and to some extent I agree with the good doctor. Confession released the tensions and some of the guilt, although it would take more than this particular confession to alleviate the guilt I will always feel for all the lies, the infidelity, the cruelty I inflicted on the decent man I should never have married. That, I suppose, is the greatest guilt of all. I do not feel guilty about loving another man, only grateful that I did and that he loved me. I could, of course, have gladly killed the editors and journalists who gave me such a hard time when this biography first appeared, but not now. On reflection I can shrug indifferently. They recognized they'd got a nice juicy story, and by exposing it and exaggerating it out of all proportion, they were only doing their job. I trust it will give them some comfort to learn that they did me no lasting harm. I am not bitter or twisted. I'm amazed, looking back at the furore, that those unfriendly rivals didn't destroy my career, which, touch wood, seems to be in good enough nick. Indeed, they inadvertently enhanced it. They gave me what's known in the trade as full exposure in the media and as a result, I guess, they helped to sell even more copies of this book. They put the spotlight on me – a journalist like themselves – and revelled in the fact that this journalist turned out to be as flawed, as human, as fallible as they are. I am delighted to have this opportunity to thank them for their help.

— INDEX —

Abse, Leo, 206, 229–33
AIDS, 253
Alexandra, HRH Princess, 122
Alexandra, Theatre, Stoke Newington, 8
Althorp, Charles, 316
Andrews, Eamonn, 205
Anne, HRH Princess, 100, 221–3, 318
anti-semitism, 4, 15–16, 26–7, 53–4
Arthritis Care, 218
Austen, Jane, 4, 222
Australia, 52, 124, 128, 152, 168–70, 189

Baddeley, Jean, 275–6
Bardot, Brigitte, 123
Barer, Joseph, 12–14
Barnes, 20, 202–4, 240, 269, 312
Bartholomew, Harry Guy, 48
Bass, Brian, 234
Battell, Kenneth (hairdresser), 177
Bedford, Duke of, 142
Belsen concentration camp, 26
Bergman, Ingrid, 122
Bevan, Aneurin, 164, 228
Birk, Baroness Alma, 324
Blackmore, Ted, 270
Blackshirts, 26, 54
Bliss, Mr, 24–5
Bogart, Humphrey, 135
Boram, Tony, 82, 305
Bourne, David, 61, 90
Bourne, Josephine see Rayle, Josephine
Bourne, Judith, 90
Bovis company, 32, 40, 54, 134, 212
Boy George, 273
Brando, Marlon, 126, 138
Brayshaw, A. J., 87
Brief Encounter, 145
Brighton, 154, 268, 288, 302
Brown, Mary, 173
Browning, Elizabeth Barrett, 25, 134, 148;
    Sonnets from the Portuguese, 25
Brynner, Yul, 142–3
Buffalo Courier, 176
Burma, 92
Burrington, Ernie, 82–3, 112–13, 205, 245–6
Bygraves, Max, 234

Café de Paris, 62
Caine, Michael, 234
Cairns, Julia, 64
Callaghan, James, 27, 238
Campaign for Nuclear Disarmament, 138
Canada, 124, 168, 274
Carl Rosa Opera Company, 11–12

Caron, Leslie, 138
Cartland, Dame Barbara, 43, 199–200
Cassandra (William Neil Connor), 48,
    49–51, 69, 165, 174, 193
Castle, Dame Barbara, 48
Castle, Edward (Ted), 165
Ceylon, 58, 92, 93
Chamberlain, Neville, 45
Chanel, Coco, 74
Charles, HRH Prince, 121, 148, 244,
    268, 318
Chesser, Eustace, 86, 178
Childs, Vicki, 206
Churchill, Winston, 48, 209–10
City Studios, 23
Clissold Park, 2, 9, 27
Cole, John, 246
Coleridge, Lady Georgina, 190
Collins, Joan, 72
Committee on One-Parent Families (Finer
    Committee), 207–11; see also Finer Report
Common Market, 220–21
Concannon, Dr, 61
Connor, William Neil see Cassandra
Conservative Party, 216
Conteh, John, 235
Cooper, Jilly and Leo, 316
Corrie, Hugh, 145–6, 150, 153, 194, 301–2
Council of Industrial Design (later Design
    Council), 73
Courier-Express (US), 176
Crofte, Helen and Tony, 186
Crossman, Richard, 192, 207
Cubitt, Kirsten, 141
Cudlipp, Hugh (Lord Cudlipp), 46–9, 51–3,
    65, 68–9, 85, 87, 111–15, 118, 122, 124–6,
    131, 133, 137, 158, 161–3, 173–4, 176, 181,
    189, 194–5, 203, 206, 264, 273–4, 284;
    retirement, 213; Publish and Be Damned,
    173; Walking on the Water, 174
Cudlipp, Percy, 69, 83, 87

Daily Express, 25, 74, 184
Daily Herald, 68–87, 88, 111, 116–17, 189,
    258, 324
Daily Mail, 25
Daily Mirror, 16, 21, 26, 45–6, 59, 62, 68–9,
    71, 75, 79, 82, 87, 103, 111–33, 134–9,
    142–83 passim, 188–97, 200, 204–5, 212–13,
    216–19, 221–2, 224, 226, 228, 233–7, 239,
    241, 243–6, 249–50, 257–9, 261–3, 265–85
    passim, 287, 290, 292, 298, 303, 306–7, 309,
    313–14, 321, 325, 329, 331, 334
Daily Telegraph, 34, 114, 259

Dalston, 1–2, 6, 19, 35
Dalston County Secondary School, 3, 6, 19
Dear Marje, 222–3
Devlin, Bernadette, 191–2, 316
Dexter, Ted, 141
Diamond, John, 313–14
Diana, HRH Princess, 244, 268, 316, 318
Dior, Christian, 73–4, 124
Disher, Margaret, 73, 269–70
Dix, Dorothy, 84, 178, 259
Dors, Diana, 163
Dunmow Flitch, 171

Edwards, Ann, 74
Edwards, Mrs, 4
Edwards, Robert, 264, 267, 281
Edwards, Suzanne, 244
Elizabeth II, Queen, 72, 79, 274, 316
English Law Commission, 210
Ennals, David, 192
Erik (milliner), 51
Evening News, 330

facial prejudice, 16–17
Fath, Jacques, 74, 81
Ferrari, Dan, 205
Field, Emma, 308, 323, 333–4
Financial Times, 182–3
Finer Report (of the Committee on One-
  Parent Families), 209–11
Finer, Sir Morris, 207, 209, 210–11
First World War, 7
Flatau, Annie (grandmother), 1–2, 6–7, 254
Fleet, the (Hampstead pub), 2, 3
Fleet Street, 24, 48, 70, 129, 130–31, 189,
  265, 281, 282
Foot, Michael, 79
Fortune Theatre, Covent Garden, 12
Frith, Michael, 268
Frost, David, 188, 316

Gaitskell, Hugh, 225
Galli-Curci, Amelita, 12
Garbutt, Christine, 325
Garland, Ailsa, 122, 124
Gascoigne, Paul, 317
Gay News, 98
General Medical Council, 271
Germany, 45, 53–4, 168, 180
Gibb, Ian, 317
Gillick, Victoria, 270–71
Golders Green, 27, 33, 41, 53, 55, 68, 75,
  91, 107, 134, 144, 159
Goodman, Geoffrey, 113, 132, 158–9, 279
Good Taste magazine, 64
Grange Farm (Slough), 58–62, 63
Grant, Cary, 118, 143–4, 313
Grapes, the (Windsor pub), 61, 62–3, 65
Greaves, Jimmy, 138
Green, Felicity, 113–14, 122–3, 130, 132,
  189, 191, 204–5, 217, 225, 263
Green Lanes, 9, 27

Gray, Thomas, *Elegy in a Country
  Churchyard*, 59
Greenslade, Roy, 281–4, 287, 306–7,
  313–14, 332
Greer, Germaine, 56, 252
Griffin, Charles, 313, 317, 333
Griffin, Fiona, 243, 288–9, 296–7, 308, 310,
  313, 333
Grimond, Joe, 164
Guardian, 191, 259, 269

Hackney Technical School (later Hackney
  College), 19–20, 22, 74
Hagerty, Bill, 235, 242–3, 261–2
Haines, Joe, 224, 225–6, 314
Hamilton, Willie, 229
Hampstead, 2–3
Hancock, Tony, 138, 183
Haverstock Hill, convent at, 3
Hawke, Mary, 177
Hawkins, Jack, 118
Hayman, Suzie, 259–60
Heath, Edward, 192, 214, 239
Hefner, Hugh, 187
Heim, Jacques, 124
Helga, 57–8
Hillside Tennis Club, 27, 28
Hitler, Adolf, 26, 45
Home, Evelyn (Peggy Makins), 84, 87,
  178, 259
Hopkirk, Joyce, 236
Howard, Lee, 163, 167
Howard, Trevor, 145
Howerd, Frankie, 183
Hoxton, 2
Hurst, Keila, 138
Hutton, Betty, 72
Hyland, Jodi, 176

India, 58, 88, 93, 101, 269
International Publishing Corporation (IPC),
  184, 194, 213
International Women's Year (1975), 214
Israel, Abraham *see* Rayle, Abraham
Israel, Josephine (Jo-jo) *see* Rayle, Josephine
Israel, Martha *see* Rayle, Martha
Israel, Rebecca Marjorie *see* Proops,
  Marjorie

Jacobs, David, 92
James, Henry, 238
Jennings, Paul, 258
Jewish Chronicle, 39
Johnson, Celia, 145
Johnson, Sarah, 316
Joseph, Sir Keith, 193

Kaufman, Gerald, 115, 192
Kennedy, Jackie, 177, 274
Kennedy, Robert, 126
Kersh, Cyril, 82
Khrushchev, Nikita, 48, 125, 274

Killing of Sister George, The, 187
King, Cecil, 48, 122, 161, 181, 194
King, Francis, 182–3
King, Tom, 247
Kingsway Hall, 11
Knight, John, 113, 275, 279–80, 284, 303
Kraft, Dr Tom, 68, 91, 144, 198, 288, 290–97, 303, 310–11, 322

Labour Party, 33, 69, 117, 164, 165, 191, 192, 214, 223–5, 245, 248, 266, 272, 275, 315
Lancet, 72, 182
Langan, Peter, 234–5
La Rue, Danny, 124, 206
Las Vegas, 125–8
Lean, David, 145
Leslie, Dr Francis, 61
Levin, Bernard, 223
Levy, H. Phillip, 146–57, 166–8, 194, 268, 287, 288–9; compared with Proopsie, 299–301; death, 291, 301–2, 308–9; *Press Council, History, Procedure and Cases, The*, 146–7, 287, 293–4, 302
Lewis, Arthur, 193
Lewis, Cissie (cousin), 8, 22, 34
Lilian (aunt), 1, 10, 22, 33, 57, 90
Llewellyn, Roddy, 316
London Palladium, 12
Loren, Sophia, 163
Los Angeles, 128
Lyons, Des, 234, 263–4

McConnell, Brian, 71–2, 132–3, 219
McGregor, Professor O. R. (now Lord McGregor), 209–11, 318
March, Frederic, 52
Margaret, HRH Princess, 115, 316, 317–18
Marryat, Mrs, 259
Marshall, Mary, 84–5, 86, 178
Marshall, Mr & Mrs, 58, 59
Marquis of Lansdowne, the (the Stoke Newington pub), 2, 27; Marje and Proopsie's wedding at, 33, 34–5
Married Women's Property Act, 232
Marx, Groucho, 126, 168
Maxwell, Elizabeth, 332
Maxwell, Ian, 278, 329
Maxwell, Kevin, 278, 329
Maxwell, Robert ('Bonzo'), 265–84, 287, 304–8, 313–16, 318, 329–31
May (aunt), 6
Meeting Point (BBC programme), 180
Megève, 123–4
Mexico, 189
Miles, Anthony, 205
Mill, John Stuart, 209
Milligan, Spike, 163
Mirror Group, 82, 112, 205, 245, 265, 280, 284, 303–4
Mirror Group News, 236
Mitchell, Austin, 226
Mitchum, Robert, 126–9

Molloy, Mike, 160, 162, 235–6, 238, 242, 262, 266, 276, 281, 306–7, 313
Montand, Yves, 123, 141–2
Moscow, 124, 125, 152, 168
Mosley, Oswald, 26, 53–4
Mount, Douglas, 25, 39, 45
Murdoch, Rupert, 189
Myers, Mrs Hilda, 166

National Association of Health, 199
National Council for One-Parent Families (formerly National Council for the Unmarried Mother and Her Child), 207
National Health Service, 77, 187, 228
National Marriage Guidance Council (later Relate), 77, 86, 87
National Society for the Prevention of Cruelty to Children (NSPCC), 72, 251, 270
National Union of Journalists, 70
Neill, A. S., 100
Nener, Jack, 114–15, 118, 163
Neue Blatt, 180
News of the World, 258
New Statesman, 223
New Zionist Organization, 54
Nixon, David, 118
Northcliffe, Lord, 47
Nova magazine, 324–5

Observer, 223
Odhams Press, 69, 71
Oh Calcutta!, 188–9
Okubadeju, Fay, 110
Okubadeju, Olumade ('Made'), 107–10, 135, 206, 315
Open Door Association, 67

Packington Street LCC Elementary School, 3
Paris, 49, 51, 122–3; fashion and, 72–6, 80–82, 120, 122–4
Pearcey, Kathleen, 49
Peck, Gregory, 118
Peel, John, 185
People, 83, 235, 261
Petticoat, 260
Philip, HRH Prince, 33, 148
Phillips, Captain Mark, 221, 318
Pizzey, Erin, 321
Playboy, 187
Pogerelski, Mr, 20–21, 25, 30
Poland, 54
Pole, John, 331
Press Complaints Commission, 209
Press Council, 287, 302
Pride, Prejudice and Proops, 222
Proops, Anya, 191, 206, 213
Proops, Daniel, 20, 191, 206, 213
Proops, Joe and Dinah, 30–31, 39, 42–3, 94, 97
Proops, Marjorie:
    background, characteristics, opinions:

family, parents and, 1–14, 18, 51;
appearance, 1, 3, 15–17, 20, 39, 42,
82–3, 116–17, 132, 150, 155; education,
3–6, anti-semitism and, 4, 15–16, 26–7;
artistic talent and, 4–5, 19–20, 39, 46–8;
socialism and, 5, 28, 33, 36, 39, 69, 77,
98, 164, 228, 237, 271–2; singing voice,
9–12; boyfriends and, 9, 13–14, 20–21;
sports and, 17, 27, 28; further education,
19–20; smoking and, 22, 24, 41, 75, 79,
82–3, 142, 191, 241, 294; housework
and, 29, 32–3, 39, 42–4; Jewishness, 30,
35, 67; sex and, 36–9, 54–5, 92–4, 102,
134, 149, 294, 299; animals and, 41, 135,
139–40, 160–61, 203, 240, 251, 319, 325–6;
feminism and, 44, 77–8, 120, 129, 187–90,
229, 233, 244–7, 273; flying, fear of, and,
51–2, 152, 235–6; driving and, 136–7, 148,
167; SDP membership and, 246–7; family
relationships *see also* Proops, Roberts,
Sidney; and Rayle, Abraham, Jo-jo,
Martha
health:
retroverted womb, 57, 136; hysterectomy,
57, 136; thyroid operation, 83–4;
back trouble, 167, 329; arthritis, hip
replacements, 167, 217–21, 240–44, 301,
329; blocked artery and surgery, 241–2;
stroke, 242–3; mental illness, 286–98;
310–12; fall, 327–9
marriage and personal life:
meeting and marriage to Sidney Proops
(Proopsie), 28–35, pregnancy, birth
of son Robert, 39, 55–8, sex and, 41,
54–5, 92–3, 102, 134, 153, 204; marriage
breakdown, 92–102 *passim*, 121; 'Sonny'
and, 103–7; 'Made' and, 107–10, 206;
'ceasefire', 134ff; relationship with H.
Phillip Levy, 146–57, 166–8, 194, 268,
287–9; care, companionship, support
from Proopsie, 204–5, 217–18, 268–9,
303; Phillip Levy's death, 291, 301–2,
308–9; Proopsie's death, 90, 95, 291, 297,
308–12; 'double marriage' and, 293–5,
298–312; comparison between Phillip and
Proopsie, 299–301
professional life:
first job with May Rose, 22–4; freelance
artist, 24–5, 39, 45; to the *Mirror*: fashion
artist, 45–9, as 'Silvaine', 49, 51–9,
61, 63–4; travels, 51–2, 76, 122–8, 138,
167–70, 176–7, 189, 191, 235; as writer,
64–5, 70, *You and Your Children*, 65; to
the *Daily Herald*: fashion editor, 68–87,
woman's editor, 69, stone-subbing
incident, 70–72, agony aunt, 85–7; back
to the *Mirror* as columnist, 87, 111–33,
138–46, 150, 151; as 'Dear Marje',
Woman's Mirror and *Daily Mirror*,
158–83, 184–206; *Ask Proops* TV show,
182; awards, 184; *This Is Your Life* and,
205–6; serves on government committees,
207–12; books *Pride, Prejudice and Proops*,

222, *Dear Marje*, 222–3; campaigns
to change law on abortion, divorce,
homosexuality, 187, 228ff; in Madame
Tussaud's, 233–4; sums up decade as
'Dear Marje', 249–58; Robert Maxwell
and, 265–84, 287, 304–8, 313–16, 318,
329–31; director of *Mirror*, 280, 284,
303–5; possible retirement and, 303–4,
308; 35 years with the *Mirror* and
onwards, 313–34
Proops, Olivia, 170–71, 203
Proops, Queenie, 29
Proops, Robert, 20, 31, 39, 53, 56–7, 58–61,
63–5, 68, 75, 77, 79, 88, 91–4, 103–4, 120,
135, 137, 143, 149–50, 156–7, 173, 180–81,
203, 287, 299; father Sidney and, 31,
39, 57, 89–103, 106–7, 301, 303, 308–11;
mother Marjorie and, 53, 60–61, 75, 77,
79, 88–102, 213, 236–7, 292–3, 296–7, 301,
310–11, 327, 331–2; broken leg, 90–91;
measles, 91–2; schooling and, 97–100,
121, 134, 138, 143; 'Sonny' and, 103–7;
'Made' and, 108–9; marriage, 170–71
Proops, Sidney, 21, 28–31, 65, 73, 119–20,
135, 140–42, 145, 146, 148–52, 154–6, 159,
166, 168, 170, 193, 202–4, 206, 245–6,
294–5, 303–4; meets and marries Marjorie,
28–45; appearance, 28, 41–2; Jewishness,
28, 30–31; socialism and, 28, 33–4, 89,
98; character, 29, 31, 33, 36, 40–44, 55,
92, 100–102, 155–7, 204–5, 212, 294,
296, 302–3, 308–9; relationship with son
Robert and, 31, 39, 57, 89–103, 106–7,
301, 303, 308–11; background, 32–3;
Bovis company and, 32, 40, 54, 134, 212;
religion and, 33, 40; sex and, 36–9, 41,
54–5, 92–3, 102, 134, 153, 204; study,
qualifications, 40–41, 44; animals and,
41, 135, 160–61, 240; housework and,
42–4; volunteers Royal Engineers, war
service, 54–6, 58–60; Marjorie's pregnancy
and, 57–8; post-war homecoming and
after, 68, 88–110; health, 92–3, 100, 217,
240, 287, 303; marriage breakdown and,
92–100 *passim*, 121; 'Sonny' and, 103–7;
'Made' and, 107–10, 206; 'ceasefire',
134ff; care, companionship and support
for Marjorie, 204–5, 217–18, 268–9, 303;
retirement, 212–13; death, 90, 95, 291,
297, 308–12; comparison with Phillip
Levy, 299–301

racial prejudice, 4, 15–16
Rainone, Nanette, 187
Ramsey, Dr Michael, 163
Rayle, Abraham ('Alfred'), 1–14, 20–22, 24,
29, 33, 46, 49, 59, 61, 63, 76, 93, 94, 97,
136, 207, 228, 239, 290–91; as publican,
2–3, 5 6, 7, 9, 22, 61, 228; 'Jack the Lad',
7; as punter, 7–8, 46, 49, 207; accident,
death, 65, 66–7, 68, 136
Rayle, Jo-jo (later Bourne), 3–10, 14, 18,
20–22, 25–7, 29, 30, 33, 35, 49, 59, 61,

64, 66–7, 90, 136, 205, 234, 287, 290–91;
  agoraphobia and, 67–8, 297
Rayle, Martha, 1–19, 23–4, 27–34, 37, 39,
  43, 49, 51, 57, 59, 61, 63, 90, 97, 150,
  290, 298; dressmaker, 7; timid character,
  8, 12; agoraphobia, 12, 65–8, 136, 297;
  death, 136
Rayle, Rebecca Marjorie *see* Proops,
  Marjorie
Rayner, Claire, 197–8, 260–61, 264
Redgrave, Vanessa, 138
Reed Group, Reed International, 194, 265
Relate (formerly National Marriage
  Guidance Council), 259
Richardson, Jo, 315
Robb, Andrew, 74
Robinson, Ann, 236, 284, 314
Robson, Bobby, 317
Rome, 125
Rook, Jean, 184
Rose, May, 22–4
Rosen, Harry, 18
Rothermere, Lord, 26, 47
Rothschild, Lord Victor, 207, 208
Royal Commission on Gambling, 207–9,
  211–12; Report on, 208–9
Royal Oak, the (Clissold Park pub), 2
Royal Standard, the (Hoxton pub), 2–3, 7
Russell, Bertrand, 138

St John's Wood, 159–61, 202–3
Saint Laurent, Yves, 74
Salvation Army, 181, 263; *War Cry*, 181
Sanders, Deidre, 258–9
Sanders, George, 144
Scottish Law Commission, 210
Sex Discrimination & Equal Pay Act (1975),
  187, 214, 229
Sidey, Arthur, 326–7
Sitwell, Dame Edith, 139–41
Skinner, Dennis, 227
Smithfield meat market, 22
Social Democratic Party, 246–7
'Sonny', 103–7
Spooner, Doreen, 139, 219, 243–
  244
Stampa, La, (Milan) 180
Steel, David, 171, 232
Stephens, A., 304
Stocker, Mary, 192
Stoke Newington, 2, 8, 27, 33
Stoke Poges, 58–9, 62
Stoppard, Miriam, 333
Stott, Mary, 191
Stott, Richard, 267, 281
Stourton, Lord Charles Edward Mowbray
  Segrave and, 239–40
Summerskill, Lady Edith, 139
Sun, 189, 190, 258–9, 260, 274
Sunday Mirror, 82, 214, 222, 260, 264, 267,
  281, 298
Sunday Pictorial (later *Sunday Mirror*), 48
Sunday Telegraph, 258

Sunday Times, 85; magazine, 180–81

Taylor, Elizabeth, 74–5, 112
Thaw, George, 162, 189, 197
Thatcher, Margaret, 5, 188, 214–17, 227,
  237–8, 262, 271
Thompson, David, 239–40
Times, The, 101, 114, 141, 156, 215, 233, 259
Townsend, Group-Captain Peter, 115, 316
Toynbee, Polly, 269
Trades Union Congress, 69, 164, 273
Trump, Donald and Ivana, 316
Two Loves I Have, 78

United States, 51–2, 125–9, 152, 168; World
  Fair (1939), 51

van Buren, Abigail, 176–7, 178, 259
Victory, the (Dalston pub), 2
Vincenzi, Penny, 172
Voss, Herbert, 11

Waldner, Francesco, 125
Walker, Don, 234
Walpole, Captain (Concorde pilot), 235–6
Waterhouse, Keith, 193–4, 235
Welch, Raquel, 195
West, George, 86–7
Westwood, Vivienne, 82
Wheatcroft, Harry, 141
Whiting, Audrey (Mrs Jack Nener), 114–15
William Ellis School, 9
Williams, Shirley, 246–7
Wilson, Colin, 171; *Sex and the Intelligent
  Teenager*, 171
Wilson, Harold, 164–6, 188, 214, 220,
  224–6, 313
Wilson, Mary, 165–6
Windsor, 61, 64; Castle, 62
Wine Office Court, 24, 39, 45
Wingate, Mayo, 87
Woman, 176, 179, 200, 222,
  259
Woman's Mirror, 130, 174–6, 178–9, 183,
  195, 200
Woman's Own, 260
'*Woman's Sunday Mirror*', 129–
  130
Woman's Weekly, 259
Woman's World, 268, 317
Wright, Delmer and Alice, 63, 69, 76, 99,
  102, 104, 177
Wright, Dr Helena, 38
Writers and Press Club, 191
Wyatt, Woodrow, 115

You and Your Children, 65

Zec, Philip, 48, 69
Zelger, Esme, 45–6, 49, 51–2, 68–9, 73